Advance Praise for *Combustion*

"*Combustion* is not simply a tool, it is the entire toolbox. Elliott is not only a good writer, but he is also a great businessman, and that proficiency comes through in his writing. His experience is your guide, and his wisdom is generously given. *Combustion* is full of examples and instruments any leader can use today. This book deserves to be on your bookshelf, or better yet, on your desk where it can be seen and utilized daily."

—**TROY M. MILLER**, CNP, CFRE, Vice President for University Advancement, Slippery Rock University

"Whether you are an aspiring leader or seasoned veteran, this book offers valuable insights to strengthen your leadership effectiveness. Elliott is an engaging writer who masterfully connects the theoretical foundations of leadership with practical, actionable applications. The book's real strength lies in its practicality. Elliott's compelling examples make complex ideas accessible, while his emphasis on speed, simplicity, and effective solutions provides principles that leaders can readily apply. The Combustion Check sections at the end of each chapter are particularly useful. Another outstanding work by the force of nature we fondly know as Elliott Haverlack."

—**KAREN RILEY**, PhD, President, Slippery Rock University

"*Combustion* is a must-read for anyone in management. Elliott's blending of outstanding business practices and lessons learned during his extraordinarily successful career provides a compelling book on how businesses should operate to thrive. *Combustion's* focus on 'unbundling' is a bold model for every organization to follow."

—**PETER PANTUSO**, Former President & CEO, American Bus Association

"*Combustion* is a powerful and practical guide for leaders who are ready to move beyond inspiration and deliver lasting results. Through compelling business examples, actionable frameworks, disciplined practices, and thoughtful reflection questions, this book turns leadership insight into purposeful action. It equips readers to strengthen teams, expand organizational capacity, elevate performance, and lead meaningful change with clarity and confidence. Combustion is essential reading for students studying leadership, managers aspiring to lead at a higher level, and experienced executives determined to create enduring impact."

—**PRASAD VEMALA,** Dean, Haverlack College of Business, Slippery Rock University

"*Combustion* is a thoughtful reminder that the best leaders simplify rather than complicate, focusing their teams on what matters most. Elliott Haverlack combines timeless leadership principles with practical wisdom drawn from real operating experience, making the book relevant for both new and seasoned leaders. Its greatest strength is challenging readers to clarify priorities, strengthen culture, and lead with greater discipline and intention. If you lead people, own a business, or want to become a more effective leader, you'll find ideas that are immediately applicable and worth revisiting. I highly recommend *Combustion* to anyone looking to cut through complexity and build a stronger, healthier organization."

—**MICHAEL WYNN,** President, Sunshine Ace Hardware

"This is a great read for anyone in a management or ownership position. Leaders will gain valuable knowledge and essential techniques to overcome obstacles. Elliott shares valuable insights from his professional career."

—**BILL DAUBMANN,** Founder and President, My Shower Door, My Architectural Glass

COMBUSTION

COMBUSTION

Simplification That Ignites Success for Leaders in Business

C. ELLIOTT HAVERLACK

GOLDEN ACORN
PRESS

NAPLES, FL

Published by Golden Acorn Press, Naples, Florida, United States of America
www.goldenacornpress.com

ISBN: 979-8-950207-08-2 (print)
ISBN: 979-8-950207-09-9 (ebook)
Cataloging-in-Publication Data is on file with the Library of Congress.

Developmental Editing by Heather Davis Desrocher
Line Editing by Boris Boland
Proofreading by Jennifer Doody
Cover and Interior Design by Jessica Angerstein

Printed in the United States of America

Dedicated to the devoted educators
of Slippery Rock University,
past, present, and future, whose passion and sacrifice
ignite the extraordinary in their students
and sustain a legacy that continues to burn
far beyond the classroom.

Scan this code to see other books by

C. ELLIOTT HAVERLACK

Contents

A Note to the Reader

Firestarter, my previous book, launched the reader into the world of servant leadership. It answered foundational questions about why servant leadership matters, how it becomes systemic, and how it unlocks true significance. It was about awakening. It challenged leaders to think differently, to lead differently, and to recognize that meaningful impact begins from within.

Combustion is the natural and necessary next step. Spontaneous combustion becomes a logical deliverable.

Where *Firestarter* created the spark, *Combustion* provides the fuel, structure, and discipline required to sustain it. It is a tactical guide that transforms inspiration into repeatable, practical excellence. It answers the questions that leaders begin to ask the moment they feel that initial ignition: How do I build this? How do I sustain it? How do I scale it? Where *Firestarter* awakened the desire for change, *Combustion* equips leaders with the tools, frameworks, and disciplined actions to actually achieve that change.

Why *Combustion*? Because ignition alone is fleeting. A spark left unmanaged dies as quickly as it appears.

Combustion is about what happens next. It's about how leaders take that initial energy and create a sustained, accelerating force that drives meaningful, lasting success.

At the heart of *Combustion* is a simple but often overlooked truth: Complexity smothers growth. Organizations, products, and strategies naturally accumulate layers over time. Features, processes, approvals, and exceptions initially feel necessary but ultimately create friction. That friction slows decision-making, dilutes value, and weakens execution. The most effective leaders don't win by adding more; they win by stripping away what doesn't matter. However, simplification is not reduction for its own sake. It is the deliberate act of clearing a path so that what truly matters can move faster, and hit harder.

Unbundling is the companion to simplification, and together they create the conditions for combustion. When leaders break apart systems, value chains, and business models, they begin to see clearly where significant benefits truly live. Effective leaders isolate what creates impact and separate it from what creates noise. That kind of clarity sharpens focus, improves resource allocation, and allows precise execution. In practical terms, unbundling creates focus, simplification creates speed, and speed, applied with discipline, creates a controlled intensity that fuels sustained growth.

Make no mistake – combustion is not chaos. It is not reckless expansion or unchecked scaling. It is a controlled burn – it is the intentional alignment of value, clarity, and execution that produces momentum over time. Leaders who understand combustion know how to remove friction without losing structure, how to accelerate without losing control, and how to scale without reintroducing the complexity they worked to eliminate. They don't just start fires; they build engines that keep them burning.

Parts of this book were originally published in 2013 under the title *Unbundle It: Simplify Your Perspective to Live a Better Life and Release the Power of Your Team*. In the years since that book's release, the principles of unbundling have been tested, refined, and proven across a wide range of real-world applications. The core concept of unbundling remains as a powerful metaphor for simplification, but the tools, frameworks, and insights have evolved. What follows is not just a continuation of that work. It is a significant expansion – shaped by experience and sharpened by results. It is designed to help leaders build healthier teams, overcome obstacles, and achieve greater levels of performance.

PREFACE

The Unique Simplicity of Water*

When business leaders confront the most daunting challenges of our time, our minds instinctively drift toward a world of overwhelming complexity. We convince ourselves that the solutions to existential threats must lie within intricate processes and solutions to formidable enigmas. But what if we trained our minds to do the opposite – to search first for the simple, the elegant, the obvious? What if we would only migrate to complexity when the straightforward path proves insufficient? Perhaps the greatest breakthroughs can emerge not from adding layers, but from peeling them away.

When we reflect on forces that shape our existence, water inevitably rises to the top of the list. It is elemental, essential, and profoundly simple. So, what if we allowed water to become our greatest teacher? What if its clarity, its humility, and its quiet

* When watching the Artemis II Launch on April 1, 2026, I heard the commentators discussing the ice caps on Mars. One commentator pointed out that those ice caps – if composed of water – would be vital for generating the energy needed to propel a safe return to Earth. That conversation was the living representation of the second-to-last paragraph of this preface.

persistence could show us a better way to live? Perhaps our lives could be deeply enriched by mastering the art of simplicity by learning – like water – to flow where we are needed, to yield without breaking, and to sustain without demanding attention.

What if…
In the simplicity of water, we could discover answers to the most challenging issues facing mankind?
The solutions to generational dilemmas could be found in a tiny drop of dew resting on a blade of grass?

Water is a universal molecule. Its simplicity belies its existential importance. Without water, life as we know it would cease to exist. Composed of just two hydrogen atoms and one oxygen atom, it is exceptionally basic in design. Yet, it displays a remarkable set of unusual and essential properties. Water's traits arise primarily from two structural features: its polarity and its ability to form hydrogen bonds. Together, these characteristics make water behave unlike almost any other small molecule.

One of water's most unusual features is that it expands when it freezes, becoming less dense as a solid. Ice floats because its molecules lock into an open, hexagonal structure. That property is critical for life on Earth: Lakes freeze from the top down, allowing organisms to survive beneath the ice.

Water is a polar molecule. Oxygen attracts electrons more strongly than hydrogen, creating a slight negative charge near the oxygen atom and a slight positive charge near the hydrogen. This polarity allows water molecules to attract one another and to interact with many substances, laying the foundation for water's most important behaviors.

Because of this polarity, water molecules form hydrogen bonds; weak individually, but extremely powerful collectively. Hydrogen bonding gives water an unexpectedly high boiling point and melting point for such a small molecule. It also gives water a high specific heat, meaning it can absorb large amounts of energy before changing temperature. That property stabilizes climates and helps organisms maintain consistent internal temperatures.

Water also has a high heat of vaporization, so it takes substantial energy to convert liquid water into vapor. That quality allows sweating and evaporation to be highly effective cooling mechanisms and helps moderate global temperatures.

Water's polarity makes it the "universal solvent." It dissolves more substances than any other liquid, including salts, minerals, gases, and many biological molecules. That solvent ability enables chemical reactions inside cells and allows water to transport nutrients, waste, and dissolved gases throughout ecosystems.

Hydrogen bonding also gives water high surface tension and strong cohesive and adhesive forces. Water molecules stick tightly to each other (cohesion) and to other surfaces (adhesion). Those properties enable capillary action, allowing water to climb plant vessels and move through soil.

Finally, water remains a liquid over a wide temperature range, is transparent to visible light, and can participate in chemical reactions without being consumed. All of those traits make Earth's oceans, rivers, and living cells possible.

To sum up, water's unique combination of polarity, hydrogen bonding, density behavior, thermal properties, and solvent power makes it **the** foundational substance for life and the environment.

But there is much more to water's story. Its impact on energy production is significant. While roughly 15 percent of global electricity is generated directly from hydropower, an additional 60 to 65 percent of power generation relies on water in some indirect fashion – such as cooling, steam production, or turbine operation.

What about the future? Many believe that solutions to tomorrow's energy challenges may also be found in the water molecule. Today's hydrogen-energy technologies face limitations, but future scientists may unlock hydrogen's enormous potential. When hydrogen is used as fuel – whether through combustion or in a fuel cell – the reaction is intensely powerful; yet, the by-product is water. Notably, no carbon dioxide is produced, making hydrogen a potentially transformative contributor to reducing carbon emissions and mitigating climate change.

How can something so simple be so vital? Have you thought about applying the simplicity of water to your life, or to your business?

INTRODUCTION

Complexity and Simplicity A Battle of Wills

Simplicity isn't the absence or opposite of intelligence. Simplicity is intelligence at its most refined. Reflecting on the simplicity – and intelligence – of water and its obvious ability to douse fire, one can easily overlook the deeper correlation between water and combustion. In its simplicity, water is composed of two elements, hydrogen and oxygen. Each of those elements, by themselves, are combustible or can sustain combustion. When bonded together, however, they form the universal molecule that defines life itself.

What an incongruity – two volatile elements unite, and rather than intensifying flame, they extinguish it. Rather than destroying life, they sustain it. What appears contradictory at the elemental level is harmonious at the molecular level.

Water remains among the simplest of molecules – uncomplicated in structure, profound in implication. Perhaps the lesson is this: Complexity is not always the answer. Sometimes power is found in the bonding.

Intelligence is a blessing, but it can just as easily become a burden. It's one of life's great paradoxes. When confronted with a challenge, we are naturally drawn toward a complicated way to meet it. The same brainpower that fuels our successes often drives us to complicate even the simplest parts of life.

We convince ourselves, *This is complicated. It requires deep, intellectual contemplation.* Certainly, complexity is sometimes necessary. But more often than not, the solution is embarrassingly simple.

Why then, do we gravitate to the complex path? Our minds crave stimulation. We get bored with the obvious. We lust for the thrill of solving difficult problems. We start believing that if our solutions are complex enough, our value rises with them. It's as if we are earning intellectual frequent-flier miles. Humans are wired to admire what's scarce, and complexity feels exclusive. It feels sophisticated. It also feels like caffeine for our ego.

But complexity is costly.

It eats time – the one thing we can never get back. It slows down decisions. It builds frustration. It turns molehills into mountain ranges with cocktail parties at the summit.

And so, we overthink, we overanalyze, and, most dangerously, we bundle.

Bundling is the quiet art of tying unrelated items, tasks, or responsibilities together, and then convincing ourselves that these things **must** be addressed as a package. Maybe it's a human defense mechanism… or maybe it's just a bad habit wearing a tuxedo.

Bundling has existed forever, but today it has graduated to being a cultural hobby. Entire industries have built empires out of it. Consider the evolution of home services. Many of us grew up with one phone attached to a wall and a television with an indoor antenna that resembled rabbit ears. Those rabbit ears were usually adjusted by the youngest child, who was also the designated remote control.

Fast-forward a few decades. Now, we're juggling cable TV, the internet, security systems, cell phones, streaming platforms, cloud storage, music subscriptions, and, believe it or not, banking services. When your cell phone provider wants to sell you gym equipment, you know that the bundling trend has gone too far.

It all feels convenient, of course. It feels economical. It feels smart. But behind the curtain, many of us have become indentured customers bound by packages so complex that the mere thought of unraveling them causes emotional vertigo.

And complexity isn't limited to corporations. It has infiltrated government, law, and even everyday paperwork.

Consider this:

The entire United States Constitution is just 4,616 words.

Using a readable font, that's fewer than ten pages.

Now compare that to the **Affordable Care Act**, which weighs in at nearly **1,000 pages**; roughly the size of a big city telephone book, for those of you who remember phone books. Clearly, our government has developed a full-blown addiction to complexity.

The best example of contrast might be the **Second Amendment**, a model of Simplicity: *A well-regulated militia,* *being necessary to the security of a free State, the right of the people to keep and bear Arms shall not be infringed.* Twenty-seven words. Thirty-eight syllables. Short, sweet, and to the point.

You could fit the entire thing on a T-shirt and still have room for a graphic of an AK-47. And yet, those 27 words have inspired millions of hours of debate, centuries of litigation, cable news shouting matches, academic papers, social media battles, and probably at least a dozen questionable tattoos. A quick Google search for "federal gun control laws" yields almost 16 million results. That is the very definition of bundling: a simple sentence wrapped in layers of legal, political, emotional, and philosophical complexity thicker than a winter parka.

This is what we do: We take simple things and wrap them in enough complication to make the Rubik's Revenge of the Extreme level Sudoku blush.

Tragically, our own government defines this tendency. The inner workings of Washington, D.C. are so complex that even a master orienteer would struggle to chart a path through that bureaucratic jungle. And the irony is rich: Many of the leaders who scream the loudest about the existential threat of climate change generate enough paperwork to make the Amazon rainforest shudder.

During my career, I witnessed this compulsion to bundle hundreds of times. My favorite example of bundling folly came shortly before one of my many retirements. A company crisis emerged, and a large team was assembled. I joined by phone. Fifteen people were on the call; 10 minutes evaporated during greetings. Within moments, the discussion wandered off-course – pulled like a magnet toward unrelated tangents.

Eventually, I asked several participants why they were there. They had no idea, so I excused them. Others provided a single piece of information and left. What had been a 15-person labyrinth became a seven-person conversation. Productivity skyrocketed. Complexity plummeted. No magic – just unbundling.

This book was born out of that moment.

Not everything is simple. Some problems do require deep thought, detailed analysis, and sophisticated solutions. But much of our stress at work, at home, and in life comes from complexity that we ourselves create. Complexity that we defend. Complexity that we even celebrate.

Winston Churchill famously said, "The pessimist sees difficulty in every opportunity. The optimist sees opportunity in every difficulty." I offer a variation: The bundler sees complexity in every simplicity. The unbundler sees simplicity in every complexity.

So, this book is for leaders at all levels who emerge from a range of circumstances and who aspire to drive performance at the highest level. It's an invitation to become an unbundler – to ignite a spark and fuel a powerful combustion.

In the pages ahead, we'll explore how to strip away the unnecessary, challenge assumptions that complicate our lives, and recognize when intellect is serving us and when it's quietly sabotaging us. If you adopt even one idea from this book, you'll reclaim time, reduce stress, and rediscover a level of clarity you may not have felt in years. Don your flame-retardant gear – it's gonna get a bit hot.

1

Personal Health: Ignite Your Core

A healthy outside starts from the inside.

– Robert Urich, actor and television producer

Have you…

Ever questioned your ability to become the person you are meant to be?

Ever felt mentally drained, spiritually hollow, and physically exhausted?

What if…

You could embark on a purposeful journey that leads to optimized physical, mental, and spiritual health in an environment where you set the standard for fulfillment?

What Is Your 'Why'?

The first question every prospective leader must ask is "why." **Why** am I here?

The answer to that seemingly simple question can be quite complex. If your answer to this question is a thirst for power, wealth, or status, then I strongly urge you to reconsider that path.

Building the Foundation: Mind, Body and Spirit

You cannot effectively lead a business, a team, a family – or even a meaningful cause – until you first learn to lead yourself. That may sound obvious, but many people spend their lives trying to influence others while neglecting their own internal foundation. They focus on strategy, operations, growth, and execution, yet ignore the very thing that determines whether those efforts will succeed over the long term.

Leadership starts long before the boardroom. It starts with values. It starts with discipline. It starts with health. If your internal foundation is weak, external success eventually cracks under pressure. All of the strongest leaders I have known had one thing in common: they were grounded. They knew what they believed, what they valued, and how they intended to live. They led from the inside out.

The foundation begins with three areas of health:

- Spiritual health
- Mental health
- Physical health

When those three areas are aligned, leadership becomes far more effective.

Your Moral Compass

I am not writing this chapter as a call to faith. However, as a Christian, I believe in the importance of spiritual health in my life. Every person needs a moral compass. Your moral compass is your internal guide. It helps determine how you behave, what you believe, and what you stand for. It shapes your decisions when pressure rises and difficult choices appear. Without a moral compass, leadership can become dangerous.

Over the past two decades, many companies have embraced values-based leadership. Unfortunately, in many organizations, values have become little more than words on walls or slogans on posters. Values are meaningless unless they are lived and breathed by everyone on the team.

I once heard a story from a senior executive that perfectly illustrates my point. He had been hired as chief operating officer (COO) of a large family-owned company. During orientation, he was told there was a zero-tolerance policy regarding profanity. However, on his third day during an executive meeting, he happened to use profanity. After the meeting, the CEO asked him to stay behind. Calmly and professionally, the CEO terminated his employment.

Harsh? Maybe.

Would I personally enforce that no-profanity policy in that manner? Probably not. But the lesson is powerful. Zero tolerance means zero tolerance. Values only matter if they are held dearly, and consequences for those who fail to follow those values must be swift and severe. You must determine what you stand for. Then you must live it, consistently.

Goals Create Direction

Once your values are clear, you need direction. That direction comes from establishing goals. Most people dramatically underestimate the importance of personal goal setting. They drift through life, hoping things work out. Hope is not a strategy. Goals are the roadmap for your life journey. Think about it this way – you would never get in your car and start driving without at least some idea of where you were going. You would have a destination and probably a route planned. Why should life be any different? Isn't your life journey a bit more vital than your next trip to the grocery store?

Your life journey is the most important journey you will ever take. You need clarity about where you are going, why you are going there, and how you intend to get there. Keep your goals simple. If your goals cannot fit on one typed page, you are overcomplicating the exercise. And please – make the font at least 12-point. Small fonts should be illegal. Goals should stretch you, but they should remain realistic. They should challenge you without becoming fantasy. Good goals create focus; great goals create action.

The Mirror and the Window

One of the most useful leadership tools I have ever found involves two pieces of glass: the mirror and the window. First, the mirror. Look at yourself honestly. Do you like the person looking back at you? Do your behaviors align with your values? Are you living with integrity? Are you becoming the person you want to become? Are you on a path to becoming the best version of the person you are capable of being? If the answer is "no," address it. Self-awareness is essential for leadership.

Now, look through the window. What is happening around you? Are there storm clouds forming? What risks are emerging? What opportunities exist? Great leaders constantly look in the mirror and out the window. The mirror provides self-awareness. The window allows situational awareness. Together, they create wisdom.

Master Your Fear

Fear is one of leadership's greatest enemies. Two fears are especially destructive – the **fear of embarrassment** and **fear of inferiority.** These fears cause people to hide, pretend, and protect their ego. That is dangerous.

Years ago, I was walking into a courthouse for a hearing when I dropped some papers. As I bent down to pick them up, I split my pants from front waistband to back waistband. This was no minor wardrobe malfunction. If there had been a breeze, things could have gotten ugly. A quick emergency repair involving safety pins and a strategically placed briefcase got me inside. Things held together until one of the pins opened during the hearing. It was painful in more ways than one.

Here's the point: Embarrassing things happen to everyone. Embrace your mistakes. Learn from them. Stop trying to appear perfect. Transparency builds trust.

Fear of inferiority can be just as damaging as the fear of embarrassment. I once sat in a meeting where a senior executive instructed everyone to prepare an RFP. Everyone nodded confidently. I had no idea what an RFP was. I felt completely out of my league; I was too embarrassed to ask. Afterward, I quietly researched it and learned it meant "request for proposal." A few days later, I mentioned the RFP to several colleagues. To my surprise, none of them knew what it meant either. Each one of us had pretended to understand. Why? Fear of looking inferior.

Ask questions. Be humble. Learn. Confidence is not pretending to know everything. Confidence is being secure enough to admit when you do not.

Discipline Wins

Discipline is often misunderstood. In business, when people hear the word, they think of punishment. (I think of accountability.) Yet, in athletics, discipline is championed. Disciplined athletes are held in high regard. Why the disparity?

Discipline is simple. Do what you said you were going to do, and do it when you said you were going to do it. It's investing in oneself. It's when you make the hard decisions to transform yourself into an improved version of the person you are capable of becoming. That is where success lives. Elite athletes understand this. Great leaders understand this. Discipline creates consistency. Consistency creates trust. Trust creates results. Without discipline, goals are just wishes.

Stewardship of Your Body

Your body is the engine that carries your purpose. If you neglect it, everything suffers. I spent much of my life struggling with physical health. I gained and lost more than 100 pounds – multiple times. I lived in cycles of progress and regression.

Then came a wake-up call. At age 45, weighing nearly 370 pounds, I suffered a serious accident and tore my left quadriceps. Recovery was difficult. That moment changed me. It was a profound experience.

I committed to exercise as a lifestyle. It was not perfection. It was consistency. That commitment changed my life. Physical health does not require extreme measures – it requires stewardship. Move your body; eat with discipline. Create sustainable habits. Remember this: There is no miracle diet. There is no secret shortcut, despite what the infomercials promise.

The fundamentals still work. Consume wisely. Exercise regularly. Make spirituality a priority. Equally important: Remain consistent. Simple wins.

Balance for the Long Haul

Health leads to well-being. It is not about perfection; it is about balance. I learned that the hard way. You see, at one point, my consistency slipped into obsession. I became so obsessed with fitness that I overtrained – badly. My pursuit of extreme results actually created new health problems. I nearly lost my life. Hypoglycemic shock left me in an unconscious, crumbled heap. A 6'5" man, down to 201 pounds, had exhausted all the glucose in his body. Over-exercising can bring deadly consequences.

That experience taught me an important lesson.: too much of a good thing can become harmful. Balance matters. The goal is not perfection; the goal is sustainable progress. You need a program you can live with – for life. Not for 30 days; not for 90 days. For life.

Final Thoughts

Leadership begins long before someone gives you a title. It starts with how you lead yourself.

- Build your moral compass.
- Set clear goals.
- Look in the mirror.
- Look out the window.
- Master fear.
- Practice discipline.
- Practice stewardship of your body.
- Lead yourself spiritually.
- Lead yourself mentally.
- Lead yourself physically.

It's a daunting list. Master it, and you'll build the foundation for everything else. Great leadership starts with discipline. Your investment in yourself might be the most important step you take in your journey.

Combustion Check – IGNITE YOUR CORE

To fuel your personal engine for peak performance, ask yourself:

1. Is your moral compass properly calibrated to guide your flame in the right direction? If not, how might you recalibrate it?
2. Are your personal goals fueling your engine or draining your energy?
3. Do you have both short-term sparks and long-term fuel in your plan?
4. Is your mind healthy and clear, ready to ignite ideas? What is standing in the way?
5. Are you ready to stop stalling and eliminate excuses from your fuel system?
6. Will you start or maintain your exercise routine to keep your engine running?
7. How's your fuel intake? Is your diet sustainable for long-term burn? What changes can you make?
8. Are you in balance? If not, are you committed to stabilizing your combustion system? How might you find balance?

Answering these questions helps prime your personal combustion chamber so that you're ready to convert fuel into forward momentum.

2

Team Health: Fuel Your Crew

We may have all come on different ships,
but we're in the same boat now.
– Martin Luther King Jr., civil rights leader and minister

Have you . . .

Experienced the stress of associating with people whom you do not trust?

Been afraid to speak your mind?

What if . . .

You could create a culture where trust was the core value?

You could work in a nirvana where team members were aligned and energized?

We learned about good health in Chapter 1. Now that we are healthy, we are prepared to take on one of the most important tasks in business – ensuring we have a healthy team.

As we've previously discussed, pure intellect is overrated; yet, we constantly hear about how smart the men and women are over at Company XYZ. If I had my choice, I would opt for a team that is healthy and just smart enough to get the job done. People with high intellect often are chronic bundlers, and we are creating a "no-bundle zone" company.

When I refer to team health, I am not referencing the personal mental and physical health discussed in the previous chapter. The health of each person is terribly important, but team health is not focused on us as individuals; it has everything to do with how well the team functions as a group. Team health starts with **trust** and ends with **trust**. It's a trust sandwich – filled with slices of values and accountability, topped with candor and empowerment. I refer to healthy teams as having optimized organizational cooperation.

We start our team with passionate individuals who each possess their own unique set of strengths. They then are thrust into an environment where they are expected to perform. Yet, far too often, we fail to invest in the development of these people.

The question becomes: are we a group of talented individuals who we have assembled into a team, or are we a talented team that is made of unique individuals who can advance the team? These are subtle, yet very different, perspectives.

When we look at the talent of the team as a whole, we can define it as organizational capability. When we focus on organizational cooperation, great things happen.

I have an equation that I use to illustrate this point:

Optimized Organizational Capability + Optimized Organizational Cooperation = Optimized Organizational Capacity

Let's say it another way: a healthy team can accomplish far more than an unhealthy one.

Some years ago, as part of my role in presiding over a large company, I was also running a smaller, subsidiary, company. The smaller company had gone through very difficult times and was stable, but continued to underperform. So, I hired a consultant to help us with a strategy session. Halfway through the first day, the consultant announced that the team members did not trust each other.

I was insulted and surprised. These people were vigilant, and dedicated individuals of the highest moral fiber. Any charlatans had been expunged from the company years ago. I expressed these thoughts to the consultant, and she asked me what any of that had to do with trust.

She was absolutely correct.

The consultant explained that the type of trust that was missing was the belief that everyone was on the same team and working toward the same overarching goals. The fact was, at that time, we had no goals – other than to survive.

We began a deep dive into how to build vulnerability-based trust. It starts with identifying values, and ensuring that everyone on the team shares the same values. During the exercise, we found that two members of our team were not aligned with the values that were desired by the rest of the team.

Both of those team members exited the business over the next year or so. One left by her choice; the other left by ours. They were not bad people; they just resisted the company's migration to team trust. In another company, both could be extremely effective. However, in our case, wrong values = bad fit = seek another job.

We initiated a search to replace those two key individuals, looking particularly for candidates who were predisposed to sharing our values. Intellect and experience were secondary considerations.

The Fundamental Attribution Error

In the early stages of migration toward a healthy team, one of the biggest hurdles is identifying and resolving the **Fundamental Attribution Error (FAE)**. The Fundamental Attribution Error is a term first used by Lee Ross, a psychology professor at Stanford University. The term identifies the tendency of one team member to believe that another team member is a jerk because he or she has a different approach to addressing a problem or opportunity.

For example, two co-workers realize that they need to act on an important issue. But one worker believes that work conditions drive his or her actions, while a character flaw drives the suspect behavior of the teammate.

Looking at the situation from the perspective of the individual exhibiting FAE, they might believe the following: *I'm a great person, but my working conditions make it impossible for me to deliver optimal results. However, my teammate has so many behavioral issues that they continue to create problems. In fact, their poor behavior creates conditions that adversely affect my performance.*

In reality, the odds are that neither perception is totally true. Each probably exhibits some suboptimal behavioral traits, and their working conditions are probably creating some strife. It follows that it's important that we identify and understand the flaws in our behavior, and work diligently to correct them.

It is also extremely important to seek to understand our co-worker's motivations. If one of your teammates continually exhibits poor behavior and it is not an example of the Fundamental Attribution Error, it is probably because they do not share your company's values. Remember, anyone who does not share our core values must be exited from the company immediately.

Assume Positive Intent

As a default position, I recommend that everyone assumes positive intent from their fellow team members until it's proven otherwise. However, if it's confirmed that the intent is not positive or productive, swift corrective action must be taken.

Among members of every team, there is potential for passion, and also for emotion. Passion is essential if you are going to create a healthy team. Passion drives us to go to the next level and motivates others to do the same. In times of stress, passionate people carry the flag and keep morale high, even when things appear extremely precarious.

Emotion, on the other hand, is a morale killer. Emotional people tend to lose control at the worst times. Periods of stress bring out the worst in these folks. They tend to snap and then heighten the crisis.

Passion is exhilarating and empowering, whereas emotion is disempowering. Never confuse the two.

Trust

People on the healthiest teams trust each other. Once trust becomes a competency, accountability comes much more easily. When we trust, we tend to be more transparent and are more likely to share the hurdles we need to leap. When we share mistakes and experiences, everyone wins.

A co-worker may have already traveled the path you are about to follow and can provide productive insight. And when you share your own mistakes, another co-worker might be able to avoid the same difficulties you went through.

Trust gives us the psychological permission to hold each other accountable while avoiding the personality strife that sometimes happens when discussing delicate matters. When there is trust, thoughts like *You don't like me, so you're holding me to unattainable standards* are not going to occur.

Accountability is the key to delivering results. Some people have the self-discipline required to hold themselves accountable. But at times, even those individuals will slip. And in the vast majority of cases for a team, reminders about accountability are needed. Far too often, misconceptions about "respect" allow many to excuse poor performance. Team members may think it is disrespectful to a co-worker to hold him or her to a commitment; "Shouldn't we be more understanding?" becomes the mantra. Frankly, I view it as disrespectful if we **don't** hold each other accountable.

When a team member is struggling – either for understandable reasons or because he or she is simply unable or unwilling to adequately perform – they need to be told. Failure to inform an employee of unacceptable performance results in "Not in the Room Syndrome." In other words, when the offending team member is not in the room, other members tend to "pile on" about that person's underachievement, but once the offender returns, it's all smiles again. "Not in the Room Syndrome" is the epitome of a misguided interpretation of respect.

This is the sort of behavior that erodes trust. It's a delicate balance, as only the most mature thrive in an environment of accountability, but once it is established, it becomes a vital part of the culture.

I have rarely found any businessperson who will say that they allow their people to miss dates and fail to deliver results, but those performance issues happen regularly. If the concept that circumstances beyond control can make it impossible for a team member to produce is introduced, permission for suboptimal results is implied. That, in turn, creates a breeding ground for organizational cancer. When it permeates an organization, and more deadlines are missed, subpar results are the outcome.

Acts of God or Acts of Man?

Certainly, there are those times when "Acts of God" result in missed dates or less-than-ideal outcomes. I urge companies to recognize that while these events do occur, they are true exceptions. What people often claim as "acts of God" are usually "acts of man," fashioned to appear as uncontrollable.

Even when a missed deadline or failure to deliver is the result of a true "act of God," it is still a failure, and should be described as such. Allowing a team or team member to believe it is acceptable to underperform due to any reason is ill-advised. Obviously, this approach is not emotion-based. If your team is populated with mature professionals, they will not fear the embarrassment that can be caused by a missed commitment.

When I was a young man, I was exposed to a very strong union situation at a company, and it left a lasting imprint on me. We will cover unionism in a future chapter, but at this particular company it was almost impossible to terminate an employee – for any reason. On the few occasions we had terminated employment, the employee was usually reinstated with back pay.

In concert with union leadership, the company developed and installed a point system for employee attendance. If an employee reached 14 points, their employment was terminated. Half a point was given for being late; a full point was given for a missed day, and a missed day as well as failure to call in resulted in two points. Employees were given credit for doctor excuses.

It was, by all accounts, an extremely generous attendance policy. Despite that, employees regularly found themselves in jeopardy because of failing to meet the guidelines. One employee, who had been a longtime shop steward, sat at 13 points. One day, he had a no-call/no-show incident. He reached 15 points, and termination resulted.

Hold on just a minute; he had a great excuse. While driving to work, a drunk driver ran a red light and hit his car. The employee ended up in the hospital with serious injuries. As such, he was given credit for an excused absence, but there was still that no-call; that point could not be removed. He remained at 14 points, which was still grounds for termination.

We ended up in arbitration over the situation. The union representative argued passionately that it was wrong to terminate a person for an "act of God." Still, the arbiter ruled in favor of the company; in his opinion, he cited that a "pattern of behavior" led to the termination. The circumstances of the final terminating event, while tragic, were not excusable.

A "pattern of behavior" is totally within the control of the team/team member. A pattern of accountability and delivering results can significantly reduce the potential of those "acts of God" when they occur.

Rationalization

The single most dangerous psychological exercise in life or in business is the art of rationalization. Everyone does it. It is used to give us permission to engage in conduct that is in conflict with our values. It can stem from referencing a deity or someone at the mortal level:

"God, if you get me through this problem, I'll never (fill-in-the-blank) again."

"Boss, if you get me through this problem, I'll never (fill-in-the-blank) again."

Once our problem is solved, however, we tend to fall back into the same behavior that we promised we would never repeat. We rationalize recanting our promise by saying things to ourselves like, *Well, God/my boss secretly wants me to be miserable.*

Rationalizing our past actions is both unhealthy and counterproductive. But the real trouble comes when we rationalize our current behavior and make excuses for things we are about to do. Stealing, sexual misconduct, failing to meet commitments, deceit, and laziness are just a few horrible actions that can gain justification through rationalization.

Candor vs. Complaining

Candor is a term that is rarely, if ever, used properly. Bundlers regularly confuse candor with complaining. But candor is always based in reality; complaints are based on feelings. A complaint is an expression of a person or group's disagreement with an item or idea, based on a **feeling** that something is unsatisfactory. Candor is an honest expression about a situation based on the fact that something **is** unsatisfactory. When having a candid conversation, watch out for complaints in candor clothing. It takes great candor to call out the difference.

Complaint, not candor: "I don't like the new health care program because it costs me more money. I'm mad about it; I've talked to others and they are mad as well."

Candor, not complaint: "You committed to deliver a project on time and you did not. Your failure to do as you promised cost the company a large contract."

Watch out for candor charlatans. They are great at abusing subordinates under the guise of candor; but, when challenged at the slightest level, they become enraged and go into defense mode.

Candid discussions start with facts, and the data to support the facts. They require unemotional communication and a high level of resolve. Most of the time, if you find yourself having repeated candid discussions with a specific co-worker, there is a much bigger unaddressed problem. An inability to address larger, underlying problems with an individual or initiative is a failure of candor.

An absolutely genuine and wonderful co-worker of mine asked me to pick up a case of Candor wine for her at the local liquor store. She intended to distribute the contents of the bottle to team members at an offsite summit. I did not attend that session, but I believe she delivered an impassioned message. Two weeks later, I sat in another co-worker's office, and I listened as he complained about a legitimate issue with a team member. I spied the bottle of Candor wine on his credenza, and asked him if he had brought the matter to the perpetrator's attention. He explained to me the risk and ramifications of doing so, and then I asked him about his bottle of wine. "You're right," he admitted.

The Healthy Team Realized

Once we have changed our perspective, we begin filling the seats with people who share our values. What about those who do not share our values, those who are incumbents, or legacy employees? Just like any individual who does not fit in with our new set of values, these people must be exited from the company.

How we exit employees depends on why they are exited. We will review the four-square grid in depth in a later chapter, but employees fall into one of four grids, depending on the axis:

1. **The employee shares our values, but does not perform** – This employee should be coached out of the business, but only after being given the training and nurturing we would give a close friend. This is the most difficult employee issue. The good news is that this person will probably find a better situation down the road, and will be happier in the long run.
2. **The employee shares our values and does perform** – This employee is championed and rewarded. He or she should be challenged and stimulated.
3. **The employee does not share our values and does not perform** – This should be easy. Exit this person, and make sure everyone knows why.
4. **The employee does not share our values, but does perform** – Greed or other spurious consideration can cloud our judgment with this employee. We make excuses for this person. We say things like, "They have some blind spots, but we can overlook them, since they perform." You are kidding yourself. This person must be removed from the organization. In this case, it is even more important that you socialize the reasons for dismissal. Your team will applaud

you for making the tough decision. Usually, the team sees through such charlatans much sooner than the leaders do.

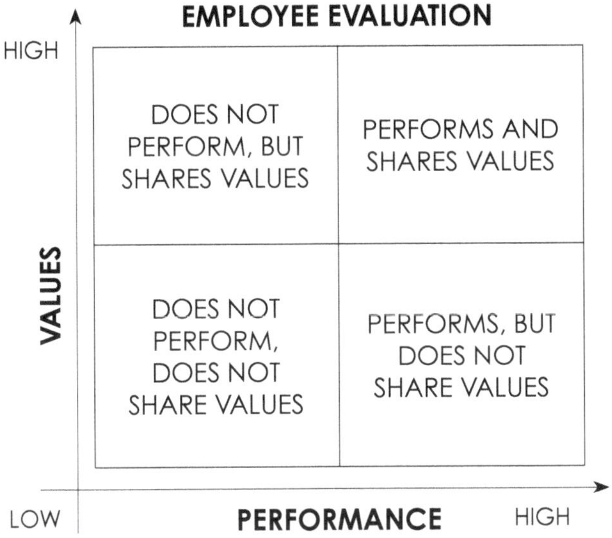

Figure 1: The Four Squares of Performance

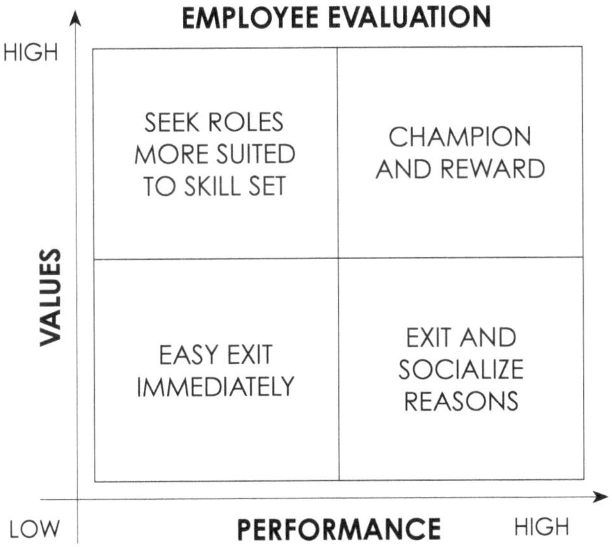

Figure 2: Recommended Action from Employee Evaluation

Now that we have a team of people who are predisposed to share our values and who perform at a high level, we need to create an environment that gives them permission to do extraordinary things. This environment rewards stretching and risk-taking, and embraces failure. Yes, mistakes are to be celebrated, provided that the responsible party gave it his or her very best. My father always advised me to "go down swinging" and never take a called third strike. He would add that if you didn't try, you would never know what might have happened if you had swung.

It is a delicate balance. Chronic failure and irresponsible risk-taking are a genuine concern, but a small one if you have the right team in place. It will be a honing process, an evolution, as your team transforms into an exhilarating juggernaut. No doubt, there will be mistakes, and costly ones at that; but the overall result will be a much healthier, more profitable enterprise.

Understanding Personalities – A Wise Investment

A highly functioning team requires investment. The first and most important investment is understanding what makes your key stakeholders tick. It is extremely difficult to become healthy without knowing how team members will react in certain environments. Proper evaluations can provide a road map into employee behaviors.

I recommend using personality typing to get to know each of the key team members. I certainly do not advocate testing every single person who is an employee, but testing core team members is essential. Not only will you personally learn a great deal about them, but they will also learn a great deal about themselves and their co-workers. Testing for personality types is a vital building block toward gaining trust.

I like the Myers-Briggs Type Indicator or MBTI.* I am far from an expert, but I am an enthusiast. I have seen the proper use of this tool liberate teams. It starts with a theory that there are 16 personality types. None are "bad" and none are "good" – they are all simply different.

A great resource for understanding and using MBTI is *Working Together; A Personality-Centered Approach to Management*, by Olaf Isachsen, PhD, and Linda V. Berens, PhD.

Isachsen and Berens propose there are four lenses, and each lens has two possible preferences. Four squared, thus 16 types. If you are unfamiliar with personality typing, that might be a bit confusing. In a nutshell, it theorizes that everyone will have a preference when it comes to the four filters. For example, people are either predisposed to be introverts or extroverts. It does not mean that an introvert cannot conduct himself or herself as an extrovert, but only that he or she prefers more introverted behavior. Such an individual will typically remain quiet rather than vocal.

> The first two preferences are Extroversion (E) or Introversion (I). People who receive energy from interacting with others are extroverts. Those who prefer quiet solitude are considered introverts.
>
> The next set of preferences includes Sensing (S) or Intuition (N). Those who prefer Sensing would be

---

* Myers-Briggs Type Indicator and MBTI are registered trademarks of Consulting Psychologists Press

> considered more practical. People who tend toward Intuition prefer hunches and are more innovative.
>
> The third set of comparable preferences includes Thinking (T) and Feeling (F). F's are predisposed to be sympathetic, while T's tend to be more impersonal. It is important to note that, regardless of preference, every individual is capable of both types of decision making. Each person simply prefers one side over the other. This is true with all comparable preferences.
>
> The fourth set of preferences is Judging (J) and Perceiving (P). Judgers prefer closure and like to have plans. Perceivers favor a more fluid environment and enjoy flexibility.*

I am an ESTP. As an extrovert, I tend to talk over people, particularly those who are introverts. This is a situation to watch out for, because perhaps that introvert who I just bullied may have a much better idea than mine. Instead, he or she was shut down by my bold personality.

Each of the 16 types will handle crises or analyses differently. And recognizing an individual's personality type will help avoid the Fundamental Attribution Error.

Understanding personality types is vitally important in business – and in life. The cost of conducting the testing is extremely low; in fact, there are plenty of free Myers-Briggs tests available on the internet. However, for business purposes, a paid approach will provide better results.

---

*Working Together; A Personality-Centered Approach to Management; Olaf Isachsen, PhD, and Linda V. Berens PhD, pp. 55-56.

Assuming you have exited the unbelievers, you should have little trouble with potential employee backlash toward personality typing. This troubling syndrome can occur when team members attempt to rationalize their personality type as superior to others. Even worse are instances when two team members with the same personality type plot together to demonstrate their personalities as superior.

In a perfect world, you would have a broad spectrum of personality types on your team. A diverse team – with a variety of personality types – allows for a dynamic and efficient exchange of ideas when problem-solving and brainstorming. You'll want to place individuals into roles that complement their personalities.

One of my first experiences with personality typing was at a company where the vast majority of our team shared a preference to be Perceiving versus Judging. I found it extremely interesting that, as perceivers, we tended to dislike lists and being bound by timelines. The company regularly missed project deadlines and had problems with members returning even simple items, such as healthcare enrollment paperwork, on time.

However, once we realized that most of us shared the Perceiving preference, we were able to put procedures in place for a more disciplined approach. The fact that we were perceivers was not a problem in itself, but the fact that almost all of us were perceivers – and that we did not recognize it – was a significant hurdle to leap over.

In my married life, there was always tension over planning. My ex-wife was vigilant about planning; there were lists everywhere. I, on the flip side, hated lists and preferred to "go with the flow," so to speak. It was not until after we were separated and we had our personalities tested that we found that her strongest personality preference was Judging – and that mine was Perceiving. As it turned out, we were not intentionally trying to drive each other crazy; it was simply the dynamic of two very different personality traits.

Understanding the preferences of the people with whom you spend time will help you in resolving conflicts. Those preferences apply to all aspects of our lives.

The Intellect–Capacity Relationship

Every leader eventually discovers that people are wired in profoundly different ways. We often talk about **intellect** – the ability to solve complex problems, to recognize patterns, and to think deeply. But intellect alone doesn't determine performance.

There is a second, equally important dimension that leaders routinely overlook: **capacity**. Capacity is the volume of information that a person can process within a period of time. It is cognitive bandwidth. Where intellect measures **depth**, capacity measures **throughput** – the rate at which a person processes or produces something. These two traits do not always travel together. Some teammates possess remarkable intellect but have limited capacity. Those people can unlock complex problems; yet, they struggle when the environment becomes noisy, fast, or high-volume. Others may not excel at abstract reasoning, but can absorb and process massive amounts of information – while producing steady, reliable output. Both profiles are valuable; both can be exceptional contributors when placed in the right roles.

Most leaders operate with above-average intellect and capacity, which, perhaps surprisingly, can create blind spots. It becomes easy to assume that everyone processes information the way you do. They don't.

Leadership maturity begins with recognizing the intellect–capacity relationship, and then adjusting expectations accordingly. Your responsibility is not to demand uniformity, but to position people where their wiring becomes an advantage. Protect those with lower capacity from overload. Give high-capacity teammates the volume they thrive on. Match complex problems with those wired for depth. Match high-throughput work with those wired for speed.

When leaders honor these differences, teams stop feeling judged and start feeling understood. And when people feel understood, they will give you their best, not because they have to, but because they trust you with it.

Other Important Investments

Equally important, but later in sequence, are other types of investments. To create an amazing team, we must invest in training, education, reward, and recognition. A "watch out" here is that no two people are motivated in the exact same way. It might be that they are predisposed to certain behavior due to their Myers-Briggs type, or their motivation might just be a personal one.

A common example of motivation for employees is recognition. Once, I was invited to play golf on a celebrated course in California. My boss at the time was very excited for me. I, however, hate golf, and was miserable the entire time. This was in my pre-candor days, and I don't think anyone knew how I really felt. I suspect that my boss realized I might not be so keen on golf when I displayed my skills – they left more than a little to be desired. One person was actually injured when a club flew out of my hand.

I was never asked to participate in golf again, but that did not stop my boss from reminding me how lucky I was to have been on that idyllic course. I appreciated being invited to that prestigious venue, but another form of recognition would have been much more motivating to me.

There is an extremely simple way to find out what best motivates your team members – ask them. Poll them about what they do to reward themselves; ask what type of rewards they find exciting. If they give you an obvious line of jargon – what they think you want to hear – ask them again until they get real with you.

Coincidentally, as I was writing this book, I stopped in to have lunch with an individual whom I had hired seven years previously. I asked him what he would say motivated him the most since being hired at our company. Without hesitation, he said, "That time you took me fishing in northern Manitoba."

The trip he referred to had been three years earlier. Since that time, he had been paid several hundred thousand dollars and had received two five-figure bonuses. A fishing trip? Really? That was what made him feel valued and made him want to perform?

He said he found it to be so important because it was something he would never have done, or even thought of doing, on his own.

The intrinsic value of a reward is higher with one that makes a lasting impression.

You and your company are making a huge investment in attracting and developing key team members. Their first day on the job is the day that they have the freshest perspective. That first day is an opportunity to get their impressions of what is truly unique about the culture you have created. Candidly speaking, you are looking for their opinion on flaws they see in the way your organization operates.

Over time, even the best teams drift. Bad habits can become acceptable routines. But new blood, if properly coached, can become a great oracle into the weaknesses of an organization. I like to refer to it as the "They haven't drunk the Kool-Aid® yet" perspective.

Recently, a company I led hired a senior manager. I intentionally spent a great deal of time with him during casual dinners. I wanted to get to know him as a person, as I saw in him an almost perfect fit with our company's values. I asked him, as a newcomer, what he saw that disturbed him most about the company. His answer was funny but insightful. "People around here don't do what they say they are going to do." He added, "You know, it's not like that at other places I've worked."

All the hard work and investment made to attract the right people is often lost as we try to bring them into our way of doing things. This is not just about culture; it is about process and procedure. It is important to attract the right people to your company while allowing them to bring their unique blend of perspective and experiences into the company. Doing that champions and enhances the organizational culture. Retaining winners like that should always be a priority.

Keeping Your Team Together

One of the most overlooked human resource endeavors is employee retention. We work tirelessly to recruit employees. We invest in all the elements to onboard the individual and conduct their training. But then, for some reason, they leave the company after a short time. Why?

It's estimated that it costs about half a year in total compensation to recruit, onboard, and train a contributing associate. When a person leaves abruptly like that, we have in effect invested the equivalent of two years' compensation to fill that position for only a few months. This might seem like fuzzy math, but the multiplicative nature of the hiring process factors into these numbers.

You might be thinking that is a rare example, but it is commonplace – particularly in the factory environment. At one company, our retention rate was less than 10 percent for those associates who had been hired in the past twelve months. In other words, 90 percent of new hires left before celebrating their first anniversary. We joked that our human resources department was equipped with a revolving door. It was far from funny; it represented an expensive tragedy. Beyond the obvious expense, our HR team members were left frustrated and felt underappreciated.

When we look at some of the company leadership positions, the costs and implications become even more dire. It might take six months or a year to source the right leader. As they take charge, they influence their team and probably are seen as people to emulate. When they leave, their team is left to wonder why.

Retaining key personnel is often a struggle. If you are doing the hiring, and if you do your job correctly, you will select the candidates that seem to fit best. They will, more than likely, enjoy the culture and share your company's values. If we continue to stimulate these individuals, they probably will remain with the company and provide great value.

Creating personalized training plans and development programs jointly with your team members will help magnify their value to the company and expand their view of the company's value to them. Work hard on these retention programs. The costs associated with them are insignificant when compared to the cost of replacing your team.

It's Not All About the Money

Many view money as the prime motivator for employment. It is certainly a strategy to throw money and promotions at people as retention tools. When done improperly, such approaches make the organization unprofitable – or less profitable than it could be. Worse, regular attempts to overcompensate particular individuals can create an overall feeling of inequity throughout the team.

If you have the right people on your team, they will understand that their wealth will grow as the company's value increases. Moreover, the broader team will embrace the rewards and recognition of those seen as essential to the company's success.

As such, it is important that team members profit when the company profits. I believe in appropriately sharing profits at all levels of the organization. No employee should expect to be rewarded when a company is unprofitable. Such an entitlement mentality should be monitored and eliminated whenever possible. Still, there are times when appropriate recognition is fitting for outstanding performance, even in the most difficult economic climate.

If implemented properly, profit-sharing programs cost the company little to nothing to adopt. They are funded from profits that most likely would not have been generated if not for the team's performance. Many attempt to overcomplicate these types of programs, but keep them simple. They will be huge aids in building trust.

Why People Really Leave

In most cases, people do not quit a job or organization over money. They quit because they have lost faith in the organization or the organization's leadership. When I first heard this theory, I scoffed. After observing employer-employee relationships for 30 years, I have found it to be true in almost all cases. Certainly, there are always people driven by greed, and they might leave for more money, but those types of people wouldn't be high on my list to join the team in the first place.

In my own career, all of my decisions to leave companies were about my fit within the organization's value systems. I would realize that I did not feel good about my name being associated with the business.

One of the businesses I led was family owned. I loved the family and deeply respected them. They were, by all accounts, a phenomenal lineage.

Unfortunately, we hired an employee who was a complete misfit. He was funny and talented, but he conducted himself in an unacceptable fashion. As president, I insisted that his employment be terminated. But one of the owners saw his behavior as simply a small inconvenience.

As president, I had a decision to make. I looked in the mirror and asked myself if I wanted to preside over a company that would allow that type of individual to represent it. I decided I could not, in good conscience, remain. To be fair, my decision was far more complex than just the situation involving a single employee, but my final decision came while standing in front of that mirror.

The Door Is This Way

As hard as we work to retain our top performers, we must work equally hard to exit those who we feel are not a good fit, or those who have developed negative, unproductive behaviors. When we decide it is time to remove a person from the team, I recommend that the action be taken swiftly. I have heard every reason that one can imagine to delay such a decision. Those reasons, while they could be somewhat valid, never seem to amount to anything material. On the flip side, almost every time there has been a delay in terminating someone, bad things happen.

Recently, a company I was consulting for had a dilemma involving a senior executive. They had put him on a three-month probationary period, and the end of that period was near. Frankly, I do not like probationary periods for senior executives. I have never seen them work effectively. Nevertheless, I was asked for my opinion on what to do next with the individual.

As I saw it, the company had three options: terminate employment, extend the probationary period, or return the person to regular duty. I asked my colleagues if they were satisfied with the executive's performance. The answer was a resounding "no." I asked if they had seen progress during the probationary period, and the answer was mixed, but underwhelming. I then asked if they thought he would be rehabilitated if the probationary period was extended. They responded negatively.

So, they actually answered the question for themselves, and really did not require my input. As it turned out, most of the other team members had been uncomfortable with the situation, and were waiting for his removal from the team. Almost everyone loved this person, but all were disappointed with his performance. The delay in his termination hurt the company and the team members. Ironically, the indecision also affected the executive himself, as he had erroneously assessed his performance as vastly improved.

Worse yet, the team had to struggle with the fallout of the termination just as they would have if it had been concluded months earlier. It amounted to wasted time for the company, the team, and the individual – and there was no change in the outcome. After the event was in the company's rear-view mirror, the feeling was almost unanimous. All were disappointed to see their colleague leave, but everyone was even more convinced that it was the correct thing to do.

Eight Point Plan for a Powerful Team

To summarize, if you want a highly functioning team, it is as simple as this eight-point guideline:

1. Engage a group that shares your core values.
2. Set aspirational, yet achievable, goals for the company and every individual.
3. Create an environment that encourages and rewards trust.
4. Empower every individual to create and achieve greatness.
5. Persuade them to stretch.
6. Love them when they fail.
7. Create an environment that encourages and rewards self-discipline.
8. Have the courage to exit those from the team who do not fit.

Combustion Check – FUEL YOUR TEAM

Before you fire up the team engine, ask yourself:

1. How does your crew look? Are all cylinders ready to fire? Who is missing? Where are the gaps?
2. Do our teammates share our fuel mix – our values and vision?
3. Do we know what type of fuel our engine (team) needs to run at peak performance?
4. Do we know where to source the right fuel and how to inject it effectively?
5. Do we know how to keep the fire burning with our team members? How will we keep them ignited?
6. Do we have the courage to remove tainted fuel that clogs the system or slows performance?

Answering these questions will ensure that your team is a high-octane unit, ready to burn efficiently toward shared goals.

3

Strategy: Kindle a Clear Flame

In real life, strategy is actually very straightforward. You pick a general direction and implement like hell.

–Jack Welch, former CEO and chairman of General Electric

Have you…

Ever wondered about your company's vision?

Ever felt that the company's vision is in conflict with what is visible in your day-to-day operations?

What if…

You could embark on a journey where your mission is known, your vision is clear, and your course is intuitively appropriate?

In my experience, I have encountered two types of companies. The first group is addicted to strategy. The leaders yearn to create voluminous sets of esoteric documents that are so complex and detailed that it sucks the life out of the organization. These encyclopedic binders are treated like religious archives. They are reviewed annually and then put aside until the process commences again the next year.

The other group spends little or no time on strategy. They do not seem to think that planning for the future is worth the effort. Because they don't plan, they often fall off course and languish. They miss opportunities, and often fail to see roadblocks obstructing the path ahead.

Each approach comes with its own set of consequences. The reality is, thinking through and debating strategy is one of the most important investments that a company can make. The process should be crisp and deliver a result that is easily socialized throughout the organization. Strategy is a living, breathing document. Let's dig a bit deeper into strategy.

Three Simple Questions

In order to be successful in business and in life, we must be able to answer three simple questions:

- Is what I want to do capable of delivering my desired outcome?
- Am I good at what I want to do?
- Am I passionate about what I want to do?

Passion: The Underrated Game Changer

In life, passion can take on many forms. People have slaved for charitable causes, and even more have fought and died for religious causes. The cults that make the headline news from time to time are unfortunate examples of passion gone awry.

In sports, it's that amazing play that we all watch over and over again. It's picking oneself up off the ground to reenter the game. It's playing hurt, or the headfirst slide.

Passion fuels our ability to deliver that extra effort to achieve our goals. Often, we forget that passion is the key ingredient that makes the difference in business. How many times have you seen an employee get a tattoo of their business logo or paint their face to support the company mission?

Actually, unions get it. If you want to see passion, just find a YouTube video from years ago that depicts the Wisconsin State House voting on collective bargaining for public workers. The melee depicted was fueled by passion. Those individuals fought in the most outrageous fashion, and all for a cause they believed in. It doesn't matter if you agree with their cause or not; the passion was extremely powerful. Harnessing that type of passion and applying it to the fulfillment of your vision is extremely beneficial.

For some reason, we business people tend to take ourselves so seriously that it feels immature or irresponsible to show our passion for our company. I would challenge you all to rethink that paradigm.

Businesses exist to produce a favorable return for their shareholders. It is as simple as that. There are countless books that preach morality in business, and many authors claim to know the ethics of business. Here is the real scoop. I have been involved with some of the most socially responsible businesses for their size in my generation. The bottom line is that **the bottom**

line created the environment that enabled the organization to take on social responsibility.

I will quote a good friend again: "Unless you win, you can't help a damn person or a damn cause."

So, how do we win? Passion! Learn to encourage it and use it to your advantage. I'm not advocating that we paint our faces with company colors or get tattoos with corporate logos. However, every person on your team – whatever their position – should be encouraged to become a company ambassador. I would urge employees to wear company emblems on clothing and learn about the brands and the messages of the company. Eventually, advocating for the company to others becomes second nature.

The Strategic Journey

Every journey starts with a step in the right direction. That's a simple statement, but so many times, we overlook simplicity as trite or not provocative. "Provocative" is a four-syllable word. I try to avoid the use of such words, because many people throw around the most ornate words in the hope that including them will make the writer or speaker sound smart. That's OK for speeches to Wall Street analysts, but it is totally unnecessary when it comes to the average person being able to understand your message. With those four-syllable words, your audience often will go away scratching their heads trying to discern what the message was. A translation may be required, but it's rarely executed, and confusion results.

Please humor me. I suspect that this chapter may be stridently challenged by established managers. Coming up is a guide for strategic planning that is simple, yet effective and empowering.

Have a Three-Day Strategy Meeting

But first, we will start by inviting company leaders to a **three-day offsite meeting**. Resist the temptation to talk about today or even tomorrow. It will be a "phones-and-computers-off" meeting; but first, we should define strategy.

What Is Strategy?

The word strategy elicits a high response from almost every businessperson. Many junior managers lust for the opportunity to participate in strategic planning, particularly those who work for companies that have overblown the strategic planning process. To those younger managers, the process is a rite of passage; from it, they can gain influence and power. But strategy is nothing more than choices. It's the **why** and **what** of the company plan.

The Journey Begins: Who Are We?

If we start with our end goal in mind, we can take the first step with confidence. I would challenge you to prepare both a mission statement and a vision statement.

Many have said that there is no difference between a mission and vision statement, and then they assemble a group of individuals intended to craft a complex statement that appeals to the group's egos. Sometimes, the assembly gets very emotional about the wording and the form of the statement.

Questions like "How will this look?" always come up. In many cases, it takes weeks and even months for such a group to create the perfect statement.

These complicated statements, and their lengthy creation processes, are examples of bundles of the most ridiculous proportions. In most cases, mission and vision statements have three things in common:

- They sound really sophisticated and thought-provoking.
- No one in the company ever remembers what they say, unless they are forced to memorize them.
- They become merely words on paper that hang in the lobby or on a website.

A mission statement should reflect what your company **is and what it stands for.** It should be as simple as you standing for something that everyone on the team can rally around.

The vision statement is **what you aspire to become in the future.** Usually, a five-year horizon is a good frame of reference when crafting a vision statement. As with the mission statement, strive for simplicity. The vision should be easily understandable, with no explanation needed. It also should clearly demonstrate that you are stretching to achieve the next level.

You should communicate both the mission and vision continuously. Make sure every team member understands what the company stands for, and where the company is going.

Core Values

Once we have completed our mission and vision statements, team members should immediately agree on core values. As you'll remember, values are those ideas that guide your company's direction. In other words, they explain how you run your company. As with the mission and vision statements, a statement of core values should be very simple and short. Five to seven words will do. If you like, you can add a supporting sentence, but I prefer to go with highlight messaging.

These are words that everyone in the organization will learn; they will strive to conduct themselves in accordance with them. When executed correctly, the values will become rallying cries for the entire team. They become woven into the fabric of the company.

It is extremely important that executives at the highest levels not only buy into your values but also conduct themselves in a way that all team members can clearly see these values come to life every day.

Far too often, company executives select buzzwords for values – buzzwords that sound great on paper. However, these executives either have no intention of following them, or simply do not understand their intent. Worse, in many cases, written values exist only for appearance. Those values will often be ignored in crisis situations because they are merely words on paper, and do not truly reflect the conduct of the business.

Some will refer to the creation of an organization's values as a "beauty pageant." Some will say that stated values must "look good" and "sound good." I refer to that kind of thinking as "form over substance." Frankly, I see little value in that kind of form, particularly when it comes at the expense of substance.

For example, we could say that one of our values is integrity. We could also add the tag line "We Do What We Say." That would be an extremely concise, straightforward message.

On the other hand, Dow Chemical also says that they value integrity, and this is how they communicate it: "Integrity – We believe our promise is our most vital product – our word is our bond. The relationships that are critical to our success depend entirely on maintaining the highest ethical and moral standards around the world. As a vital measure of integrity, we will ensure the health and safety of our communities and protect the environment in all we do."

Is that statement effective? It sounds very nice and is extremely well written, but how can we rally around such a tedious paragraph? In my view, Dow's statement is a prime example of form over substance.

Yet another favorite example of form over substance in a statement of values comes from the following excerpt from a well-known company: "Integrity – We work with customers and prospects openly, honestly, and sincerely. When we say we will do something, we do it; when we say we cannot or will not do something, then we won't do it."

That particular value of integrity is brought to you by Enron, circa 2001. Not only is the statement cumbersome, but they obviously did not read it or follow it.

It's important to create value signage and other similar reminders for the team; they should be pleasing to read and in places of high visibility. Most people react positively to enticing visual stimulation. I would also recommend that you assign one creative person to complete that work.

When selecting values, think about those characteristics that best describe how you want the company to be viewed by your team members – and also by people in the community. You want them to think, "Company XYZ is known for (insert value)."

Values that I find particularly appealing are:

- Trust
- Speed
- Candor
- Curiosity
- Creativity
- Celebration
- Education
- Integrity

We have now taken the first steps toward creating our culture. Make sure the team is aligned, and ensure that you have created something you can embrace and socialize throughout the organization. We can distill all of what we've discussed here into three key points:

- Mission Statement – Who We Are, What We Stand For, and Why We Matter
- Vision Statement – Who We Aspire to Be
- Values – How We Will Conduct Ourselves

Mission

Enhance the Lives of Our Customers through Education

Vision

Become Recognized as a Trusted Educator for Business people

Core Values

Simplicity	Unbundle everything for enhanced results
Trust	The keystone for a healthy team and healthy business relationships
Candor	Only through open and honest exchange can a team excel
Discipline	Self-discipline and team discipline drive performance
Education	The best way to educate is to be educated
Balance	Find yours and well-being soars
Individuality	Unique solutions for unique teams

Figure 3: Example of Visible Mission Vision and Values

Achieving the Vision – The Long View

The next step is to create objectives or strategies, but before you move forward, make sure you have the mission, vision, and values written on paper and hanging on the walls.

Many gurus will preach the OGSM model, which stands for Objectives, Goals, Strategies and Measures. I have used this model multiple times, and it can be an extremely effective tool. Unfortunately, in my experience, I have found that a team typically gets gummed up in thc formality of the OGSM process.

I have been part of teams that have literally spent hundreds, if not thousands, of man-hours trying to fit the right statements into boxes on the traditional OGSM model. I view that kind of process as the epitome of a bundle with little or no value. The process of defining what each category entails, the explanation of cascading objectives into the goals, and then into the strategies, is mind-numbing. If you are interested in learning more about the OGSM model, find another book. There are plenty of them out there.

Strategy = Choices

I like the term "objectives." The biggest reason I prefer it is because it's not the word "strategy." That may seem to be an odd motivation, but the problem with using the term "strategy" is that it can create great, unproductive debates. In a team discussion on "strategy," someone – usually a chronic bundler of high intellect – will challenge the strategy as not strategic enough. The team will then spiral into a hypothetical debate about the strategic value of the strategy, and will question if it may actually be a tactic. My answer? "Who cares?"

If we can ever get out of never-ending meetings and debates over unimportant fluff, we can actually start to decide how we are going to achieve our vision. I recommend that a team come prepared by doing a bit of homework before the meeting.

Questions Need to Be Answered

Each member should look into a mirror and out through a window and ask the following questions:

- What are we good at?
- What are we bad at?
- What is the competition doing?
- What is the consumer doing?
- What are the hurdles?
- What opportunities exist in the marketplace?

This is a great deal like a SWOT analysis (Strengths, Weaknesses, Opportunities, and Threats). As with the OGSM, this is a very good model. However, it is cumbersome and it, again, puts form over substance. That costs both time and money. Delivering effective SWOT-like results can happen naturally when a group has already deliberated on the above questions before coming to the meeting.

Select a scribe and start creating; write your ideas on a whiteboard or easel pads. Just remember that your team is a group made up of individuals who have varying personalities. It can be a good idea to prompt individuals who are more introverted with an opening, so they are encouraged to share their ideas. Try to always be mindful of your team members' Myers-Briggs personality types.

It is important that all ideas be posted in a place where the team can see them and use them as stimulus. Strategy is nothing more than a collection of choices; and the best way to evaluate choices is to see them.

Once the strategy is developed, the team should start to build on the ideas and concepts discussed. The team should take those ideas and concepts and come up with four to six simply-defined objectives that the company will act on. The objectives should have one uniting focus – to make sure that the company has the best chance of winning in the long term.

It is perfectly acceptable, and even encouraged, that you craft as many initial objectives as the team feels comfortable with. Encourage debate and have champions of each objective explain why they believe that theirs is worthy of consideration. You can have an enormous amount of fun with the team during this debate. I promote an open exchange, with some time limitations.

The Vote

Once the debate is completed, it is time to vote. Every participant ends up with four votes. The objectives that receive the top votes move to the next filter. I recommend selecting four or five objectives, total.

Of those objectives, the team should pick one goal for which the company will not be beaten. Usually, this goal has a quality, service, or operational excellence element to it. This goal will become the company's strategic anchor. The objective will define the company's point of difference with respect to the competition; it will be socialized both internally and externally. If it is presented and handled appropriately, everyone will know what your company stands for – not only because you communicate it, but because you live it.

Usually, the strategic anchor falls within one of three categories:

- Customer satisfaction
- Product or service quality
- Operational superiority

A good example of having a strategic anchor is McDonald's. The restaurant chain is known for consistent quality. You know exactly what you are getting wherever you see those golden arches. When entering the doors or the drive-through lane, one knows exactly what they are going to see, taste, and smell when they receive their order and unwrap the paper. I'm not advocating McDonald's food, but I am advocating their proven business model. I think it is safe to say that McDonald's owns the product consistency space in fast food.

Scenario Planning

After we have decided on our strategic anchor and our remaining objectives, we are ready for scenario planning. This exercise validates the worthiness or resilience of the objectives. Proper scenario planning requires the team to examine a variety of economic, governmental, consumer, and customer futures.

You may wish to consider other factors as appropriate to your business, but I urge you to keep it simple and light.

The objectives that pass the scenario planning filter are ready for prime time – almost. You just need to check a few things:

- Have the objectives been clearly written down?
- Do they include the Mission, Vision and Values?
- How does the entirety of the work look?
- Ask the team members to read through all of the objectives aloud. How does it sound?
- Does it flow?

Take a 15-minute break. When the team returns, ask them if they have had time to digest the work. How does it "taste" and feel? Once you have alignment, request that each team member stand and state, "I'm in."

Everyone's in? Congratulations – you are almost done! There are only two steps left in this exercise. The first is to determine how the team is going to know when it has achieved its vision. We must align on how we are going to keep score and clearly define the objective's completion. You will be looking at large bucket trends for a five-year horizon. These trends should be no more than three measures examined at longer time intervals, possibly quarterly or annually, that gauge if the company is moving toward its vision.

Socializing the Five-Year Plan

The final step is to agree on how to communicate all these objectives to the broader team. It is vitally important that all of the information sinks into the skin of every employee. Our objective sheet needs to become a living, breathing document. A warning: if you end up with more than three or four pages, you have overthought the process.

I suggest one or two pages with the mission and vision statements in large format print; one page with the list of your values, again in large format print; and finally, one page with your five objectives. The reason for a large format is so that team members (and visitors to your facility) can easily see, read, and understand the content.

You are now done with your five-year strategic plan. While it will be a document that you will see, hear, touch, feel, and taste every day, the team is now done with formal long-term strategic planning for the year. Note: If you are measuring properly and the results still do not fit the objectives, you may have to return and make modifications. If you did your work well the first time, it will be a rare exception.

Building the First Span of the Bridge: Year One

After a great meal and some time for the gym, assemble your team for the final formal strategy session of the year. You read correctly: **The final formal strategy session of the year**.

During this session, the team will decide what the company will work on during the next 12 months. I like to refer to it as building the first span of the bridge to the future. The work is vital to the long-term success of the company.

Identify the Biggest Hurdles

I like to start by asking the team to describe the biggest hurdle that must be leapt in the upcoming year. Then, try to craft a short phrase, addressing the hurdle, that everyone in the company can rally around. An example might be "Get Healthy." With that phrase, it is evident that the team is not healthy and that the company intends to correct that situation. A short explanation to the entire team on the definition of healthy is required; but once the team understands the definition, it does not need to be added in print.

Once the team has something to rally around, it is a fairly straightforward exercise to create five or six statements that describe what the team will do over the next 12 months. Each statement should state clear expectations. *This is what we intend to do*, and this *is how we will do it.* And *this is when it will be completed.*

Example: Grow share of "XYZ" Brand by five points.

Your annual plan will be similar to the five-year horizon, although it will be much more specific. Developing the annual plan should take less time, not only because it is for 12 months rather than 60, but also because a majority of the planning concepts have already been agreed upon. Your mission statement and company values were already established in earlier meetings.

Keep Objectives to a Minimum

As with your five-year plan, the team should be urged to share ideas when creating yearly objectives. Each idea should be supported by answering the question of "How will doing this help the company achieve its vision?"

Four to six annual objectives should do. However, it is important that at least one of your objective statements describes how the team will enhance the **strategic anchor**. Your strategic plan must describe how the company plans to ensure that no competitor overtakes the organization's leadership status in its chosen area.

Once completed, the team should have a one-page document that clearly outlines what the company will focus on for the next 12 months.

Key Performance Indicators (KPI)

As an equally important part of the annual plan, the team will create a scorecard that will allow team members to easily gauge progress toward the goals. Elements of the scorecard should be carefully selected and kept to a minimum. These will have a closer feel and be much more tactical in nature. I prefer the use of Key Performance Indicator trackers for the scorecard.

Watch out. Key Performance Indicators tend to become overdone. Often, large decks are created; they look great, but only serve to make all involved feel good. When creating a deck, keep the number of slides to a minimum. Make sure that they clearly demonstrate the company or team status in achieving stated goals. All depictions should clearly show if the progress is on target, behind target, or ahead of target. There are a few essentials to keep in mind when selecting them:

Does the content accurately reflect the health of the activity being measured? Once again, we may see the "beauty pageant" presentation raise its ugly head. Nice charts can be created that show us delivering some measures on a regular basis. But when you take a closer look, the result of the efforts fell short of the mark, and team performance suffered. We simply chose to measure the wrong thing.

Are the measurements captured at the proper time frequency? There will be some measures that should be recorded daily, or even in shorter time frequencies, and others that should be measured only annually. One company I worked with used the results of the employee survey as a measure. We reviewed the survey results monthly, though we only conducted one survey a year. Interestingly enough, the indices remained the same. Unpacking the survey with actionable tactics would have been far more effective. An alternative might have been to wait for the next results and look for trends.

Do the objectives "stretch" us enough to move the company to the next level? Are they still achievable? Putting a goal on paper that is unachievable only serves to demoralize the team. Let's say that we are going to cut the electric bill in half. However, if there has been no realistic indication that the electric bill can be cut in half, we fail to meet the objective.

Are we measuring items the team can impact? Far too often, we decide to measure items that the team has no control over. It may look nice on paper, but when we can control neither the failure nor the success of the item, the measure provides nothing.

Example: We live in the tropics and want 30 days without any rain, so we decide to measure rainfall. Good luck.

Are we presenting our measures in an understandable way? Far too often, we focus on creating a flowery description of the items to be tracked, so they sound sophisticated. I prefer a clearer and simpler approach. For example, the United Way wants to receive $100,000 in donations. So, they put a thermometer in the town square with 20 levels that represent dollar thresholds. When ten levels are blocked in, everyone in town knows that $50,000 has been donated - clear and simple.

I recommend that you focus on three core performance indicators at an appropriate frequency – daily, if possible. Collate that data into a weekly performance report, and add two or three more indicators if you are able. Repeat that same method with a monthly report, again adding one or two more indicators if appropriate. All of that will give you a great measuring stick.

Three Days Invested

At the end of your three-day session, the attendees will communicate the new one-year plan to the rest of the organization. Each department will then craft its own plan that will ensure that its team delivers support needed to help the company win.

I believe that strategic planning is one of the most overblown and misunderstood things in business. Teams are often torn apart by strategic debates that rage on and on in meetings. Countless hours can be wasted. Worst of all, somewhere in the Amazon, another grove of trees quakes as mountains of paper are created to satisfy the appetite of the strategic effort.

Why do we do it? I have some thoughts.

Smart People Love Strategy

As I climbed the rungs of the corporate ladder, I realized early on that if I could get onto the strategic planning team, I could gain power. I coveted the honor of being selected to participate, and I set out toward that end. When the day finally arrived, I learned the meaning of the phrase, "Be careful what you ask for, you just might get it."

After over 30 years of participating in strategy sessions, I have come to realize that they are mostly about form and have little to do with substance. There is no question that transformative ideas, great decisions, and considerable wealth have been created from such sessions – but at what cost?

Every strategic planning session that I have participated in could have been conducted with far less effort. Moreover, I believe they would have been much more productive if the "beauty pageant" could have been *exchanged* for a simple *exchange* of ideas. Unproductive debates on whether a statement is transparent enough for the document continue to drone on at planning sessions. The irony is that the "document" usually ends up in a drawer and never sees the light of day until the **next** strategy session.

We treat strategy like religious rites, with all the requisite pomp and circumstance. It makes us feel smart. It gives us something to talk about at our country club. Not unlike teenagers who seek to belong by having the right clothes or haircut, business people enjoy telling their friends that they were in on a powerful strategic planning session.

I suppose I am simply not smart enough to understand it all, and I am thankful that I have never "gotten it."

Focus and Alignment

We must remember that the success of the broader team must outweigh any team or individual desires. If a team or a person has objectives that infringe on those of the broader organization, then the individual or team must be either redirected or given a subordinated priority.

Each team leader should be aware of this MBOs (Management By Objectives) approach, and should be assigned objectives that help the company achieve the one-year plan. Those objectives could also help the organization prepare for the five-year plan. If created effectively, every incremental objective will support achieving the overarching objective.

When creating individual business objectives for executives, see that they are written in such a way that there is some interdepartmental tension created. Assuming you have the proper leaders in these roles, that tension will stimulate productive debate and force tougher decisions to be made. The result is a much healthier company.

Also, be on the lookout for "mission creep." At many points during the year, there will be new stimuli introduced to the team. This is the "shiny new object syndrome." It's a different concept, fresh and enticing, so many will flock to discover its appeal. The effect of "shiny new object syndrome" reminds me of when my son started playing soccer. The young players darted back and forth across the playing field, chasing the ball. It was a chaotic and unproductive situation. The same happens regularly in business.

Certainly, new ideas and concepts all enrich the plan. And of course, we will utilize fresh information and emerging tools to our benefit. But if that new input does not truly enhance the plan, then we must resist its temptation. With any new idea, ask yourself one simple question, and ask it regularly: How does this help me achieve my one- or five-year plan?

Strategy or Tactic

One of the most frequent – and unproductive – topics I have ever participated in is determining if a statement is a strategy or a tactic. More times than I care to remember, I have seen groups of more than 20 people debate that question for over an hour. It is pure idiocy.

This is the real question: How will deciding whether or not to do something help the company win?

Trust me, I have had plenty of strategic gurus attempt to indoctrinate me. I have listened politely. And I have participated in, and even led, some extremely tedious and unproductive strategic planning sessions. It is all part of playing the game. Always in the end, I looked at the final work and realized that the outcome could have been produced using a much easier approach.

Strategy Is Choices

In an unbundled, simplified world, strategy is just… choices. It is really that simple. We decide what choices we are going to make to help us win.

Often overlooked, and in my view equally important, is the fact that our choices also outline what we will **not** do. How many times do companies get distracted by fads or unessential actions? It happens all the time, in almost every company.

Please do not overlook what I've just stated. It might be the most important thought of the chapter. Bundlers will drag you into the morass of complexity, and you must be vigilant in order to escape. Using a blatant steal from the Reagan years, I recommend that you "Just Say No." Unless you have agreed as a team that a particular strategy is consistent with the company's vision, it should not be discussed further. Repeat after me: **What we will not do is as important a part of our strategy as what we *will* do.**

Simplifying strategy is one of the most important time-savers and organizational capacity enhancers. Still, businesses tend to hold firm to the old rigid processes that create the strategy time sink, year after year. It takes a bit of a leap of faith to depart from the conventional approach, but once you make the jump, you will never return to the old methods.

As I remarked earlier in the chapter, making strategizing simpler is one of the most difficult concepts for traditional business people to embrace. If you can honestly buy into this concept, let's take a break, and enjoy a glass of wine or your favorite libation. This is a time for great celebration!

Combustion Check – IGNITE STRATEGY

Before you ignite your company's strategy, ask yourself:

1. Can you break free from the old fuel mix – the classic strategic habits that stall progress?
2. Are you willing to inject three days a year of high-octane effort to revamp your company? When and where will it happen?
3. Are you ready to fuel a living, breathing mission, vision, and values system that powers every decision? How will you socialize them within the enterprise?
4. Are you committed to keeping the pressure gauge in check – tracking performance, and holding the team accountable?

Answering these questions means your strategic engine has the spark it needs to drive sustainable combustion in the marketplace.

4

Execution: A Spark That Lights Everything Up

Vision without execution is hallucination.
– Thomas Edison, inventor and businessman

It has been said that you have to say something seven times to someone for it to sink in. If that's the case, then we should say "execution" 700 times. If strategy is the most overblown thing in business, then execution is the most underrated and underappreciated.

Have you . . .

Ever felt uncomfortable in your factories or retail outlets?

Ever experienced a disconnect between the plan and the execution?

What if . . .

You could become a leader who felt as comfortable in the factory or retail outlet as you do in the board room?

You could productively engage with all team members within your organization?

Learn to Love Execution More than Strategy!

I have struggled to understand why business leaders gravitate to strategy at the expense of execution. Ask almost any business leader about execution, and they'll all agree that it is vitally important to a business's success. They will usually also agree that it is rarely focused on with the same enthusiasm as strategy.

I have come to believe that business leaders are not as likely to appreciate execution because they simply do not understand it, and it scares them. The most highly intelligent people who become business leaders are taught to think about the "next great idea." In some cases, leaders feel that if they get distracted by **actually doing things,** it will stifle their ability to **think about how to do things.**

That sounds almost contradictory, but it is absolutely true. Executives will rarely admit to it, but I am convinced it is the case. There is no shame in this "think vs. do" dilemma; and frankly, it is an extremely powerful reality – as long as we can embrace it. We will cover that concept further in a later chapter.

Bundlers will assemble a team – or multiple teams – to examine and understand the failures of execution. They will create complex theorems and implement classroom sessions, dragging all the employees into unproductive gatherings. Think about the irony of the situation. We tend to bring people into a room to solve a problem, but rarely choose to gather at the site of the failed execution. Certainly, there is a time and a place for classroom-style problem-solving, but when trying to understand an execution failure, can't much be learned on the site where the issue occurred? Think about a detective, attempting to solve a crime – but never visiting the crime scene.

Consider this, too. Every sports team practices on the field, court or venue where the game is played. In business, however, we almost never do this. How can we expect to win if we don't practice in the forum where we will execute?

Execution happens in many different places and takes on many forms. It might be in an office, it might be in a factory, it might be on a golf course. In business, execution can happen almost anywhere. Too often, businesses forget that execution makes or breaks most opportunities.

Project Management

One of the most easily identified areas for flaws in execution is project management. Your project management team might be approaching a new product launch, a reformulation, or a packaging change. Regardless of the initiative, there are usually conflicting priorities and not enough clarity about the exact objective of the project. Such a lack of structure will result in errors being made, timelines being missed, and money being wasted.

After a failure or two, management normally commissions a cross-functional task force to prevent future failures. Usually, the team's first priority is to give the team a proper name. I have no particular problem with team names or project names, but they tend to become way overdone. In some cases, the team loses sight of its objective while coming up with an essentially meaningless name.

These task forces – more often than not – are created with groups of 10 or more people. Since the meetings usually become tedious, the department managers often assign junior team members to attend the sessions. Problems occur because the junior members often do not feel empowered enough to challenge problematic suggestions; they frequently see those ideas as mandates. That's inefficient and unproductive.

It is amazing to watch these teams work through their project lists. Usually, the department that thought to send an "influencer" representative is the winner in task force situations. This person will drive the agenda and will twist the outcome to his or her department's benefit. In effect, he or she rides roughshod over the team and forces his or her perspective.

While that scenario may not be a major issue during every project, it very often affects cost and timing, and rarely allows for optimal output. If you are satisfied with suboptimal results, then it is probably not a big deal to you.

These meetings are huge opportunities for those who promote dysfunctional bundling. By definition, such meetings are bundling incubators. Just the fact that multiple projects are bundled into one meeting creates wasted time, stress, and confusion. Attendees, who may only have one project to discuss or may only be involved in one peripheral part of the project, are forced to sit through a multiple-hour session. They have plenty of real work to do, but they are "meetinged to death" and their available work time shrinks.

More disastrous is the fact that all affected projects slow down as artificial, formal stage gates must be cleared. Every project must now go through every stage gate, no matter what the topic. It is the epitome of dysfunction to assume that all projects have the same requirements and involve the same level of attention. **One size does not fit all.**

The reason we like these one-size-fits-all project management protocols is that they are easier to control and monitor. But that ease of control ironically clogs the project pipeline and creates an onerous bureaucracy that slows things down. The structure creates more work than is necessary, results in more mistakes, and overwhelms the responsible parties with the process.

Introducing the Director of Growth

I have found that there is a much better way to effectively manage projects – create a position of project manager, project leader, or even project czar. You might want to find an even more creative or cooler-sounding title; you are looking for a very special candidate to fill the role. Perhaps we could call it the Director of Growth.

You are looking for a person who is well-liked and respected by most of the organization. This would not be a person who just employs bravado, but rather someone who exhibits a quieter, controlled approach. This individual must be able to influence others and should be extremely self-disciplined.

This Director of Growth will be the project gatekeeper. He or she will be responsible for keeping the score for all projects. Instead of holding large summits with dozens of people, this individual will schedule one-on-one sessions with designated stakeholders. Then, the stakeholders will communicate any feedback to their departments.

The Director of Growth will build lasting relationships throughout the organization, and will become very well versed in the implications of various factors for the departments. That knowledge will, in turn, prevent disasters before they have a chance to damage the organization.

Understanding the Effort / Impact Relationship

The Director of Growth will also quickly be able to gauge the effort/impact relationship of projects. Simply stated, no two projects or opportunities will require exactly the same effort. Neither will they have identical impacts. The Director of Growth will be able to get simple projects moved through the process quickly, and will allow more complex projects to get the attention they require.

The meetings with stakeholders are essentially virtual team meetings. They will become incredibly effective and efficient by avoiding the time sink required to hold large task force sessions. Certainly, there will have to be small group meetings from time to time, but they will not need to be as frequent. The time freed up will allow team members to create wealth by focusing on their "day jobs."

A company's investment in a full-time Director of Growth role would be significant, as it would require a robust compensation package to attract the right person. However, depending on the size and scale of your organization, it could be a part-time job. In larger organizations, this person may need a support staff;

however, I would resist the urge to assign multiple people to the role. Finding one good person will be challenging enough.

An unintended positive outcome of this approach is that the successful Director of Growth becomes an interdisciplinary expert and one of the organization's most valued resources. He or she will be very promotable and should be able to assist executives in identifying areas ripe for opportunity and cost savings.

It's OK to Remain Conventional – If You Must

By all means, the conventional team or task force approach is very tempting. If you cannot pull yourself out of that model, please be mindful of two important factors to address to ensure the best results.

Firstly, make sure the team has the expected outcome of the task force in front of them, written and visible at all times: "This task force has been created to accomplish the following task: (insert task)." The team needs to be challenged to evaluate whether the task force is truly working toward the expected outcome. Way too often, task forces get blown off course by the hot air in the room.

Secondly, early on, conduct an effort to impact review of every project. Far too often, projects that require almost no effort to complete are held hostage to the process. It might be as simple as just do it and move on.

Some projects – which could easily be executed – are delayed for weeks or months because they are not deemed as urgent as other competing projects. The team can get so tied into the formality of the process that they forget to reach for the easily-grasped $100 bills that are flying by.

I have seen projects that are worth hundreds of thousands of dollars annually be delayed for over a year because the team just couldn't get it done. When the team finally gets to evaluate the opportunity or proposition, it only takes less than one hour to complete. The real tragedy is that the team member who was responsible for the project may have known from the beginning that it would take less than one hour, but he or she was unable to get the project addressed.

You may think that my previous paragraph might be overblown or exaggerated. Trust me – these types of examples are more frequent than anyone wants to admit. They end up being covered up, for fear that those responsible will be embarrassed. There's that old fear of embarrassment, raising its ugly head again.

Execution in the Supply Chain

Executives are always in search of the silver bullet, the panacea, that will make all the problems in the operations area go away. Billions of dollars are spent, and millions of hours are invested in such initiatives. Most of us have heard some of the manufacturing buzzwords: "Lean," "Total Quality Management," "Six Sigma," and more.

Let me define those terms, because we will use them.

Lean is a rather ubiquitous term in industry that describes the effort to eliminate waste in the supply chain. Often the words "manufacturing" or "enterprise" are added to better describe the effort.

Total Quality Management (TQM) is another rather common term, but was used more widely in the 1990s. It stands for continued improvement in the quality of every task or endeavor in an organization. I was trained in the Philip Crosby school of TQM and even became a certified trainer myself. It was one of the most overblown endeavors I experienced in my career. I'll cover the subject in more detail later in this text.

Six Sigma is yet another term that describes a quality-focused approach using measurement to eliminate errors. From its humble beginnings at Motorola less than 45 years ago, it has become an industry in and of itself.

Where Are the Real Savings?

The results of the initiatives are impressive. The return on investment, when executed properly, is noteworthy. The problem is that, in most cases, the approach is flawed.

Here is what often happens. Your company's CEO or supply chain leader, hears about Lean, or a similar system, at a seminar or reads about it in a book. He or she likes the concept, and hires a team of gurus (outside consultants). However, the mission of those consultants is to return a huge bucket of money to **their** company. Yes, their company is no different than your company. They are in business to make a profit and return better-than-average results to their company shareholders. Yes, they will show you the Promised Land, but they will bundle on unneeded training and procedures. They will make it more complex than necessary.

You will get improved results. Unless, of course, there is an issue with corporate advocacy. If there are too many failures, it will be far too easy to excuse them as flaws in corporate oversight. Then, your gurus will recommend remedial consulting, and that, of course, requires additional investment. But since you are in so far, why not dump another pile of cash into the exercise?

I cannot even count the number of times that "efficiency gurus" have blamed lack of leadership support as the reason that their project failed. That's probably the case in many instances, but shouldn't we strive for a solution that is much more resilient while also improving performance?

Go It Alone

Improved execution seems like the simplest thing to realize, yet it often is viewed as the hardest thing to complete. When you unbundle the drivers of inefficiency, there are almost always obvious, easy fixes that are revealed. Improving execution is hard, because it takes discipline and presence on the plant floor – an approach that makes most executives queasy.

Simply stated, most executives are uncomfortable on the plant floor. They are out of their element there, and prefer to avoid such situations.

I have found that when you go it alone, without external involvement, while employing the proper discipline with management support, the results are much more dramatic. And, the savings will be significantly more meaningful. If you are uncomfortable in the plant, find a person on your team who enjoys interaction on the floor. Put them to work to deliver your objective.

The added bonus is that the team develops a sense of ownership by adopting this approach. The empowerment of creating internally driven solutions to challenging dilemmas is liberating. In contrast, the use of outside consultants is often viewed as dictatorial and makes the team members feel inadequate and disenfranchised.

The Management Challenge

I have offered a management challenge to over two dozen different managers on over two dozen occasions. The challenge? Stand in an area of the plant and observe – for a full day. Managers laugh at that simple suggestion, but no one has ever made it through a complete day. In fact, most can barely make it through an hour.

A decade ago, I was convinced by some managers to dispatch a maintenance expert to a struggling plant. We were having difficulty with a specific type of equipment. I agreed that he would stay in the plant the entire time and watch, to find out what led to the equipment breaking down. We all knew that the equipment was breaking, but we just kept sending people in to repair it. In my view, the only way to remediate the situation was to watch the apparatus in operation and see how and why it was breaking.

When he arrived, I happened to be visiting the facility. He and I spoke, and he agreed to "hit the floor."

But an hour later, I went on an unguided plant tour and found that two of the three units were down. I asked where our expert was, and no one seemed to know.

I found him in the office. I advised him that two pieces of equipment were down; he seemed surprised, and indicated he had been on the floor an hour before and everything was running smoothly. He had decided to come to the office to check his email.

Some of the best and brightest managers I have ever worked with find that just observing for long periods of time is an impossible task. I suspect that it has to do with boredom. Nevertheless, if you don't see what led to the failure, you can't correct the situation. Observation is the best approach that I have found to determine root causes of breakdowns. Once the cause is found, corrective action can be taken.

Ask an Expert: They Are in Your Plant

Normally, your operators will be extremely engaged in plant activities, and they can provide valuable insight. And keep in mind that the people who actually do the manual work in your company may be more loyal than you might think.

However, if there has been mismanagement, they can become disgruntled. Huge chasms in management-labor relations may need to be bridged. Talk to your people; treat them with the same dignity and respect that you expect, and watch what happens.

People at lower levels of the organization want their jobs to go as easily and smoothly as possible, so they are interested in streamlining processes. They are also fonts of knowledge about operations. However, because most executives feel they cannot identify with the hourly workers, they will allow surrogates to speak with those on the floor. Beware – far too often, surrogates have their own agendas and do not allow the flow of information to move upward.

Remember, in most cases the hourly mindset is: "This is a job, I get paid to be here; if they want me to stay over, then they will pay me extra." Simply stated, it is a very transactional relationship. Still, the workers want their hours to be as free of frustration as possible. Moreover, deep down, they do care, but frustration and lack of empowerment stifles their enthusiasm.

If you want improved execution, it requires three things:

- Focus
- Discipline
- Measurement

Assign a "champion" who connects with the "people." Give them a goal to deliver the results you are looking for with detailed expectations. You must give this champion the opportunity to assess and evaluate drivers of performance. In my experience, failures on the plant floor are often the result of decisions or perceived mandates from third parties that drive cost overruns and waste.

Rather than a defined position, this is a person who loves digging in and enjoys the challenge of solving problems. They delight in keeping score and winning. You might have twenty of these people working on their own specific issue. It's not a role; it's a way of life.

Give the effort a snappy name; that usually gets people excited. I personally do not believe that a name for the initiative is essential, but if it helps make the effort successful, so be it. You might even want to put in some sort of gain-sharing program that allows the team to benefit from the progress made.

If handled properly, such programs cost little. The accelerated results will more than pay for the program costs.

Once you know the landscape of what you need to fix, corrective action can begin. That will require a high level of discipline, because Fetal Position Syndrome (covered in a future chapter) is a huge risk. Having discipline will drive a change; and the people on the plant floor – if they understand and have some "skin in the game" – will respond. This "skin" can be a positive reward or negative consequences. Both approaches work, and a good combination of the two will keep employees engaged.

Measure It

Almost everyone likes to see a tote board. As a child, I remember watching the Jerry Lewis Telethon all night long to see how high the number would rise. We keep scores at sporting events; we sit and watch election returns. As part of the process of measuring your initiative, use a visual measurement system.

If your champion did his or her job correctly, there will be motivation and momentum. The goals will be achieved, along with significant bonuses. Never underestimate the value of momentum on the plant floor.

Some remedies are easier than anyone could imagine. Once, a few days after I joined a company, it was clear to me that they were throwing a lot of money into the garbage by leaving supplies and tools out in the plant to be lost or stolen. I simply went out on the plant one evening with some buckets and collected items from garbage cans and work areas. I captured thousands of dollars worth of oils, sprays, tools, gloves and wipes; five large buckets in all. Included were two tools worth several hundred dollars each.

The next day, I brought every hourly employee into the lunch room and showed them where all their profit sharing was going. Ten years later, hourly personnel still talked about that crazy manager – me – who dug through the garbage.

More importantly, the plant's operating costs started to decline as efficiency increased. One might challenge the correlation of the garbage collection to efficiency improvement. Still, many of the hourly personnel noted that, for the first time, someone really cared about controlling waste. While many other modifications were made during that plant's improvement process, the garbage collection is the one that is most remembered.

Another example of an area to work on is safety. Years ago, I attended a holiday party at a company that I had had the pleasure of leading for almost a decade. The team was days from completing a full year without an accident. When I mentioned that feat in my comments to the group, the entire assembly erupted with enthusiasm. It was exhilarating. Powerful, I thought. I am convinced that measurement fueled the enthusiasm and excitement. It's been fifteen years and I can still feel that energy.

So raucous was the response a catering manager from the hotel entered the room to see what was going on. He commented, "Wow, they love you." I responded, "Maybe so, but they love winning even more and this is what winning sounds like."

External Support Can Be Valuable

If you cannot figure out how to fix a problem yourself, then go to one of the gurus. They will definitely help move your company toward a more efficient plant environment. It is far better to go the route of a third-party facilitated effort than to not address the opportunity at all. If you do choose to engage a third party, get all the cost details up front, and agree on measures and returns before you start. If possible, put some of their compensation at risk.

Remember, the gurus have a very different objective than you do. They want results so that you are satisfied, but they also seek a sustained assignment that will lead to more work. You, on the other hand, want optimal performance as quickly as possible. The paradox is that many companies will happily spend $200,000 or more per plant to implement a program like Lean, but will not fund $75,000 for an internal champion to get sustainable results that are achieved faster.

General Operations: Tips for Better Execution

With over 45 years of operational experience, I have learned some easy tips:

Walk the plants, work sites, retail outlets and distribution centers – and not with an entourage. Go out alone and talk to your people; connect with them. They will love it and will happily share areas of opportunity for improving execution. Dress appropriately; that means wearing what the team is wearing. Showing up in a suit or dress will only widen the perceived gap between you and the hourly employees. When you become real to your people, they will be motivated and deliver great results. If you can't get out to the plant floor, hire an executive who can.

One year, my company was having significant struggles. There was not going to be any profit sharing or bonuses; any raises would be small or nonexistent. Looking to find something to celebrate, the brand team decided to recognize a milestone for one of the brands. The fact that the milestone had been achieved six months late was lost on them. Nevertheless, the brand team decided to have a huge cake made and have a party to celebrate the accomplishment. After the party, the leftover cake was placed in the lunchroom for the hourly people to enjoy, but with no explanation of the milestone. The overwhelming response from the plant was that the company's poor performance was the fault of the "fat cats." And instead of fixing the problems, they were partying. Throwing the leftovers in the lunchroom insulted the plant workers. As they saw it, they did the work but got the scraps.

I brought my concern to the brand team, and they seemed baffled by the outrage from the plant workers. They simply couldn't understand why half-eaten cake left on a break room table with no other communication could be construed as demeaning by a group of hourly employees who were not getting raises or bonuses. As they saw it, they were sharing the fruits of the celebration with the entire company.

Check the quality, sanitation and human safety records of the operations; these are *the intangibles.* If those areas are in check, the odds are that you have a fairly efficient operation.

If they are not up to standards, then you probably have a great deal of improvement to be made in your core operational areas.

Plant scheduling can make or break an operation's ability to be efficient. Simply stated, if your company hasn't focused on scheduling, you will probably discover there are ways to improve operations. Use a visual tool to be able to see the schedule. Once you can see the schedule in blocks or a similar fashion, you can quickly understand where the opportunity for improvement lies. Numbers on a piece of paper can't deliver that clarity.

Most processes have multiple steps. Trying to create a plant's scheduling in one step will be a failed effort. Unbundle the schedule into distinct steps, and the results will be significant.

Never implement a program that is simply being done to "check a box." If you implement something, make sure you stick with it. Keep it fresh and get feedback from the employees. Long-tenured employees have seen the "management fads" come and go. They are very skeptical and see them as wastes of money that could be shared with the underappreciated workers. We as managers have so much going on that our perspectives become clouded. We check our boxes and fill filing cabinets with reports that never get read.

At one job early in my career, we were asked to walk through the plant and make observations. The observation report had to be filled in every day. The intent was that management would read the reports, and then do something about any deficiencies. After it was clear to me that nothing was being done as a result of the reports, I tested the system. In my report one day, I wrote,

"A $50 reward if anyone asks me about my report by close of business today." I wrote this every day for 30 days… and I was never called. So, I presented my reports to the senior manager to demonstrate the flaw in the program. It was eliminated immediately.

Operations are almost always very simple when you unbundle them. I mentioned to a co-worker that I had been doing a certain task for 30 years and that it was really quite simple. He responded that he had been doing the same task for 20 years and that he found it extremely complex. I responded, "You are not doing it right." Often, individuals want to make things appear to be complex, so management stays away. Do not be fooled. The saying, "It's not rocket science" is usually very appropriate.

Determine three or four key measures that drive operation performance; make sure everyone knows what is being measured, and why. Ensure that everyone knows what the goal is, and put a means of measuring daily performance in place. Almost everyone wants to win; but if you're not keeping score, how will you know if you win?

Try to make it engaging and enjoyable. Some of the best execution improvement programs I have seen in my career have been taken from our everyday lives. Safetyland, an unlicensed version of the game Candyland®, was one such program. The previous year, the group had used Wheel of Fortune as their safety program basis. In both cases, the workforce was divided into teams and took weekly turns "playing" the games that the programs were based upon. Playing the games quickly became popular with employees, and teams reveled in the experience. The facility in question – using fun and unique methods – went almost 1,000 days without an accident. The plant then followed that performance with another 300-plus accident-free days (and counting).

They had no expert safety gurus in the facility. They simply set a goal, engaged the workforce, and kept the program fun and visible. In doing so, they had created a culture where accidents were unacceptable. Those who were injured due to poor work habits were viewed in an unfavorable light.

The results spoke for themselves. Of note is the fact that the lone accident at the facility during the four-year span involved a temporary employee who had been on the job only three days. That spoke to a different hurdle for the management team.

Six Sigma or One Sigma?

As mentioned previously, Six Sigma is another operational measurement system used to tighten tolerances and ensure that consistency and reliability are core competencies. It definitely has its place and is an extremely powerful tool.

Unfortunately, not unlike many "best practices" in business, Six Sigma is overblown. It often takes us to a level of precision that is not sustainable or is extremely costly to make sustainable. When applied to a process or a specification that does not require that level of tolerance, it is a waste.

Six Sigma uses the following example, which I have heard over and over in my career: "If we were in the business of giving birth to babies and we dropped one out of every hundred, it would result in terrible consequences."

The reality is, unless you are in the baby birthing business, that is a ridiculous notion. It has no business in a conversation about business, and simply does not apply to our efforts to execute better. If we put the same controls and expense into making toothpicks as we do in "birthing babies," very few people would be able to afford to enjoy a nice bacon-wrapped scallop at a cocktail party.

To bring the 99-percent-baby-birthing metaphor to life in business, I suggest that Six Sigma is vitally important when applicable, but I believe that One Sigma is optimal in 99 percent of instances. The notion of measuring is key; however, the notion of measuring precision levels that exceed a process's ability to commercially repeat is a fool's errand.

Try this exercise; you probably need a break from reading, anyway. Grab a piece of paper. Place it a few feet away from you. Now toss a penny on the paper. If you have placed it properly, you probably can hit the paper every time. Take the paper and fold it in thirds and then in half again. Attempt to throw the same penny. My experience is you will rarely ever hit the paper. It has not just become six times harder; it is now six times 60 times more difficult.

Certainly, that reference is metaphorical; however, tolerances or specifications that are tighter than what is commercially viable are real concerns. The fact that a scientist can replicate something in the laboratory has little bearing on what will happen in the real world. And, specifications that can be achieved on brand-new equipment might be impossible to meet after that equipment has been used in commercial operation – even when best-in-class maintenance is performed regularly.

Balancing Act

Frankly, it is a bit of a balancing act when considering what tolerances or specifications to follow. Obviously, we must consider a number of factors, including customer expectations, safety, and the cost of waste. If the equipment or the process is incapable of delivering the desired outcome, an organization must decide where the tipping point is.

Specialized equipment or processes that can achieve the desired outcome must be considered, but can you afford them even if they do exist? It's easy to either overtax your operation with unreasonable expectations or to under-challenge your operation, allowing opportunity and savings to go out the door with the garbage. I don't believe there is a textbook solution. Finding the proper balance takes a person with a good gut instinct and a bit of an edge.

One organization that I was associated with had a long-standing product formulation that had been produced successfully for over a decade. It was mandated, by the rarely seen but often enabled ***They***, to implement a new artificial tolerance, and the company found that it was incapable of meeting the new specification. The scientists cried foul, insisting that it was a plant issue. Yet, after significant investment in process control equipment, the results were the same.

The scientists again called on the operations team to deliver. In a gutsy move, the operations turned the plant over to the scientists – and interestingly enough, they could not meet the new specifications either.

The phrase "commercially viable" is an important one to consider when creating specifications and tolerances. All the Six Sigma rhetoric in the world will not change the viability of a process or specification. If your business requires a Six Sigma level of precision, so be it. Hopefully you are in a market segment that will allow the cost required to execute such precision to be factored into profit margins.

Excuse Management

There is an old saying: "Excuses are like assholes; everyone has one." I would revise that saying by adding, "And assholes have excuses for everything." Failures in execution usually end up wrapped in excuses. Much like the Fundamental Attribution Error that we discussed earlier, responsible parties tend to search for ways to blame others or the environment. That debilitating word, "rationalization," comes into play here. We rationalize that the expectation did not meet the realities. I would urge you to consider the fact that professionals should fully understand the realities of the expectations before making a commitment.

The most frustrating excuse is that there was a misunderstanding of the expectations. The more chronic the excuse-monger, the more aggravating and debilitating are the impact of his or her failures. Usually, an excuse-maker's conversations start with, "Oh, I thought…" or "I misunderstood what you wanted."

The best way to avoid excuse management is to eliminate those chronic offenders from your team. There will always be noise and a lack of clarity if you allow them to hang around. Expel them, and the entire organization will breathe a sigh of relief.

The following guidelines will eliminate the opportunity for excuse management:

- Clearly write what the expectation is.
- Agree on milestones that may be needed to successfully ensure that the project's progress can be accurately monitored.
- Agree on who is going to be the responsible individual.
- Agree on a date or dates when results will be delivered.
- Make the responsible party read the previous four steps back to you.
- Ensure that the party responsible and the accountable party are the same person, or at least that they are two people in the same reporting line.
- The number one excuse for a project miss is "external factors." Advise project teams that any such events must be brought to your attention as they occur. No surprises.

The above seems very simple, and may seem unnecessary to put into print. When you unbundle, just about everything is trouble-free. And it should be unnecessary to adopt this kind of overt handholding. So, in a perfect world it wouldn't be needed, but realistically, it is required if you seek optimal performance. It might feel a bit draconian, but when you put it through a filter of clear communication so that neither party forgets, it becomes very powerful and empowering.

Gumby-ism

The best executors are like Gumby®. They are very flexible. To become great at execution, we must be able to make changes on the fly. Being nimble is a virtue that is touted by many, but some people are simply not good at it. People love to "talk the talk," but when they are stretched, they seem to fall well short.

Some simply do not have the street smarts or edge to pull off seemingly risky and unproven modifications. Others are afraid of failure or become confused. If you have created the correct culture where failure and risk-taking are embraced, you'll be able to flex.

Complete Everything That Can Be Done Now

We tend to live in a world with "to-do" lists. I am a big advocate of writing things down, and an even bigger believer in project and KPI (Key Performance Indicators) trackers, but "to-do" lists can become overblown and clutter our lives. We tend to write everything down, even simple tasks. I find that, more often than not, getting simple tasks **off my plate before they get on my plate** lets me avoid plate-clearing exercises.

Once, an associate of mine had requested approval to proceed with a project. I stopped by his desk and advised him to call another associate, Bob, for coordination. He pulled out a sticky-note, wrote "Call Bob," and then added Bob's phone number.

I asked him, "Why did you just write that down?"

"I didn't want to forget," he answered.

"What are you doing right now?" I asked.

"Nothing."

"Why don't you call him now?" I asked.

"I guess I could," came the answer. He picked up the phone and began dialing.

I returned five minutes later, and my associate had concluded his call and had his answer. I could not resist asking him why he wrote down Bob's phone number on the Post-it.

"I always do that, so I have the number with the note." He smiled.

"But you clearly knew his number from memory," I stated.

"I guess it is just a habit. Normally, I don't know the phone numbers, so I have to write them down so I don't forget."

This is one example of how "to-dos" can clutter our lives. Yes, reminders are important, and lists are essential, but making those lists as short as possible lets us eliminate confusion in our lives.

Efficiency consultants are always talking about plate-clearing exercises and time management tools. These might be great ideas for some – maybe even you – but assuming that your co-workers or subordinates think exactly as you do is a big mistake. We certainly would not buy an associate who was six feet tall the same company logo coat that we would buy for an associate who was only 5'4". It's obvious that their sizes are different; they do not look the same. Newsflash: they probably do not think the same either, and they probably operate in different ways to be effective. Again, one size does not fit all. We'll cover more on that in a future chapter.

Create a culture where "Gumby-ism" is fostered, and your team will ramp up execution and make it a core competency. That will go a long way in creating the unbundled environment you seek.

Combustion Check – FUEL EXECUTION

Before lighting the execution fuse, ask yourself:

1. What would it look like if you gave execution the full burn?
2. Can you keep the fuel mix simple and efficient, avoiding unnecessary complexity?
3. Can you resist igniting task forces that drain energy without adding power?
4. Are you committed to maintaining a stable combustion chamber – finding balance in execution?
5. Are you ready to embrace a flexible, stretchable culture where "Gumby-ism" fuels innovation?

Answering these questions ensures that your execution engine burns cleanly and efficiently, propelling initiatives forward with controlled energy.

5

Communication: Conducting the Spark

Communication is the most important
skill any leader can possess.
– Richard Branson, founder of the Virgin Group

Have you…

Ever experienced the confusion that results from miscommunication?

Suffered the consequences of incomplete or inaccurate messaging?

What if…

You could transform into a communications Olympian?

Your company could thrive, using straightforward, purposeful communication?

In my 45 years of experience, and in talking to other business executives, an almost universal perception is that communication is seen as a weakness. In some cases, this perception is a reality; in others, it is more of a crutch. It's used by some people to justify blunders. There is almost always room for improvement when it comes to communication. Yet, when we attempt to optimize communication, it's easy to achieve the point of diminishing returns. To define that point, it's when the benefits of improving something is far outweighed by the investment required.

Criticizing or challenging communication enhancement programs is often considered heresy. The fact is that the need may not be enough to warrant the perceived urgency, the cost, or the drag on the organization. Ironically, I have found the cure for a communication issue often can be worse than the problem itself.

I find it interesting that an individual can employ the best communication practices, while being both engaging and articulate, and yet still have their message unheard. And then, another individual, with nothing but a juicy piece of gossip, will have their message run through an organization or community at top speed. That phenomenon has much more to do with passion than it does with actual communication.

Right People, Right Communication

Getting communications right can be a struggle, but that struggle can be greatly avoided by having the right people on the team. When we create a productive culture within our organization and staff it appropriately, we win most of the communication battle.

I think a great example can be found at your local university. Most universities are a mix of young traditional students, fresh from high school, and non-traditional, more mature adults who are expanding their education. Those non-traditional students seem to grasp the subject matter being communicated by the professor much more easily than many of their younger counterparts. Is it a language barrier or an age issue? I think the answer is "neither." The fact is, almost all of the non-traditional students are there to learn and better themselves, while many of the traditional students are not as motivated. Same communication, same intellect levels – but with different motivation, and different results.

Recently, I was shopping at my local Wegman's supermarket. I go to that specific store because I enjoy the experience. The company has created a culture of empowerment, and dealing with their staff members is enjoyable. Notably, Fortune magazine has just named Wegman's to the list of 100 Best Companies to Work For.

As I checked out, I congratulated the cashier, wondering if she would even have a clue what I was referring to. She knew all about the award, and the twinkle in her eyes demonstrated the pride she felt. Two other employees in the area came over and joined the conversation; they beamed as they shared their excitement with me as well. These were all entry-level workers, but they already knew the news and were energized by it. There was no question that the passion these folks had for their company was extremely powerful.

I thought that this organization must have, within its culture, a fairly robust communication program fueled by passionate employees. I then wondered if Wegman's paid a premium to attract and retain these folks. As I researched the company a bit more, I found that the market's success had very little to do with compensation and everything to do with culture.

Throughout my career, I have been fortunate to be part of many wonderful organizations. One thing is very clear: Communication, people, passion, and morale are directly linked. The more passionate people are, the more effective the communications program is, and the better the morale. I believe the elements are symbiotic. Poor communication leads to bad morale, but even the best communication will not fix a morale problem if the people are not passionate about the company.

The Wrong People Kill Effective Communication

Great companies that have passionate people often make one key mistake that kills communication. They allow misfits to remain part of the organization for too long. Misfits are those individuals who don't fit the company's culture or don't care enough to try. These malcontents are morale killers, and they create communication challenges.

In the past, I worked for an absolutely wonderful company that had an extremely parental culture. The vast majority of their employees were both loyal and engaged, but we allowed laggards to hang around under the guise of fairness and of being family. These slackers polluted the employee pool, and the entire team suffered as a result.

We introduced a new health care program. We planned it properly and created a communication protocol that was extremely robust. It started with face-to-face, midsize group meetings where I explained the highlights of the program. Every employee signed in and was given pertinent information, both in writing and verbally. The final part of the meeting was a Q & A session. One of the key elements was to have small group meetings where employees could bring their spouses in to speak with an advisor about the changes in the program.

These meetings were followed up with voicemail reminders and fact sheet articles. Additionally, every supervisor was given in-depth training so they could effectively answer questions from employees. By almost all accounts, the communication program met its objective.

However, a small handful of employees claimed to have not understood the program and added that communication had been poor.

Every employee in that group had three things in common:

- Each had attended the introduction meeting and had signed in.
- Each had failed to sign up for a small group session.
- Each had been rated "Needs Improvement" by their reviewer in their most recent evaluation.

If a company wants to improve communications, the first step is to make sure they have the right people in the organization. But having the right people is only the start; the wrong people must be exited from the company. It is up to management to create and maintain an empowering culture of communication.

Poor Leadership Kills Effective Communication

My first job out of college was with a company that had serious morale problems. The fact that it was a union plant made the situation more difficult, but not impossible to rectify. Management decided that something needed to be done. They brought in a third party consultant to talk to the plant employees and find out what was driving the poor morale. (As a young, naive person, I wondered why we in management didn't simply ask the employees ourselves.)

After a survey and a number of analyses were completed, we determined that the perception of the workforce was that management did not care about them or the output of the plant.

Actually, management was scared to death of the union workers. Other than the managers whose jobs involved actually working in and around the plant, members of the management team avoided going anywhere near the plant or the workers.

The fear and lack of trust between the two groups created the perception that management did not care. As a fairly new addition to the team, I definitely came to believe that management would have much preferred not even to **have** a plant – except that they needed products to sell.

In an amazing feat of utter stupidity, the plant's general manager, Art, decided to buy pencils for all workers that said, "Art Cares." Every employee received a pencil. A few days later, Art decided to actually enter the plant to ask the employees how they liked their pencils. He donned a red hard hat – and quickly found that no one knew who he was.

Committed to connecting with the employees, Art returned to his office and had his assistant arrange to have the hard hat engraved with his name. After a few days, Art returned to the plant. Although that attempt to relate with the workforce was deemed a failure, Art was not ready to give up. A mandate came down to the supervisors; we were to meet with each member of our team and tell them how much Art cared.

Most of the senior supervisors had, years before, lost any motivation to have a dialogue with the workers. As such, they ignored the request. But I and one or two others actually fulfilled the request. To say the results were disappointing would be a huge understatement, but I did learn some new words to describe management that have remained with me through my entire career.

The chosen communication method between the union and management was a formalized grievance. The money and time wasted discussing, defending, and negotiating these grievances paralyzed the company. It also served to further erode communication and widen the chasm between management and labor. It was no surprise when the company decided to close the facility seven years later. The only shocker was that it took the company so long to do it.

It was publicized in the media that the union had forced the closure due to their unwillingness to cooperate. But the closure had as much, if not more, to do with poor management than anything the union ever did.

The parent company had huge union problems. I believe the vast majority of those issues were the result of a weak management team. Management had implemented poor communication programs due to deeply flawed and adversarial relationships. The company had filed for bankruptcy protection twice in 15 years.

That company's example is certainly a stark one. While it is the most outrageous specimen of poor communication I have ever experienced, there are plenty of others out there that cause disruption and erode trust. Poor communication typically creates bundled scenarios that adversely affect company performance.

If we are going to create a good communication program, there are a few principles that need to be understood and followed.

Words Carry Less than 10 Percent of the Message

At least half of communication is body language. Eye rolls, smiles, and furrowed brows all speak volumes. Your posture, hand gestures, and even the clothing you wear all contribute to the communication experience. When you decide not to engage in face-to-face communication, you risk confusion of your message, particularly if you are communicating a delicate topic.

The advent of the video conference has made it extremely convenient to have an "almost in the room" experience from halfway around the world. But it is still important to make sure that you are aware of your body language, since it comprises over half of the communication experience. When your body language is poor, even in a video conference, communication suffers.

Over 40 percent of communication is tone and tenor. People are great at adding their own perception of tone and tenor to written communication. This is particularly true when the receiver is predisposed to dislike or not trust the sender of the message.

Try this test: Grab a piece of written communication – perhaps an email that was sent from someone you don't particularly trust. Read it, and then change the name on the email to a person you admire or revere. Re-read it. Chances are that you will see the narrative in a far better light.

To illustrate this theory, I did this with political speeches. During a planning meeting, I read a couple lines from a State of the Union speech from Barack Obama, making sure to mention the author. The team was about half conservative and half liberal; understandably, about half liked it and agreed with the statement, and the other half did not. I then read a very similar statement from an anonymous source. I asked the team for their reaction, and the response was about the same. I revealed that the anonymous orator was a stalwart of the right-wing mentality, Ronald Reagan. My point was made.

Back when emails started to become a standard part of our lives, my typing skills were limited. Because of that, I opted to use ALL CAPS. One day, someone asked me why I was always yelling in my emails.

That's a bit of a joke, but misreading the intent of a document is a very serious matter. In many cases, misunderstanding the intent of a written document can result in significant organizational conflict and disruption.

When putting something in writing, the author of a document should review it through the eyes of their sharpest critic.

While written communication usually is fairly clear, it only takes one instance of misunderstanding to create serious implications.

A simple filter of review will ensure that the wick of the powder keg is not unintentionally lit. Whenever possible, communication should be face-to-face. That offers the opportunity for 100 percent accuracy of the communication's dynamics, and it allows for immediate feedback. Anything less than a face-to-face meeting can result in a misunderstanding; yet, electronic communication is what many prefer. People tend to hide behind technology; they'll send emails, or choose to call into a meeting rather than to be present or video in.

Since we do not know people's motivations, we are left to draw our own conclusions as to why a person chooses a particular communication method. As such, when we tend to like a person, we assume positive intent. Conversely, when we're predisposed to not like a person, we interpret their communication in the worst possible light.

Communication Is a Web

Many of the experts advocate that communication should move up and down in the organization. They specifically cite the need for executives to drive communications down to the lowest level of the organization and also to allow for communication to bubble back up to the highest level.

I personally like to look at communications as a web that goes up, down, across and diagonally. It is equally important that communication occurs across the organization in addition to going up and down.

A healthy web of communication starts with awareness. You need to make sure each employee in your company understands that their ability to communicate, both as a part of a team and individually, is crucial. Stress that their ability to clearly convey their thoughts is essential, not only to the success of the entire business, but also to their own success with the company. Once each person understands that they have a vested interest in how they communicate, they will become much better communicators.

Harnessing the Power of Informal Communication

It is also essential that we understand the perceptions of other groups when it comes to communication. How do we engage them to get them excited about our project or topic? Keep in mind that the other party is most motivated when they, too, have a personal stake in the outcome. Reaching out to other groups can be quite simple, and it starts with understanding the power of informal communication.

Informal communication happens everywhere. Interdepartmental and intradepartmental communications are constantly occurring. Weekend plans and updates on the wonderful things in our personal lives are common discussions. Favorite sports teams' performances and children's activities are other topics of informal communication.

Informal conversations happen during and after work hours. They happen in offices, break rooms, hallways, parking lots, restaurants, bars, and just about everywhere else. However, these conversations can become rumor mills that clutter the communication system. Most people find juicy gossip far more exciting than mundane, work–related topics.

Rumors in the workplace need to be quelled immediately and replaced with business-related facts and constructive dialogue. I recognize that people will want to talk about their outside lives at the office; that type of communication is also part of a healthy work-life balance. Nevertheless, it often consumes communication within the office, and we must ensure that it stays in its proper place.

One morning, as I sat in my office, I overheard conversation after conversation from the office next door. My co-worker loved to fish – as do I – and I heard all about his weekend fishing activity. He tends to have a rather boisterous voice, so even an office away, his open-door conversations were easily overheard. At 10:30, almost three hours into the day, I entered his office and questioned if he had anything to talk about other than fishing. He looked at me perplexed and said, "What?" I honestly believe he failed to realize that he had accomplished nothing that morning other than superfluous banter about his angling skills. That is an example of informal communication overwhelming the workplace. It happens all too often.

Certainly, some co-workers are more apt to engage in these types of exchanges than others. An efficient way to help regulate this type of informal conversation within the office is to have employees on the floor to help control it.

Appoint your most popular, influential (and probably very talkative) associates as informal communication ambassadors or cheerleaders. Be sure these ambassadors understand how important it is that non-work-related conversations be kept at an appropriate level. Also make sure they realize that they are now responsible for helping maintain a level of informal communication in their respective team or department.

Teach these team members creative skills that will help with their new responsibilities, like how to weave important company messages into informal conversations. This new talent can be an effective communication management tool. Before you know it, all the unproductive chatter will become opportunities for loyalty-building.

I learned to make sure I screened my assistants to confirm that they could be an advocate for the organization. I found that these individuals could make a huge difference in the attitude of the team.

There will be no better person in the organization to become your voice than your administrative support employee. These individuals hold a vital role in communication, because they tend to be viewed as approachable. Due to the fact that they are privy to sensitive information, they become viewed as influencers. The trick is to make sure that both you and your assistant actively champion the effort.

External Communication

Every company should have a formal external communication plan. Depending upon your type of business – and your goals and objectives – you can tailor such a plan to your specific needs. You can either select an in-house communications team, an external communications consultant, or a combination of the two for a hybrid approach. There are plenty of experts in the field.

There are three important, often overlooked, pieces to external communication.

1. Every company should promote themselves. Ask yourself: What is your company good at, and what makes you different? Make it a priority to let the world know. There is a contrasting school of thought that it's better to stay under the radar, but the only reason I see to stay under the radar is if you're doing something you're embarrassed about. If that is the case, I urge you to re-read Chapter One.

Twenty seven years ago, I was heading logistics and customer service for a large consumer product goods company. We never talked about our service record other than to demean it, or make excuses for our poor results. While there was certainly room for improvement, I always felt that our service was better than our customers' perception of it.

I regularly heard from sales personnel and customers alike that our service was subpar, and these people would cite a specific competitor as "best in class." When our company bought that competitor, we discovered two important facts. Fact one: They had been positively marketing their service, both internally and externally, for years. Fact two: They had started an objective to talk about their cutting-edge approach to customer service. But a quick peek at the numbers revealed they had far worse service metrics than we did. They had more late trucks, more errant orders, more shorted products, and more damage than we did. But their intentionally self-promoted "best in class" image masked the reality – poor performance.

They had a great strategy. Bundle up an impressive story, put a bow and ribbon on it, and start talking. It was a self-fulfilling prophecy. (The power of "controlled bundling" will be covered in the final chapter.) We, on the other hand, had engaged in our own self-fulfilling exercise – but it was far less productive, since it started with excuses.

Remember that self-promotion will generate positive results in many areas. In addition to promoting brands and services, publicizing the company's culture – along with its social and environmental efforts – should help bolster the company's image in the community. Self-promotion will also help attract new employees. When a company needs community support, the organization that has a truly positive public image and is viewed as a caring company will be treated much more favorably than one that is perceived as putting on an act.

2. As long as you have one employee, you have an opportunity for an in-house company ambassador. Who better to trumpet the great qualities of your company than your own people? I advocate instituting a formal program – sign up individuals who will be charged with getting the message out.

I like to refer to these people as evangelists. Unlike the religious variety, these folks will engage others in whatever topic the company wants to communicate. It can be championing specific products and brands, or talking about the great things the company is doing for the community.

We spend huge amounts of money formally marketing our brands; why not informally market the brands and the company as well? When the employees truly believe in their employer and are urged to talk to others about them, great results occur.

3. There is immense power in the use of the internet and social media. I use Facebook, not because I love Facebook, but rather because I know it is a phenomenon that has great influence. It does not stop with that particular social media super-giant either. Online platforms such as Twitter (X), Instagram, Pinterest, and TikTok are being rapidly embraced by consumers of all ages. By gaining an understanding of these online applications and how they influence people, businesses can both gain a competitive advantage and avoid a competitive disadvantage.

The Internet: a Powerhouse of Good and Evil

It is important that all your employees understand the power of the internet and recognize the benefits as well as the risks. The internet and all social media sites are public. When you elect to post sensitive material, it is there for all to see. Just ask Anthony Weiner. If you are not familiar with Congressman Weiner's plight, you might want to Google him to get the details of his escapades. He was forced to resign from the House of Representatives for accidentally posting naked pictures of himself in a public forum on the internet.

Around the time of the Anthony Weiner scandal, I found that one of our company executives had posted a rather inappropriate comment on Facebook; I felt it could reflect poorly on the company. After some discussion, the executive apologized, promised never to do it again, and then promptly "unfriended" me on Facebook. Unfortunately, we were not effective in changing this executive's behavior. Instead of cleaning up his act, he chose to continue engaging in improper conduct. Ultimately, he and the organization were named in a lawsuit with one of his subordinates over inappropriate Facebook exchanges.

Hopefully, you can learn from my experience. Set a strict internet and social media policy and do not deviate from it. The internet is very powerful; it can make you and it can break you. Make sure you control it. Your social media and online conduct policy should be stated in writing, and it should be signed by all employees. Appropriate online behavior starts at the top of the company and should be embedded at every level. There is nothing personal or secret about the internet.

As social media programs have developed, companies increasingly use these tools to promote their products. Frankly, in most cases, the approach is too clinical or not entertaining enough. The companies that win are the ones that go out on the edge and create buzz for their products. I feel that if you want to use Facebook, Twitter (X), TikTok, or YouTube as promotion tools, you ought to consult with a person who is proficient with them. These people are usually young, tech-savvy, and passionate about social media. If you have teenage children at home, you might even have an expert sleeping in the bedroom down the hall.

The Words We Choose

Most leaders examine formal communications through the lens of how it will sound. They act as if an organization's messages will be engraved on a tombstone for all to see for all eternity… or until acid rain dissolves the stone.

They carefully choose the right words; the words that send the right message. The problem is, those words are usually not part of the average person's vocabulary. Before choosing your words, understand your audience. If you are speaking to Wall Street analysts, there is a semantic expectation that must be met. Failure to play that game correctly can result in eroded price-earnings (PE) multiples. On the flip side, when you are talking to the third-shift production team, different vocabulary words are probably more appropriate.

I find that the best approach in both instances is to "dumb it down," unless you know that your specific audience expects more intellectually stimulating language. That is particularly true when having internal discussions. Choose the simplest, most direct set of words possible. You will seem much more real to your audience, and that will yield better results.

Before any readers accuse me of being elitist, I proudly consider myself a master of the "dumb it down" approach. Frankly, I strongly prefer listening to a dumbed-down style speaker. He or she is direct, concise, and easy to understand. When I was a child, my father used very basic words with the appropriate tenor and tone to get his point across. There was never a question about his message.

Use Four-Letter Words with Great Regularity

I often joke about using four-letter words instead of four-syllable words. Some of the most powerful words in business are of the four-letter variety.

My favorite four-letter word is the **'F'** word... **free.** I love free stuff, and I love the fact that I live in a free society. My second favorite four-letter word is **love**. Simply stated, I love "love." I love it so much that I turned it into an acronym:

Live
Our
Values
Everyday

Another powerful four-letter word is **team**. Teams get things done, and a properly motivated team can achieve the seemingly impossible.

Inappropriate Four-Letter Words

There are some extremely detrimental four-letter words as well. The two worst four-letter words in business are **they** and **them.** These words are used to cast blame or to shift accountability. I have outlawed these words in my business, but amazingly, they continue to live on. A sample conversation:

"What went wrong?"

"They forgot to call the customer."

"Who are they?"

"Them."

"Who are them?"

"I guess I don't know."

"Go find out."

"They will get mad at me."

"Who are they?"

Think I am kidding? Watch for it. When you come across these words, eliminate their use from your company's lexicon. "They" or "them" should never be the answer to a question.

The other four-letter words I dislike are the four-letter contractions **can't** and **don't**. Typically, I find that the most common misuses of "can't" and "don't" are when an employee really means **won't**. "I can't do it" usually means "I won't do it." Likewise, "I couldn't" usually means "I didn't bother to."

My advice is to put a contract out on contractions.

Getting Emails Right

During my career, the most transformative changes in communication have been the advent of the internet and email. These innovations have made worldwide communications instantaneous. As with many productive innovations, people find methods to use them to their advantage. But often, there are disastrous outcomes.

My informal survey of business people suggests that many get an average of 100 or more emails per day. I am no exception.

I decided to catalog all of my emails for a month. I found that over 50 percent were emails that should not have been sent. These included many "reply to all" messages with the thought-provoking, one-syllable content of "Great!" Of the remaining emails, approximately one-third were "cover-your-ass" carbon copies. While it is important to cc people sometimes to ensure they're in the loop, it has gotten out of control.

In the end, I found that less than 20 percent of my daily messages actually contained content that was pertinent to me.

"Reply to all" and cc emails often go hand in hand. They create a logarithmic explosion. Let's say you send an email to 10 people and need a response from each, but only you need the information. If each of your recipients sends a "reply to all" message, a minimum of 90 unnecessary emails are immediately created. There would probably be more than that, as additional "reply to all" emails will probably be generated as further replies.

I have asked multiple people why they feel compelled to "reply to all" in emails. Most often, I hear, "It's just easier," or "I wanted to make sure everyone knew I replied." Thus, the continuation of the "cover-your-ass" mindset.

Even more concerning are what I call "firebomb" emails. These are the ones that create chaos within the organization. Oftentimes, the sender sends such an email intentionally, but with unintended consequences. Examples include: a message that addresses a sensitive subject; an email that criticizes or questions the competency of a different department, or a communication that challenges a decision made by a co-worker. Unfortunately, sometimes addressees may include superiors or third parties who should not have been copied (or at least, did not need to be copied).

People tend to become defensive when they feel like they are being attacked. Whether the email attack was intentional or unintentional, the inability to understand the immediate goal of the email creates stress on the team. Usually, such an email will result in a recipient sending a defensive firebomb email of their own.

What will make the situation worse is if the recipient decides to discuss the email with co-workers, reading it aloud and adding an offensive tone and tenor. Very possibly, the escalating conflict could have been avoided by re-reading the email with a more neutral tone.

Tips for Excellence in Email

Here are some simple rules for emailing that will help your organization:

Never send an email when you are angry. I advocate a cooling-off period before ever addressing any dicey topics. As we learned earlier in the chapter, text alone accounts for only 10 percent of communication; with emotions flowing, 10 percent isn't going to cut it. Take the direct, face-to-face approach. It always works best.

Never address a sensitive or emotionally charged topic via email. Email is never the appropriate format to discuss a sensitive subject. Such communication can create significant organizational strife. In addition, the tone, tenor and body language that the recipients use to read the email to their friends is usually exaggerated.

Eliminate the use of return receipts. They have no place in the business world. Does anyone actually send them back?

Mandate that "reply to all" emails are not allowed. It is far too easy to hit "reply to all" and clog the email server with unimportant gibberish. If it is important enough to send, make your employees type in each recipient's name. Today, the autofill feature makes this an easy task. Cultures that allow "reply to all" emails create drag in the organization. Inevitably, because someone is so used to emailing that way, embarrassing mistakes occur.

Recently, an employee and his wife filled in their paperwork for our new health care system. Out of habit, he replied to all with his response to this companywide message. We all had fun with it.

Eliminate one-word emails. I am perplexed as to why these would ever be sent, but I get them regularly.

Be cognizant of string or multiple-message emails. End users will often go back into the history and find sensitive or inflammatory information. Once, my organization was in a dispute with a less-than-savory customer and we received a flowery email from them explaining their situation. At the end of the message, they mentioned what an important partnership we had. But a simple scroll down through the email chain revealed a directive from one of their executives that stated, "Tell them what you need to, so they will ship the order. We just won't pay them."

Ensure that emails requiring a response are addressed promptly. Often, receivers of emails forget to respond to requests in a timely fashion. There are a myriad of excuses that I have heard. The fact is, a failure to acknowledge an email creates a number of problems. It can leave the sender wondering if the email was received; it can result in needed information not being received in time; and it can cause the sender to feel that you do not respect them enough to respond. All of this erodes trust and creates drag. It is vital that messages get timely attention. One of three types of responses is acceptable:

- Question answered
- Request clarification
- Acknowledge receipt and advise timing for a reply

Do not expect answers on emails from cc (carbon copy) recipients. This sounds obvious, but I have been amazed by the number of times individuals will ask me if I received their email and wondered why I didn't respond. When I advise that I rarely respond to cc emails; they seem surprised.

Technology Can Mask Underachievement

Fifteen years ago, when smartphones made the scene, many scrambled to find a way to use the revolutionary technology as a tool to enhance performance. Still others found a darker side; they used it to create a facade to deceive. They found ways to game the system with it.

Today we live in a world of artificial intelligence – smartphones on steroids. Those same bad actors have a new tool to mask their shortcomings. AI is an amazingly powerful tool when used properly. We must remind ourselves that it is the user, not the tool, that leads to the untenable. As pointed out in Chapter 2, if we discover such negative individuals in our organization, we must expunge them from our midst. He or she who will cheat to gain advantage is not to be trusted – and when trust is broken, our existence is hollow.

Conflict – Difficult Conversations

All of my clients and the companies I led had one glaring shortcoming in common. None of them significantly educated team members on conflict resolution. Some provided some rather generic language, usually in a handbook that was rarely read. But all failed to adopt meaningful programs to train team members to become good at de-escalation. Why? To me, there are two probable root causes. The first is that the matter is an uncomfortable topic, and training would confirm that unproductive behaviors exist in the enterprise. The second – and probably more common – reason is that they simply do not think about it.

Conflict is ubiquitous. If there are two people in a relationship, conflict will undoubtedly make an appearance. Think about your most intimate relationships – maybe your spouse. Have there not been times when conflicting views created tension?

In a company, even a smaller one, there are hundreds – if not thousands – of distinct relationships. Co-worker to co-worker, associate to customer, associate to vendor, and of course, leader to team member are but a few. Conflict is hard-coded into our business. How we decide to address that reality can be a game-changer.

One could draft an entire volume on conflict management and resolution. I'll include some of my favorite tools as stimuli here, but I also challenge readers to incorporate formal evaluation and training into their enterprise.

Discovery

Many businesses adopt a standard of perfection. It is very black-and-white, and it morphs into right or wrong solutions. This creates winners and losers. Now, the perfection standard is appropriate in many situations; quality assurance comes to mind.

But when dealing with our team members, the perfection standard can result in animus. Most people do not like to lose, and in a world where only two outcomes are acknowledged, there will be plenty of losers.

Adopting a discovery standard, one that seeks to truly understand motivations and root causes, creates opportunities for more productive outcomes. Questions and the answers introduce new data points into the matter. When we probe for solutions, we create an environment where there are **winners** and **learners**.

Active Listening

The use of active listening allows one party to state their position. The other party asks questions in a genuine attempt to understand the details. After the topic is fully explored, the listener will restate what they heard.

Restatement achieves two vital results. First, it guarantees that the listening party clearly heard the position of the other party. Second, the party speaking reaffirms that his or her opinion is worthy of the listener to record.

When executed properly, there is no ambiguity, and a productive solution is the result. The psychology of getting to state a position – and having it discussed – usually results in enhanced well-being, even when the matter is not concluded as hoped. The truth is that people just want to know they have been heard.

Cooperative Power

Cooperative power is an excellent tool when facing resistance; it seeks to explore positive outcomes.

When faced with a daunting challenge, it is reasonable for team members to become disenchanted. They may even see the matter as unsolvable. But looking for the positive and seeking feedback can help to soften the implications.

A team member might say, "It's impossible."

Your response might be, "What would make it better?"

Or you might say, "What would we need to do to make it possible?"

In doing so, you place yourself into the situation and are seen as a cooperative member of the team.

Using this technique, the impossible becomes possible, the possible becomes probable, and the probable becomes reality. Well-being soars, and you have become the team's ally.

Unbundling Communications

Communication is easy to master when you unbundle and simplify. If you get your email usage under control, you will free up vital time for productive endeavors. It really is not that difficult to fix.

You can transform communication from a huge weakness into a considerable strength simply by taking a proactive approach. Create a culture of excellence in communication by initiating a **best-in-class** communication program. Discipline yourself – and those around you – to use proper communication tools (and to use them properly).

Leading by example is a key element to optimizing communication. Mobilize your employee base, reward them when they've championed the cause, and give them gentle reminders when they slip. Get that right, and you will greatly enhance your communication base. You'll transform your team into a communications juggernaut.

Combustion Check – IGNITE COMMUNICATION

Before sending communication sparks across your organization, ask yourself:

1. Are you committed to mastering the spark of communication and making it a core competency?
2. What is the right fuel (people) to ignite the fire of effective communication?
3. Are you willing to ignite your personal brand and promote yourself with energy?
4. Are you committed to harnessing the explosive power of social media for impact?
5. What will your email policy do to power productivity (rather than drain it)?

Answering these questions ensures that your communication channels ignite clarity and influence, fueling momentum across your team.

6

Meetings: Simplify to Ignite Action

The meetings can be a lot of fun
or they can be frustrating.
– Bob Weir, rhythm guitarist, the Grateful Dead

Have you . . .

Ever dreaded meetings?

Found meetings to be an unproductive distraction that keeps you from your "real work"?

What if . . .

You could become the master of the meeting?

You could create meeting protocols that enable, inspire, and unlock hidden ideas?

I have yet to meet a person that has not complained about how many meetings they have to attend and how unproductive meetings are. These same people schedule or mandate the very meetings they claim to hate. Of course, everyone thinks that the meetings they call are more productive than the meetings called by others that they are forced to attend.

Newsflash! Chances are that your meetings are every bit as boring and laborious for your attendees as others' meetings are for you. To take it a step further, even with the most careful planning and execution, your meetings are probably full-fledged bore-a-thons.

I had fallen into the trap of thinking that my meetings were an exception to the mundane for nearly two decades before having a sort of epiphany.

What makes meetings so unproductive? My belief is that there are simply too many of them. They are attended by too many people or by the wrong people. They are not planned properly. We allow unproductive behavior during them. Yes, they are boring.

Do We Need That Meeting – Really?

There are some basic tools that we can use to eliminate unproductive meetings. Start by resisting the automatic, conventional wisdom that "We need a meeting" and question that with "Do we really need a meeting at all?"

It's all about perspective. We are so ingrained in the habit of calling a meeting that it is our first inclination. Before calling a meeting, ask yourself **three questions**:

- **Why** are we having this meeting?
- What is the **purpose** of this meeting?
- What are the **expected outcomes** of the meeting?

If you cannot answer these three questions honestly, then do not schedule the meeting. Then, ask yourself honestly if there is any way you can achieve the answers you seek using another method. If the answer is still no, proceed to plan your meeting.

Ground Rules – Your Meeting, Your Rules

Before you even consider having a meeting, you should create ground rules that are to be followed by all attendees. Ground rules are simply how you expect all attendees to conduct themselves – before, during and after the meeting.

Yes, conduct before and after the meeting is every bit as important as conduct during the meeting. For example, you should set a clear expectation of what each attendee should have prepared before the meeting. Each attendee should understand what their role in the meeting is. If they are presenting, they should have a clear understanding of the content of their presentation, the length of time they have to present it, and the expected format.

Attendees should clearly understand what they should do with the information they gather from the meeting. If there are assignments or action items, each attendee should understand their scope and expected execution.

During the meeting, clear expectations of behavior are necessary. Some of my favorites are:

- Arrive on time.
- Be respectful of other attendees.
- No phones or computers.

- No leaving the meeting or getting up to walk around until scheduled breaks.
- No eating (consuming beverages as appropriate is acceptable).
- No side conversations.
- Good posture.
- Listen intently (even if you don't want to).
- Ask questions at the appropriate time.
- No filibustering.
- Take notes.

Fear Not: Discipline Makes for Great Meetings

Some of those rules may sound a bit harsh, but if you prepare properly for the meeting and create a reasonable agenda, they are perfectly appropriate. When I get complaints about my ground rules, I usually refer to movie theater etiquette. What behavior do you hate most from others at the theater? I guarantee that your answer can relate to at least one item on the list above.

It's amazing to me that the same people who seemingly cannot sit still for a one-hour meeting have no problem staying seated in a theater for two hours or more. Maybe we need to charge team members $10 to attend, and then their behavior might improve. $12.50 if the meeting is going to contain 3-D effects.

A chronic complaint is "I have to use the bathroom." How did these people make it through school? I recognize that as we age, our bodies create needs that previously were not there, but these same folks seem to be able to keep their bodies in check when it suits them. I refer to this phenomenon as **Convenient Meeting**

Incontinence Syndrome. For fun, you can call it CMIS. (This is breaking a later rule about acronym use, but rules are made to be broken.)

I was in New York City at a conference with executives on teambuilding. An hour into the presentation, someone began to leave the room. The speaker stopped and queried the person; the dialogue went like this:

"Excuse me, where are you going?"

"To the bathroom."

"Couldn't you have gone before we started?"

"I guess."

By that time, the disrupter was completely embarrassed, but the speaker continued.

"Did you want the entire group to take a break now, or should we just wait for you to return?"

The individual slunk out of the room, and I'm not sure he ever returned. But one thing was certain – throughout the remainder of the two days of meetings, not one person left during a session. I found the tactic of the speaker remarkable.

Agendas

After you have decided to conduct a meeting but before calling it, commit to making a detailed agenda. The effort it takes to create an agenda sometimes persuades a potential meeting creator from doing so! Still, creating an agenda will significantly decrease both the number of subsequent meetings required and the length of those meetings.

Agendas should go out as far in advance as possible, in order to allow attendees to prepare for the meetings. A week is ideal. Obviously, crisis management meetings are an exception.

Why Are We Having This Meeting, and What Are We Going to Do?

Unprepared meeting attendees waste more time and energy than almost any other event in business. But it is inaccurate to believe that the attendees' lack of preparedness is the fault of the attendees. Really, this is the leader's failure. Remember, you are responsible for making sure your attendees know what is required from them – before, during and after the meeting.

There are two main driving factors for lack of preparedness. The first is extremely straightforward: attendees simply do not know how to prepare, or what to prepare, for the meeting. The meeting organizer or leader needs to make sure that what attendees are expected to contribute is clearly communicated and understood.

The second factor is a bit more complicated to identify. This is the failure of the meeting organizer or leader to create an expectation of participation for the attendees. If attendees believe that it is acceptable or allowable to simply show up to a meeting, chances are they will just show up – and that's all.

They will probably arrive, grab a cup of coffee and settle in for what they believe to be a preordained unproductive session. These bad examples permeate the entire organization; in fact, it is usually the higher-level attendees of a meeting that display the most overt lack of preparation. Underlings are normally too frightened to fail to prepare, but they are quick learners. They can become participants in this same behavior if they are not guided properly. Agendas and ground rules are the perfect tools to eliminate such issues.

An agenda should state both the purpose and the expected outcome of a meeting. The purpose is the reason for the meeting being conducted. If the purpose is weak, the meeting will most likely be ineffective, and it should probably not even be held at all. (Remember the three pre-meeting questions we are supposed to ask ourselves.)

Expected outcomes are the specific and tangible results we seek to realize as a result of the meeting. An example of an expected outcome might be to educate the staff on a particular topic. A test on that topic, following the meeting, could be a barometer of that meeting's effectiveness.

Another example might be to educate you, the leader, on a topic or to gather input that will lead to a decision. Obviously, if you walk away and feel like you fully understand the subject, you can consider the meeting a success.

One of the easiest and most common expected outcomes of a meeting is a decision that needs to be made about a specific topic or initiative. The purpose of such a meeting is to make the decision. If no decision is made, the meeting should be considered a failure.

It is essential to get the concept of purpose and the expected outcomes philosophy right. If attendees assume something specific will be achieved in the meeting, but you, as the organizer, had no intention of that outcome, confusion ensues.

Confusion can often lead to disappointment and an erosion in trust. And an erosion in trust is a sin that cannot be allowed.

Visibility Deters Mission Creep

Make the purpose and expected outcomes of your meeting visible; moreover, continually check to ensure you have not suffered from **mission creep**. Mission creep is the tendency to get off course in a meeting. The likelihood for meeting attendees to veer off topic during a conversation is a frequent reality, and it's unproductive.

Allowing mission creep to go unchallenged is an unacceptable risk to an otherwise productive meeting. Furthermore, every attendee in a meeting should have the right and the obligation to be vigilant for mission creep. A visual reminder is a fantastic facilitation tool; it can be pointed to by attendees to call out instances of mission creep.

That visual reminder can be as simple as the printed agenda that includes the purpose and expected outcomes. A good idea is to print the agenda on a large poster-sized piece of paper that can be hung on the wall in a spot that is easily viewable by all attendees.

Guess Who's Not Coming to Our Meeting

Based on the agenda and purpose, determine who the attendees should be. Use a discerning eye. If you cannot come up with a legitimate reason to have someone attend your meeting, do not invite them. In fact, you should take a contrarian approach. Ask yourself if you can have the meeting and get the results you desire without inviting the person. If the answer is "no," definitely invite them.

Make the agenda relevant while encouraging involvement from all attendees. Sometimes, in an effort to win an imaginary stylistic competition of making the agenda look or sound professional, we insert confusing prose that distracts from the purpose or the expected outcomes. Keep it basic and accessible.

Also remember – we have up to 16 different personality types in our meeting. Some may try to monopolize the meeting, while others will need prompting to participate. Spell out the times for attendee feedback in your agenda. Scheduling feedback times will let your more introverted personality types know they are expected to contribute.

We Need a Break

Equally important on the agenda is the time for breaks or meals. Failure to properly allow for ample breaks is a fatal error. Just as we, as individuals, need mental breaks to increase productivity, we need group breaks as well. Assuming that you have a team that adheres to your guidelines, more frequent breaks can create much more productive meetings. They also help avoid legitimized CMIS.

Assuming you have the discipline to reconvene at the agreed-upon time after each break, I advocate more breaks versus less breaks. People tend to get antsy after 90 minutes in a meeting. On the other hand, if you lack the discipline to reassemble your attendees, then you will probably need to have a more traditional schedule – a break every two hours.

Meeting Must-Haves

Each attendee should have a role in the meeting. It might be as simple as providing input, or listening and taking great notes. Regardless of each person's specific role, once there is individual ownership in the meeting, its productivity will improve dramatically.

The Facilitator

There should be a facilitator for every meeting. This person has an important role. He or she makes sure the meeting flows properly, and also keeps the attendees on task and engaged throughout the meeting.

Good facilitators know that different personality types will each conduct themselves very differently in meetings, because they are inclined toward a particular type of conduct. Some attendees will tend to talk over others, and jump in and monopolize the meeting. These individuals need to be coached to allow other people some time to add their input. On the flip side, others might tend to remain quiet and not add much to the conversation. A good facilitator will draw input out of those individuals.

A good facilitator will use a variety of tools to gain the most participation from attendees. Tools could include a round-robin-facilitated discussion where each person asserts his or her view on a certain topic, or a gallery walk where attendees get to walk around and view various poster sheets. The gallery walk might include voting dots (self-applying stickers that can be affixed to show one's support of a statement or thought) or sticky note suggestions to enhance the work being viewed.

If you are struggling with facilitation of meetings, pick up a book on the subject and try a few of the ideas. Better yet, the American Management Association has a great course on meetings. Plan to attend one.

Often, the role of facilitator is filled by the meeting leader, but that should be avoided if at all possible. Instead, try to use one of your team members who have expertise at facilitation. If you do not have any team members who are accomplished facilitators, find a team member who is interested in learning about it and send them to a training session. A good facilitator is a key member of the meeting and finding a qualified one is essential.

The Meeting Police

When it comes to meetings, there are two important roles that often go unfilled. These are the roles of timekeeper and scribe. Many times, meeting attendees prefer not to fulfill these roles, as they require additional work and are generally considered thankless positions. However, with no timekeeper or scribe, meetings will be less effective.

I recommend that the meeting leader find two individuals for the roles and then give them immense power, raising their status to that of a police officer. The concept of policing at a meeting can introduce a bit of fun into the roles. The timekeeper could hand out citations for those who bloviate beyond one's scheduled time allotment. The scribe's citations could be for a failure to follow up or to turn in action assignments. Introducing fun into some of the more traditionally tedious assignments is not required, but it adds an interesting element to the roles, and I have found that it can have a positive impact.

The timekeeper makes sure that presenters stay on time. Reminding attendees how much time the team has to discuss a topic, and making sure the team does not go overtime, is an essential part of the timekeeper's role.

Every meeting needs a timekeeper. I have yet to attend a really productive meeting without one. I've tried meetings both with and without a timekeeper; the timekeeper is a keeper.

The scribe takes notes and records action items. At the end of each meeting, the scribe will review what has been decided upon, who has agreed to complete each task, and when they have agreed to have the tasks completed.

The scribe is also responsible for seeing that notes get circulated to the team, along with action items. Action items should be clearly stated – what is to be accomplished, who will accomplish them, and in what time frame. The scribe, in police officer mode, can send out reminders to attendees to see that assigned tasks are completed. I recognize that this type of continuous follow-up should not be required; but, unfortunately, you will find that it's needed.

Regarding the position of scribe: The role is often viewed by attendees as subordinate or inferior. First, if your team is healthy, members will no longer fear being seen as inferior. Second, the scribe can use a clerical person to assist in the assembly and distribution of the notes. But the scribe oversees the distribution and can become extremely powerful, as he or she will have the meeting leader's permission to demand compliance on follow-up items.

Remember, you are allowed to have fun in meetings. Just don't annoy the police officers in attendance.

The Parking Lot

There should be a "parking lot" in every meeting. A parking lot is a sheet of paper or a board that is visible to all attendees. On it, all items and thoughts that come up during the meeting that are not germane to the meeting are recorded. The parking lot serves three purposes.

First, good thoughts are not lost. Second, time is not wasted discussing peripheral or unrelated topics. Finally, the attendees will feel valued; that their ideas are important. When they see that their ideas are noted, they are less likely to take up important meeting time to discuss them. They know that the thought will be addressed in a later forum.

Meeting Decision-Making

Frequently, meetings are called in order for a team to make a decision. Decisions can take different forms. At one end of the continuum there is the **tell decision**. The tell decision is when you have already made your decision, and you are simply calling a meeting to tell the team what you have decided.

Tells are, as the word suggests, mandates. These are not up for debate, and though a tell decision might seem a bit heavy-handed, you simply must execute these. Tells have an important place in the decision-making hierarchy; you should not avoid making them. A meeting might be called to simply explain why you made the decision and afford the attendees the opportunity to ask questions. Be careful not to allow attendees to challenge the decision; but rather let them ask questions to understand it.

On the other end of the continuum, there is the **collaborative decision**. Usually, these decisions end up in a vote. There are a number of ways to conduct a vote; but you, as the leader and final decision-maker, need to make sure you can live with the outcome of the vote. There is nothing more infuriating to a team than to have its vote overturned by a leader who wanted a different outcome.

Votes should be public. If attendees do not have the courage to allow their teammates to see how they voted, they simply do not belong on the team. Oftentimes, I have successfully used the **top-three vote exercise** to arrive at a complex decision. This works well when the team is deciding which projects to prioritize. In this exercise, each team member is given three votes, and they cast their vote for their favorite three projects. After all the votes are tallied, the entire list is automatically prioritized from top to bottom.

Making Sure All Attendees' Voices Are Heard

Leaders need to keep in mind that junior team members – who might only be periodically invited to meetings – often are extremely nervous when giving presentations to executives. We tend to forget that, and sometimes we unintentionally create unproductive environments. If you have taken the appropriate steps in planning your meeting and inviting attendees, every member of the team will know that they are valued. It's good to make sure that your junior team members realize this.

That Darn Discipline Again

Following the guidelines that we've discussed requires intense discipline and it can be difficult. However, if you commit yourself to executing the steps properly, you will experience much more productive meetings. I really do not know why, but it appears that the element of fear drives most of us to adopt more productive meeting behaviors. I like a nice combination of fear-based discipline along with positive reinforcement for those who embrace and champion the ground rules.

An example of using fear as leverage might be to advise employees that if they are late or unprepared for a meeting, they will be asked to leave. I like to call it the walk of shame. In contrast, all employees who attend and participate will be given a nice memento or will be invited to a fun after-hours event. Many have challenged me that the **stick** portion of this **carrot-and-stick** approach is unduly harsh; I disagree. Provided that every attendee knows the rules and consequences, there is never a need for the stick.

I look at meetings as very similar to college classes. When I was in college, you did not dare arrive at some professors' classes late. And if you wanted to pass, you made sure that assignments were completed on time and completed satisfactorily. Likewise, in business, employees should arrive on time and be prepared at meetings. As we assume leadership roles in business, we seem to unwittingly forget some of the basic rules of conduct we learned years before.

Lateness is Disrespectful to Everyone

Ground rules are great examples. Everyone is expected to arrive on time for the meeting. But how many times have we heard someone apologize for being late? "Thanks, OK," is the usual response. The reality is, the perpetrator is probably not really sorry, or he or she would not have been late. And their tardiness is definitely not OK. We have wasted all the other attendees' time, and it enables poor behavior from others.

At one company I worked for, lateness became so chronic a problem that we all committed to arrive five minutes early. That newfound discipline lasted about a month before we were back in our old rut.

I have seen leaders charge offenders a $5 penalty for their lateness. I find that tactic a bit juvenile. And it can get out of control. In one case, a really bad offender pulled out a twenty, and claimed that he would also be covered for the next three times he was late.

I prefer a more direct approach. When the meeting starts, the doors are closed and not reopened until the break. This allows those individuals who were late to explain their lateness to you after the meeting, preferably in your office. It is a great way to **gently** reinforce your point. I promise you that this approach will eliminate lateness in all but the most legitimate cases.

Once, I was heading to an offsite safety meeting, and, as a result of being detained, I was running late. I was to speak at the meeting to show my commitment for the program. Our safety results had plummeted, and we needed to get people's attention.

As I drove, I decided to tell the attendees I didn't have enough respect for the program to arrive on time, hoping to demonstrate unacceptable behavior.

I walked into the meeting four minutes late, and found that not one attendee was in their seat and ready to go. They were drinking coffee and talking about every topic other than safety. It took another five minutes for the team to assemble.

I addressed the crowd in a loud and passionate voice: "While I was driving over here, I was so annoyed at myself for being late that I decided to fall on my sword. I was going to tell you that my lateness showed my lack of commitment to this project and that it was at the core of the eroded performance. It is now obvious to me that none of you care enough about the safety program to be on time either, so we are all responsible." I added, "Maybe if we took a bit more time to ensure our own conduct was acceptable, our safety results would be acceptable."

The entire assembly was shocked. There were attendees from many levels in the organization, and most had never seen me that animated. The message was delivered, and I received great feedback from many afterward.

Paying Attention Pays

Another fairly obvious expectation is that attendees should listen to what is being discussed. How many times have you seen someone at a meeting texting or reading emails while others are speaking? Actually, as mentioned in my list of meeting conduct expectations, you should require that electronic devices be turned off. This is one of the hardest things to get accomplished, although it should be among the easiest.

Try this tactic the next time that someone is on their smartphone in your meeting: Stop the meeting and have everyone watch intently as the violator completes his or her work. Call the individual out by name and announce to the group that you will all begin again when he or she is done.

Missed Commitments Invalidate Effectiveness

The only thing more disturbing than a ground rule-breaker is the person who does not meet his or her commitments. Missed commitments are usually wrapped in superfluous excuses. These excuses usually include references to those four-letter words, "they" or "them." Because "they" and "them" always show up in excuses, we've outlawed the use of those two words.

Are some of the previous suggestions harsh? *Maybe.*

Are they unduly harsh? *I think not.*

Will they promote better meeting results? *Absolutely.*

Unasked Questions

One component that meetings always seem to be missing is questions. Either due to lack of interest or fear, people tend to fail to ask questions at meetings. At the beginning of every meeting, presenters or facilitators should clearly set the expectations on questions. They should either be asked during the presentation or afterward. Regardless of how you choose to handle questions, they should be encouraged and embraced, provided they are relevant.

Failure to ask questions and poke into the rationale behind a decision will often result in missing an important perspective. The person who failed to ask their question might have had a valuable insight on the potential success or failure of a project.

Each member was invited to the meeting by the leader. Therefore, if the leader has prepared for the meeting properly, each attendee knows that they are there to provide some input. The bigger the project, the more important it is that all appropriate questions be asked, investigated and answered.

Blah Blah Blah

As much as I embrace the art of the question, there are some individuals who simply ask questions because they want to seem provocative or intelligent. Hopefully, you have exited these types of folks from your company. You do not need showboaters in your organization, but if you cannot seem to ferret them all out, call out their bad questions. The people who ask unfocused and irrelevant questions are self-absorbed, and any hint of embarrassment sends them reeling.

I recall attending a large meeting of a Fortune 500 company. The president was discussing a new product launch. In attendance was one of those showboaters. The president asked for questions, and this individual stood up (a dead giveaway that the question was going to be carefully worded, with at least one vocabulary mindbender in it) and asked, "Will the rollout be ubiquitous?"

The president answered without hesitation. "It will be done with great ubiquity," then added, "Are there any **real** questions?"

All in attendance learned the definition of slinking back into one's seat.

The After-the Meeting Question

On the other end of the scale is the person who approaches you or another attendee after the meeting with a question or an idea. It usually starts with, "I didn't want to say anything in the meeting, but…" (Depending on the frequency of this behavior, it might be appropriate to explain to the employee how much more productive it would have been for them to comment in front of the team.) Ironically, I have often found that the perspectives shared in such after-meeting conversations are usually insightful. They may have you, as the leader, rethinking some of the decisions agreed upon in the meetings.

Failure to speak up during a meeting is normally a fear and personality issue. As a result, I advocate an empathetic coaching approach to correcting this situation. I always have plenty of energy for working team members through fear issues. They are commonplace, but if they're addressed, you will optimize your team dynamics.

Summing Up a Meeting's Elements

Productive meetings involve great discipline. Once you get into the habit of properly preparing for meetings and effectively executing them, they will become much more useful. You will find that you will eventually require fewer meetings. But every member of the team must commit to the same level of discipline, so standards do not fall. Demand a higher standard, and you will enjoy the fruits of the seeds sown.

All of this may sound extremely complex, but it really is not. It is simply about discipline and planning. The investment is worth it and the framework you create will quickly become part of the normal conduct of business. Not only will you have more productive meetings, but the standards will permeate the entire culture of the organization.

Combustion Check – IGNITE MEETINGS

Before lighting the fuse on your next meeting, ask yourself:

1. How will you cut the dead weight from meetings, eliminating the unessential?
2. Are you committed to fueling meetings with proper planning to make them productive?
3. How will you inject discipline, so meetings burn brightly instead of sputtering?
4. Are you ready to ignite collaboration, ensuring that input from all attendees fuels the discussion?

Answering these questions ensures that your meetings burn with high energy, delivering maximum output with minimal waste.

7

The Redcoats Are Coming: Simplify to Ignite Innovation

Question your paradigms, your perceptions of reality.
– Daniel N. Robinson, psychologist and professor

Have you . . .

Ever underestimated your competition?

Ever been caught up in chasing red herrings?

What if . . .

You could learn to see around corners?

You could foster a mindset that discards the noise and gets to the heart of the matter?

In the late 18th century, the greatest fighting force the world had ever known was the British army. They were well-trained, followed the rules of engagement, and crushed their enemies. Their red uniforms were among the most feared sights of the day. Yet, a ragtag, under-resourced set of militias exploited the British army's egotism and defeated it, transforming the way wars were fought forever. The unlikely victors were units of what became known as the Continental Army, and the war they won secured the independence of the British colonies in America – the new United States. This lesson continues to resonate in today's business world: past success does not guarantee future victories, and overconfidence can be exploited.

Are You Your Own Worst Enemy?

In business, our success often can create dire weaknesses that get exploited by the competition. Or a success can result in myopic thinking that ultimately leads to failure. Certainly, past practice is a good indicator of the future, but it is only one indicator. We can become set in the way we do things because it worked in the past. So, we should evaluate all factors that can impact success. And we should ask ourselves: Is there a complacency born of past success hidden within our culture?

Frequently, transformative events occur that make everything we knew before obsolete. The most noted are technological advances. I can remember the first time I saw a fax machine. That was less than 40 years ago, and the fax is all but obsolete now. Other, more efficient ways of sending documents have replaced it. Unfortunately, most advances are not as obvious as the fax and its successors. It takes a watchful eye to understand the implications of seemingly unimportant events.

The government is another source of transformative events. One area of government that affects business is environmental regulation. Administrations can make or break industries with a stroke of the pen.

Many businesspeople suggest it is best to stay out of politics. I agree that becoming a candidate is not for most of us in the business world, but failure to be aware of government intrusion is just brainless.

Economic factors like the price of gasoline can drive buying behavior and lead to disruption in the marketplace. In such cases, we need to ascertain if the change is driven by short-term or long-term dynamics. If we react to rising gasoline prices, making long-term decisions based on that reality and its implications, we may see very different outcomes when the price of gasoline falls.

Success can breed complacency. Organizations become entrenched in their routines, relying on methods that worked before. But transformative events – technological advances, regulatory shifts, or economic fluctuations – can render familiar approaches obsolete.

The Consumer Is Fickle

Consumers are interesting creatures; their behavior is hard to predict. I have seen more reports than I can count where the consumer acts exactly the opposite of expectations. I am a huge believer in "going with one's gut." And when you go with your gut, it takes much less time than assembling additional data or conducting further research. It allows you to take full advantage of the element of speed.

I am not a marketing expert. In fact, I've been called out by many marketing teams for my lack of understanding. As such, my ideas on the subject are neither popular with the purists nor proven. Frankly, most of my experiences and successes have come as a result of years of suffering through many failures.

Companies spend huge amounts of money trying to understand the consumer. The conventional approach slows things down, and based on my experience, that is not very reliable. These consumer research initiatives are opportunities for bundling and complexity that create organizational drag.

Pile analysis on top of analysis, focus group on top of focus group, market trend report on top of another report – and you have created a mountain of information. But if nothing concrete comes from it, you simply have made the process very difficult and flushed cash down the drain.

Engage Where Passion Lives

I advocate a much easier approach. I like to refer to it as "walking and talking." Before you engage in it, make sure you are passionate about what you are marketing. If, for example, you are in the game-streaming business and do not like PC or video games, this tactic will not work.

It is as simple as engaging with people while they are taking part in activities that they feel passionate about. In my experience, people love to talk about what they truly enjoy or value, so reach out to them in their environment. For example, if you are in the fitness business, go to a gym and start connecting with your audience. The same thing works in churches, sporting events, nightclubs, restaurants and almost everywhere else.

I recommend you take what you learn, create a concept and start talking about it. If you get a good reaction, I would say, "Go for it." The money and time you save by not going on the conventional route will allow you the opportunity and finances to make some mistakes.

There are a couple of things about mistakes and failures that are interesting to put into perspective. First, the only person who never failed is a person who never did anything new. Since it's paraphrased from an Albert Einstein quote it must be true. Second, as long as you learn from mistakes and failures, they are not total losses. In fact, those apparent defeats may lead to the best learning experiences.

Mistakes Should Be Embraced

The fewer resources and the less money that you invest in proving your product idea, the less painful any failure will be to your organization. I am not a big baseball fan, but I draw from baseball to help me wrestle with failure rates. If a professional baseball player has a .400 on-base percentage, it means he fails in his objective 60 percent of the time; however, he might be considered an All-Star in the eyes of the team and the fans.

I have always felt that if you are successful with product launches one-third of the time, you will win long term. Of course, you must be resolute and have the buy-in from the team, along with an understanding and mature board of directors.

Frequently, successful companies who have a long track record of victory get far too set in their ways, and it stifles creativity. The more they embrace their steady success, the better chance that they will not introduce a breakout idea that shocks the marketplace. The established, successful company seems to get far too comfortable with the status quo.

The bravest companies challenge conventional wisdom. And it's much easier for a startup group to stretch into the unknown. Often, a startup has little invested, and therefore little to lose. The more successful an organization is, the more likely they take on a psychological belief that they have too much to lose. They become ultraconservative. If you trust your team, I recommend you get out of your comfort zone and create some disruption.

Innovation, Complacency and Rebirth

Apple and Microsoft illustrate how leadership and culture shape long-term performance Their combined histories illuminate the reality that even the seemingly greatest of companies are susceptible to nearly lethal failures that can extend beyond a decade.

Apple: Founded in 1976, Apple struggled after Steve Jobs' departure in 1985, faltering under John Sculley's leadership. Jobs' return in 1997 sparked revolutionary products – the iMac, iPod, iPhone, and iPad – that transformed both Apple and the industry. From 2002 to 2012, Apple delivered **nearly 5,000 percent shareholder returns**, highlighting the power of bold, unconventional innovation.

Microsoft: Founded in 1975, Microsoft dominated software but became complacent under Bill Gates' later leadership and under Steve Ballmer. Focused on incremental improvements rather than breakouts, Microsoft returned a modest **2.5 percent annually to shareholders** between 2002 and 2012. Under

Satya Nadella, starting in 2014, Microsoft embraced cloud computing, AI, and new business models, revitalizing growth and market relevance.

The takeaway: Success is not a guarantee. Companies must continually challenge assumptions, innovate, and embrace risk to avoid being overtaken.

Cutting Through the Clutter

We become so invested in the methods we use and the routes we follow, we tend not to explore new ones. Or, when we do start exploring, it has to be for something very new and very different. It seems as if we are either trying to swing for the fences or not bothering to get into the batter's box at all.

I bought a new car that had global positioning system (GPS) technology. I had a route I took regularly to the airport from my home. I knew that route was the best route, but one day, for kicks, I engaged the GPS while returning home. I noted that the GPS instructed me to take a different route. When I ignored the electronic advice the first time, the GPS attempted to get me to correct my mistake. I ignored the GPS unit three times during that trip, as I was convinced that it was incorrect. I had a number of things to accomplish that day, and did not have time for a joy ride.

But the next time I traveled the same route, I decided to explore a bit. The GPS route cut 15 minutes off a one-and-a-half hour trip. I had simply never taken the time to look at a map or consider alternatives to my traditional route.

In business, we fill our lives up with meetings and analyses. We build procedures and protocols to support our way of doing things, when oftentimes a new approach could lead to much better results. It is extremely interesting that many in leadership roles tend to consult expensive business gurus who suffer from the same kind of predisposition in their own organization.

Ask Someone who Has Traveled the Road

In almost every case, the answers are much easier to come by than anyone would think. The vast majority of us are not pioneers; we are simply driving down a road paved by others. Nevertheless, we often refuse to consider just how simple it would be to explore a bit.

I have found that asking someone who has already traveled a similar road nets amazing results. They have "been there," and because of that, they have seen, heard, touched, and felt during that journey. They have a unique perspective. Chances are that there is a nugget or two of relevant information contained in their experience. It does not always work, but the investment is rather small. And it's easier than ever to just ask – the advance of internet search engines can enhance and sometimes even replace talking to individuals with experience.

Google It – The Modern Shortcut

Today, the first step to solving a problem often starts with a simple search. In 2026, everyone – especially younger professionals – assumes that answers are just a few keystrokes away.

I remember a corporate crisis where a new product reached a multi-million-dollar cost overrun due to instability. Our best experts failed to find a solution. But a new employee, on his first day, identified the root cause. It was a simple procedural tweak and minor formula adjustment – and it resolved the issue. A quick online search later revealed that the solution was publicly documented. The lesson is clear: Sometimes, the simplest approach solves the most complex problems.

Artificial Intelligence (AI) is a rapidly emerging tool. I liken it to Google on steroids. We should ask ourselves how the use of AI can enhance our organizational capacity. At the same time, we should be ever vigilant to ensure we do not rely too heavily on its power and unwittingly tarnish company values and culture.

Creating Google Masters

I have worked tirelessly to embed a Google mentality in my company and my life. I find it amazing that any company would hire an employee without first Googling them to check on their background and any obvious red flags. This should be priority number one for every human resources team. Instead, many companies opt for professional background checks. I certainly advocate those as well, but why waste the money up front when the company can weed out problems in a free internet search? It is a simple first gate.

A new product arrives on the shelf? "Google It."

You want the answer to a crossword clue? "Google It."

Going on a date? "Google them" (before the date).

I have preached the use of Google through all of my companies and with all of my colleagues. Amazingly, I still see people retract into their old habits when they should know better. This tendency astounds me. I refer to this behavior as **Fetal Position Syndrome** – the tendency to revert to old, familiar methods, despite our awareness of more efficient new ones.

Fetal Position Syndrome: A Familiarity Trap

Fetal Position Syndrome is the tendency for people to crawl into the fetal position during times of stress or fear. It's a fairly common psychological condition. When under stress, we retract to what we know – to what feels comfortable or safe.

Fetal Position Syndrome is everywhere, and in all aspects of business. Comfortable work processes or problem-solving tools become habits that are difficult to change.

It requires great discipline to make changes to processes or procedures, and then stick with them. Individuals become so invested in the methods they have used for years that they must be continually guided in the new methods. This is particularly important when installing new technologies – operating systems or enhanced computerized planning tools.

Then, we tend to fall into the trap that our new software or process will be the panacea for all of our problems. The reality is that no new system has the ability to make sure human inputs are accurate, or even entered.

I have experienced countless complaints from co-workers that new systems just do not work. They will claim that the system is flawed. While I have certainly seen programming glitches, I have never seen a system simply make mistakes. In every case, such problems can be linked back to very uncomplicated input issues or math errors.

If your legacy (old) operating system is too cumbersome or not capable of delivering the intended analyses, a new system will be recommended. Of course, any new computer software system will come with fanfare, promises, bells and whistles. The tendency is to go with delusions of grandeur. The reality is – in most cases – after several years with the new system, the organization will settle into a very specific routine. The routine usually leverages only a small percentage of the power of the system. But then the system is deemed too cumbersome, or not capable of delivering the intended analyses, and a new system is recommended… the cycle repeats.

A lack of discipline and the bundling of needs are at the root of such failures. Request after request is made, report after report is created, and system modifications are requested to support all of this activity. It becomes too much work to sustain, and thus does not occur.

Simplifying System Integration

When implementing a new system, I recommend the following approach:

1. **Instill intense discipline right away.** Ensure that every person who will touch the new system understands expectations, and that they will abide by them.
2. **Select a provider and a system that meets your needs.** Many businesspeople have a love affair with the best-in-class

systems and believe that their popularity and perceived power are required for optimal performance. I have found that, unless you have an extremely large and robust business model, there are a number of good systems and providers that are much less costly to purchase and support. These systems will have more than enough functionality to propel and optimize your business.

3. **Focus on need vs. "nice to have."** My experience suggests that businesses adopt processes and protocols that become viewed as core to the operation of the business. In reality, many of these are either completely replaceable, or are not necessary to keep the basic functions of business intact. Yet, we tend to force established processes and protocols into an already stressful startup period. That holds the implementation hostage until every "I" is dotted, and every "T" is crossed.
4. **Keep the system's backbone untouched.** A regular problem is the customization of software to meet the perceived needs of the organization. The tendency is to embed these enhancements into the code of the software. This creates a unique operating system only applicable to your organization. As such, support over time becomes expensive or inexistent.
5. **I would opt for a "bolt-on" approach.** If you believe that there is a must-have functionality, use every available resource to minimize touch points with the core system. By bolting on, you leave the core operating system pristine and more receptive to software updates.

6. **Layer in functionality over time.** Too many moving parts integrated at startup creates confusion and leads to frustration. When we opt to layer in functionality over time, the implementation is much more manageable.

   I compare system implementation to attending college. At many universities, there are tiered courses that complement each other. At the institution where I studied, we had 100-level courses through 400-level courses. It was strongly recommended not to attempt a 400-level course without fulfilling the prerequisite introductory ones. In fact, in many cases it was not allowed without permission.

   Usually, an attempt to jump directly to the 400 level courses led to failure or poor results. Following the path using prerequisite classes produced superior results. A similar approach to system integration holds true.

7. **Resist the urge to settle.** I have found that, after a few setbacks, team members tend to give up and settle for just what is available at the time. The result is the organization never fully realizes the benefits of the system that was just purchased and the investment made to integrate it. Usually, the IT department gets the blame, and the system is perceived as unsuccessful or marginally successful. Neither characterization is fair.

Peeling Back the Onion

When we become very invested in what we have built, we kill the entrepreneurial spirit. We need to challenge our conventional wisdom to make sure we have fully thought through a challenge, or completely evaluated an opportunity.

For items we need to address, I advocate reducing them to the most simple terms. Since most things are bundled, we have to wade through layers of implications. It is like peeling back an onion to examine every surface. If you have a four-inch onion, depending on its exact shape, it will have approximately 50 square inches of surface area on the outside. But if you peel back the onion's layers, one by one, you might find that it has more than 550 square inches of surface area. That's more than 11 times the originally calculated surface to examine, question and evaluate. Before someone challenges my math, there are two surfaces to every layer… and you have not seen my onion.

When we challenge convention, we create the opportunity for breakthrough ideas. When we become too invested in the way we always have done things, we fail to see many opportunities for improvement.

The Tale of the Christmas Ham

A story I like is the "Tale of the Christmas Ham." A young girl was watching her mother prepare the Christmas ham. She questioned why her mother removed about six inches of the ham shank and carefully placed it in the pan alongside the remainder of the meat.

"Why do we remove that end only to place it in the pan next to the rest of the ham?" she asked.

"Because the fat in the end helps keep the entire ham moist," she answered.

"Why not leave it on?" asked the little girl.

"I'm not sure," answered her mother, and added, "My mother did it that way. Why not ask Grandma?"

Fortunately, the grandmother was visiting for the holiday, so the young girl sought her out, and she received the exact same answer from her grandmother. As luck would have it, the great-grandmother was alive and well and visiting also, so the girl ran to her.

Great-Grandma knew the answer. "I cut off the end because the pan I used was too short to fit the entire ham."

Because this family had been using the same method for generations, they just assumed it was the best way. In actuality, they were just adding an extra step – an unnecessary step – that had only been needed when they had less effective tools. If it had not been for the newest member of their family, they would have never questioned their method.

Under stress, people and organizations retreat to familiar habits. Legacy systems, overcomplicated protocols, and bureaucratic inertia limit innovation. Discipline, simplification, and learning through repetition and revision all counteract the tendency to stay stuck.

Not a Miracle – Just Fresh Perspective

Innovation often comes from those with different experiences or unconventional thinking. They either ignore, or are unaware of, conventional wisdom. Sometimes, they just "aren't smart enough to know it couldn't be done."

Strategic observation and adaptation are critical. Learn from competitors where possible, bend rules intelligently, and question outdated norms. Appropriately applied, these tactics foster innovation without violating ethics or laws.

Ethical dilemmas can create significant angst in the organization. What one team member might find perfectly acceptable another might see as disqualifying. This is where values come in. Provided you are certain with assurance you haven't trampled on your core values, I would advise taking advantage of any opportunity and whatever tactic you can justifiably use to support the objective.

Fresh Thinking: Rotate, Challenge, Ignite

Rotate talent, encourage exploration, and foster curiosity. Avoid becoming a "Redcoat" – rigid, defensive, and resistant to change. Fresh perspectives keep organizations agile and innovative.

> "Nothing is as embarrassing as watching someone
> do something that you said couldn't be done."
> – *Sam Ewing, Chicago White Sox*

Innovation rewards those who simplify the complex, challenge assumptions, and act boldly. The Redcoats may be coming – but those who question, explore, and ignite, change will thrive and prevail.

Combustion Check – IGNITE INNOVATION

Before lighting the fuse on your next innovation, ask yourself:

1. What could you do in a new way to fuel the fire, even if it feels foreign or uncomfortable?
2. Are you committed to using all available fuel resources, tools, and insights – to feed the blaze of progress?
3. Are you ready to spark discovery by making search engines like Google and other modern tools a core part of your toolkit?
4. Are you prepared to shift perspective, fan the flames of fresh thinking, and burn away old assumptions that may be holding your company back?

Answering these questions ensures you are ready to light the fuse, keep your innovation engine burning bright, and turn conventional thinking into combustible action.

8

Customization: Not All Fires Are the Same

You don't get harmony when
everybody sings the same note.
– *Doug Floyd, musician*

Have you . . .

Ever felt like you were being constrained or forced into a box that checks a corporate playbook?

Ever felt like some of your co-workers were working against you?

What if . . .

You could burn the playbook and create a collaborative arena where diversity of thought was championed and you could lift everyone up?

One of the more interesting miscues that business people make is the assumption that what is helpful and motivating to one person is helpful and motivating for all. The concept that one size fits all has been touched on in previous chapters, but is such an important dynamic that it deserves more focus.

For example, we have two employees: Joe and Janice. Joe is a 6' 2" golfer who loves to listen to operatic music. Janice is a 5' 4" tennis player who is a football fanatic. We would not think of giving Joe and Janice the same company logo T-shirt. It's simply stupid to think that both Joe and Janice could wear the same size.

Furthermore, we know Joe likes the opera, and that Janice likes football. We would not send Joe to the football game, nor would we surprise Janice with tickets to an upcoming opera performance. Why not? The answer is fairly simple. Janice doesn't like opera, and Joe doesn't care for football. Their rewards would not motivate them.

Forced Formality Is Folly

However, leaders often force Janice and Joe into the same type of training and development classes, without considering their respective strengths and weaknesses. It is as ridiculous to assume that the same training would equally benefit both as it would be to give them the same size shirt.

We tend to force people into frameworks that are formal. We recite the sage wisdom that formality is our friend. I believe that, in many cases, an appropriate level of formality is warranted. But it is a very dangerous thought to cram different types of individuals into the same one-size-fits-all box.

I believe that such a closed-minded approach stifles creativity, wastes time, erodes morale, and causes our teammates to question our competency. Employees watch in amazement as the next management fad comes and goes, but not before sucking significant energy and cash from the company.

Blind Spots Abound

All of us have blind spots. Blind spots are those characteristics of our personality or conduct that are thought of as negative by others. Interestingly, we seem to not be able to properly process those traits as concerns. That demonstrates a lack of self-awareness, which leads to strife in our relationships.

Most who claim that they have no blind spots are the very people with the biggest ones. Depending on the severity of the blind spot and the influence of the individual with it, the perception of a blind spot can range from slightly annoying to offensive.

I think we have all been around someone who complains about another person's behavior, yet we see the very same behavior in the person who is complaining. We'll scratch our heads, but normally we don't point it out. However, in our new world that values candor so much, a private, appropriately worded comment might actually help improve relationships.

The most severe example of a lack of self-awareness that I have seen involved an individual who led a company that was acquired by my organization. He was quick to describe the relationships he had with his team members as productive. Moreover, he was quick to praise individuals on the team for their contributions.

The company had 69 associates. Each individual had a unique perspective about the company's performance, but all were aligned on one belief. They all despised the individual who led the company. The company's performance had been extremely poor for nearly a decade, and most of the associates pointed to this same person as the root of the problem.

When I advised him that we were terminating his employment, he was shocked. After two hours of discussion, I felt that my explanation had been completely ignored or unheard by this individual. I was amazed by his lack of self-awareness and his continued refusal to even contemplate his shortcomings. I left the exchange believing that he was a very troubled individual.

Even Our Very Best Have Blind Spots

If it were only the people who are bad fits for the company that had blind spots, our job would be easy. We would exit them from the organization. Unfortunately, some of the best and brightest have blind spots – and despite their intelligence or genuine goodness, they cannot seem to realize they have those traits.

I had a very brilliant boss who was a champion of the best-in-class in just about everything. He was a voracious reader. He always seemed to be on the cutting edge of every trend. He regularly pushed me to read and expand my perspective. Most of the time, following his suggestion was extremely productive, because I discovered concepts and tools that I continue to use.

At the same time, he was one of the absolute worst follow-up people I have ever known. To this day, I remain perplexed by him. He was a paradox, because he could be – when he chose to be – one of the most genuinely caring people I have ever known. After years of having the majority of the team advise him that his lack of responsiveness was debilitating, he prodded us to consider his silence to be praise.

I think his lack of responsiveness was a result of a number of traits, but one was definitely his tendency to be extremely disorganized. He had way too much going on in his life to be able to keep up with everything.

At one point, he hired an organization guru who worked with him for over a year. My boss claimed that this individual had helped him so much that he wanted each of the senior managers to benefit from this person's sage advice. I was to be the first.

To provide some background, I was already known for being one of the best follow-up people in the company. I rarely – if ever – missed dates, and I was known for being a productive responder. To be fair, I led a quiet and reserved personal life. A big Saturday night for me was sitting on my dock with my fiancée by my side and a glass of wine in my hand, loving every minute of it.

I met with the consultant, and I found him to be an extremely interesting individual with a compelling approach to organization. The problem was that his approach simply did not work for me. I gave his system a try, and found that by the time I typed everything he wanted me to, I could not get as much done. I became inefficient.

Unfazed by my failed test, my boss forced the guru's training on all the company leaders. The ones who were efficient hated it and regularly complained to me. The ones who tended to be more inefficient remained equally inefficient, or so it seemed to most of us. As for my boss, he claimed that the new system had changed his life. Frankly, I saw no measurable difference in his follow-ups or lack thereof. Nor did any of my colleagues. If it helped him, it was worthwhile that he went through the process. For me, it was a total waste of time and money.

I want to reiterate that I continue to have enormous respect for this man. The fact is that we all have blind spots. In his case, despite the fact that he was made aware of his shortcomings regularly, he was either incapable or unwilling to change.

I will close this section where I started. Again, we all have blind spots. For those of you who do not believe that you have blind spots, they are abundant.

Unique Approaches, Unique People

I prefer a more tactical and specified approach. Examine each person's strengths, weaknesses, preferences, and long-term goals, along with their capabilities and capacity. Once you have gathered that information, create a personalized development plan that will most benefit both the person and the company. Adopting an individualized training program will enhance creativity, save time, enhance morale, and have team members coming back for more. These motivated individuals will, in turn, become more capable and create more wealth for the organization.

Capacity and Intelligence

One often-overlooked characteristic is capacity. Each of us has a mental capacity. Not unlike physical capacity, one's mental capacity can cover a broad spectrum. One person may struggle to bench-press 100 pounds, while another can easily pump out reps at 300 pounds. Variety also occurs in mental capacity, and the disparity between extremes can be as stark as in physical capacity.

Regularly, leaders confuse capacity with intelligence. They mistakenly assume a limitation in capacity corresponds with an equally limited intellect. Not true; they are qualities that should be examined independently.

In my experience, some of the most intelligent team members have had extraordinary limitations when it comes to capacity. While they were able to solve some of the most complicated problems, they simply could not do so in short time periods or dynamic environments. At the same time, I've worked with others who capably juggle an astoundingly high number of priorities simultaneously. But those same team members might struggle with basic problems.

The fact is, healthy teams need both kinds of actors, along with the full spectrum of others between the two extremes. Understanding where a team member works in relationship with others is a vital tool for success. Use of differentiation – a tactic that will be covered in the next chapter – and the four-square grid, covered in Chapter 2, will facilitate the creation of this skill set.

Wealth Creators and Wealth Dissipaters

If we examine a company's wealth creation in the form of a pie chart, wealth is created in slices. While it is true that the pie is always changing in size, there are debits and credits that contribute to the creation of the entire pie. Some slices are bigger and some are smaller. Some remain constant, while others can fluctuate month to month and year to year. It has an ever-changing circumference with a dynamic area. Interestingly, Πr^2 equals area but has nothing to do with a pie chart.

It is a straightforward exercise to examine how varying brands and customers make differing contributions to the wealth to the organization. Assuming we are not in a brand-building investment phase, Brand A delivered $5 million to the bottom line, while Brand B lost $3 million. Therefore, Brand A is creating wealth, while Brand B is consuming wealth.

For two customers of the same size and the similar growth patterns, sales to customer Y generated $1 million in profit, and sales to customer Z delivered $2 million. In this case, Customer Z creates twice the wealth of Customer Y.

There is nuance involved and we must understand all the factors in play. In an apples to apples comparison there are wealth dissipating brands and customers. They must either be corrected or removed from the portfolio. Far too often, internal stakeholders use smoke screens to cloud the realities and thus attempt to justify retaining these underperforming elements of the portfolio.

This was illustrated when a friend, who leads a rather unsophisticated business, lost his second largest customer. His profitability soared and an important lesson was learned.

We can easily comprehend these relationships. Keep in mind that a direct comparison needs to also examine future potential earning streams of each opportunity, along with the investment required to maintain and develop them.

When it comes to people, we tend to have a much more difficult time making such comparisons. I believe that there are human wealth creators and human wealth dissipaters. At some levels within an organization, it is easily understandable to make the comparison.

For example, at the most basic levels, we have two similar employees; their average output goal is 100 units per day. Employee No. 1 – we will call him Ted – regularly produces 125 units per day; and employee No. 2, Fred, produces 75. Clearly, Ted is overproducing while Fred is lagging. If the company profitability is based on achieving 100 units per day, then Fred's performance takes away from the overall performance of the organization. Therefore, Fred is a wealth dissipater. Ted, on the other hand, is not only overdelivering, but creating wealth.

The previous example is a simplistic comparison, but the fact remains that we can and should draw out such contrasts. Over time, if uncorrected, Ted will probably become frustrated with Fred, and with management. I have seen this dynamic play out in every working environment I've been in. It is not the exception; rather, it is the rule. No two people are going to perform identically. So, we need to find ways to ensure that the Freds of the world either get the training and discipline they need, or to reassign them to a role where they can excel. If either of those options is not possible, they need to be exited from the company.

The wealth creation and dissipation dynamic is often harder to see at higher levels of the company, but if you peel off a bit of the onion, you will find the same parallels. The wealth creators are typically pulling the company forward, while the wealth dissipaters are putting a huge drag on the enterprise.

The Bib and the Apron

Over time I have come to believe that most people at work fall into one of three categories: **Bib Wearers, Apron Wearers, or Baprons**.

This idea came to me after an interview I had many years ago while working for a large consumer packaged goods company. I had been with the company for over a decade and had built a strong track record. When I was asked to interview for the role of vice president of North American sales, I was surprised when the interviewer insisted that I submit a resume.

During the conversation, he remarked that I had "done a great deal" in my career, but then added something that I found astonishing. He said he was not impressed with people who do things, but with people who think about how things should be done.

I defended the results that my team had delivered – millions in revenue, and meeting or exceeding expectations in 19 out of 20 quarters. I added that in doing so, we have created some of the most innovative solutions in the category. He acknowledged the results, but insisted they mattered less than the thinking that might have produced even greater opportunities.

Finally, I asked him a simple question: "If everyone is sitting in a room thinking about things, and the light bulb burns out, does someone change the bulb or do you just sit in the dark?"

The interview ended shortly afterward. Months later, I realized what had happened. I had encountered a classic Bib Wearer.

The Apron Wearer

Apron Wearers are the people who do the work. They build the products, run the analysis, test the systems, answer the emails, and keep the organization moving. Without them, nothing gets produced, no reports are written, and no customers are served.

Because their output is tangible, Apron Wearers often take pride in what they produce. When their work is finished, something real exists.

This also explains why Apron Wearers sometimes resent Bib Wearers. When they look at executives who spend their days thinking, meeting, and reviewing reports, it can be difficult to see how the executives create value.

The Bib Wearer

Bib Wearers are different. They are fed information created by Apron Wearers and spend their time thinking about what it means. Their job is to interpret data, identify patterns, and make decisions that move the organization forward.

When a Bib Wearer glances at a report for 30 seconds and walks away with an idea worth millions, the system has worked, even if the Apron Wearer who created the report spent hours producing it.

For this reason, Bib Wearers are often highly compensated. Their value lies not in the volume of work they produce, but in the **decisions and ideas** that shape the company's future.

The Bapron

Eventually, I discovered a third type of person. I call them Baprons.

Baprons can think like Bib Wearers and work like Apron Wearers at the same time. They are energized by both activities. They enjoy building the spreadsheet and analyzing the results. They don't need a team of analysts to generate insights because they can create the analysis themselves.

While Baprons may not always be the strongest pure thinker or the most efficient pure doer, the combination can be extremely powerful. Both Bib Wearers and Apron Wearers tend to respect Baprons because they understand both worlds.

Embracing the Differences

No role is inherently better than the others. Organizations need thinkers, builders, and people who can do both. Problems arise when people are placed in roles that conflict with their natural tendencies.

An Apron Wearer placed in a Bib role may struggle to make decisions. A Bib Wearer forced into an Apron role may become bored and ineffective.

But the most overlooked problem is the Bapron trapped in an Apron role. These individuals often become frustrated because they see opportunities for improvement, but lack the authority to implement them.

It's important to recognize each of these differences and align people with roles that allow them to thrive. Once you understand whether a person wears a bib, an apron, or both, you can begin building teams that use each strength effectively.

Calling all bib wearers: Please think carefully about the unintended consequences of your actions. An apron wearer, who may have spent hours, days or even weeks to prepare a report, has probably poured a great deal of passion into his or her work. When you give it a cursory glance and it sparks a brilliant idea, remember to take the time to explain to the apron wearer how vital their work has been. It's even better if you can spend a bit of time in reflection with the report in hand. Since you are likely to be a big thinker, think about how your actions impact others.

Failure to do so results in Do Nothing Fat Cat Syndrome. Bib wearers who embrace and reward apron wearers can avoid this debilitating consequence. Remember, it is the bib wearer's responsibility to keep this from occurring as they are likely the leader.

There Is a Size for Everyone

One size definitely does not fit all – however, in business there is a size for almost everyone, and almost everyone has a size. Recognizing your size and knowing how to optimize your performance is a great first step.

Identifying the sizes of those individuals around you and encouraging them to optimize their size is a great next step.

Seeking out, attracting and retaining individuals who have sizes not currently found on your team will enhance outcomes.

In the movie *My Best Friend's Wedding*, there is a great exchange about crème brulée and Jell-O®. Julia Roberts' character informs Cameron Diaz's character that she is crème brulée, and her soon-to-be-husband prefers Jell-O®. When Cameron Diaz informs Julia Roberts that she could become Jell-O®, Julia Roberts advises her, "Crème brulée could never be Jell-O®."

Make sure that your team has both crème brulée and Jell-O® on it, along with all the other available foods, and you will create a potent buffet from which you can feast.

Combustion Check – IGNITE INDIVIDUALIZED APPROACHES

Before lighting the fuse on your next program or initiative, ask yourself:

1. Are you committed to replacing one-size-fits-all programs with tailored solutions that fit each individual?
2. What are your blind spots? Are you willing to seek the opinion of others to discover them? How will you conduct this evaluation?
3. Do you recognize the difference between intelligence and capacity, and are you committed to evaluate each team member accurately?
4. Can you identify who wears a bib, an apron, or a bapron to understand the roles people play in your organization?
5. How can you embrace differences, leverage unique strengths, and ignite diverse contributions?

Answering these questions ensures that your team burns brighter as a whole, with individual talents fueling collective success.

9

Proven Rules: Salvaging Old Wood

If you can't explain it to a 6-year-old,
you don't understand it yourself.
– Albert Einstein, theoretical physicist

Have you . . .

Ever found problem-solving to be overly daunting, physically exhausting and mentally draining?

What if . . .

You could adopt a childlike perspective with a fresh attitude, embracing the simplicity of your youth?

I pride myself in learning something new every day. The morning I finished this chapter, I found myself in the back seat of a car driven by a man who had exchanged a successful business career for the solace of his car. His day was now planned by his Uber app. Prior to becoming a driver, he had been a senior manager for a national fast-food chicken chain. What I found fascinating during our conversation was his knowledge of the intricacies of creating the perfect fried chicken dish. I had never contemplated the challenge of achieving a balance of taste and moisture, and then making sure the oil would not actually penetrate the meat – while still allowing it to flavor the coating. I found out that the chicken I've enjoyed for decades requires a rather delicate balance; and at the same time, had to hit a consumer-friendly price point and be easily replicated over millions of pieces. How fascinating!

Many times in business, we have to return to our roots to get the answer we seek. Usually, issues come down to some basic principles that we learn early in life, but for some reason, we have decided to forget or ignore them.

Differentiation

One of the principles we learn early in life is differentiation. Someone is first, someone is last, and everyone else falls in varying levels between. Differentiation is one of the most empowering and productive principles in business.

Differentiation is simply a way to prioritize. Jack Welch, former CEO of General Electric, is one of the stalwarts of differentiation. His examination of its principles in his book Winning is a worthwhile read.

Classic differentiation as applied to business usually involves the members of your team. The principle states that all people are not equal in the workplace. It forces you to discern who your best people are, and who your worst are. Someone is first. Someone is last. The remainder all are ranked in between.

Normally, you evaluate your team members through a lens of performance and potential, or one of performance and cultural fit. I actually like to trade the filters out annually to ensure that both lenses are considered over time.

One might think that the filters are not that revealing. Nothing could be further from the truth. One year, we examined performance and potential, and the next year we examined performance and cultural fit. While some individuals remained at the top in both evaluations, there were a significant number of members at the top of one list that landed squarely in the middle on the next.

Once you have ranked all of your team members, you can separate them into subgroups. Each group will fall on the continuum of the differentiation grid you have created.

DIFFERENTIATION GRID

HIGH

PERFORMANCE

B26	B17	B9	B2	A16	A11	A7	A4	A2	A1
B36	B27	B18	B10	B3	A17	A12	A8	A5	A3
B45	B37	B28	B19	B11	B4	A18	A13	A9	A6
B53	B46	B38	B29	B20	B12	B5	A19	A14	A10
B60	B54	B47	B39	B30	B21	B13	B6	A20	A15
B66	B61	B55	B48	B40	B31	B22	B14	B7	B1
F1	B67	B62	B56	B49	B41	B32	B23	B15	B8
F5	F2	B68	B63	B57	B50	B42	B33	B24	B16
F8	F6	F3	B69	B64	B58	B51	B43	B34	B25
F10	F9	F7	F4	B70	B65	B59	B52	B44	B35

LOW **POTENTIAL** HIGH

Figure 4: Differentiation Grid A=top 20 percent; B= mid 70 percent; F=bottom 10 percent

Reward and Develop Top Performers

There is a classic 20-70-10 approach. The top 20 percent are your movers and shakers. These folks are the high performers that make things happen and stand out in the crowd. We need to keep these individuals engaged and do whatever is required – within reason – to keep these folks happy and motivated.

It is important that we create formal development plans for these individuals. The first step should be to talk to the identified high performers. All too often, we as executives believe we know best; we then create plans for the high performers on our own.

It is appropriate to balance company needs with a candidate's skills and acumen, but to do so without a dialogue first is lunacy. We must first get insights into their goals and desires, discover what stimulates them, and find out where they see themselves in five or 10 years.

Young people need guidance and mentoring, but attempting to turn a person into someone that they have no desire to be is counterproductive. One time, I lost one of my best people because he was incapable of dealing with the stress of his new position. He simply was not cut out for the role. Instead of speaking to me about his angst, he simply resigned. That day I lost two people, my best operator and my new supervisor – yes, the same person.

After discussing a top performer's goals and desires, you and the top performer should create a plan that you both sign off on. The plan will be the roadmap to that employee's future; and, if completed properly, is a significant retention tool.

Make sure to reward these people with perks that motivate them, even though the perks wouldn't be included in their formal plans. An example of a perk could include a dinner for the employee and their significant other, tickets to a sporting event, or a weekend getaway. Get to know your top performers, so you understand what motivates them most.

Top performers may get off track from time to time. As part of their mentoring program, make sure you counsel them when you see the slightest weakness. Immature mistakes can quickly become ingrained, adverse behaviors if not corrected. Act swiftly and deftly when counseling these individuals. If you have executed your development program properly, they will welcome candid feedback.

The Heart and Soul

The middle 70 percent of employees are the heart and soul of the organization. They may not have the capability to lead the company to the next level – but without them, the next level is impossible to attain. They deliver results, they are loyal, but they just do not rise to the elite status that those in the top 20 percent do. Reward them and love them, but understand the economic implications of overdoing it.

These folks in the middle are often taken for granted. Make sure they know how important they are to the future of the organization. I often refer to this positive reinforcement as "showing them the love."

When in Doubt, Throw Misfits Out

Finally, there are those team members who reside in the bottom 10 percent. These are the people who drag the team down.

As previously addressed, I like to refer to them as wealth dissipaters. They are either poor cultural fits or in the wrong spot in the organization. These folks must either be rehabilitated or removed from the business. We invest significant time and money trying to rehabilitate these individuals, and in most cases it does not work. Usually, they simply need to be exited.

I can't tell you how many times I have heard that certain people "just need time" or "we can't afford to lose them; they are better than nothing." I call this Dead Man Walking Syndrome. Everybody knows what is going to happen, especially those in the bottom 10 percent.

We play the game, and we allow those designated for dismissal to hang around. Then, bad things happen. The identified 10 percent continue to perform below expectations and they spread their poor attitudes to others. Even worse, they gather information for the lawsuit they will eventually file against the organization. Using the word "will" in the previous sentence is a very strong word, but it is more accurate than the word "may." Using "will" prepares you for it. And then, if it doesn't happen, you can consider yourself fortunate. In my experience, a lawsuit gets filed or at least threatened.

I have a philosophy: Absolutes in business are rare. "Always" and "never" are hardly ever used appropriately. With that said, it is **never** a good idea to allow poor performers to linger. The best outcome of delaying the inevitable is that you continue to receive substandard service from a substandard employee.

The poor performers tend to suck all the enthusiasm out of the air. More detrimental is the effect they have on the good performers. At best, the fully effective employees feel like they have to work harder due to the poor performer's poor contributions. It's even more probable that the poor performer will impact the performance of the entire team. Moreover, they can create lasting negative attitude challenges.

In my experience, the candidate for termination is usually aware that he or she is on a short list. They go into a defensive mode and start gathering information – either to prepare for an eventual lawsuit or to discredit the company. I have had malcontents steal formulas, marketing plans, sales presentations and other materials. They justify their behavior by saying they felt disenfranchised by the company.

Misfits File Lawsuits

Lawsuits are another matter. Typically, those people who sue companies in reactionary anger have invalid claims. Most claims can be proven to be invalid on a material basis, but still, almost every company makes innocent mistakes. When circumstances are twisted by skillful lawyers, those mistakes sound horrific. There are few things more damning than having a sleazy attorney mold the facts to paint a fictitious picture of the **heinous acts** perpetrated by an **evil organization.**

Thirty years ago, I allowed a malcontent to stick around. Finally, she resigned, and within weeks armed police were at my office to serve me and the company with a lawsuit. The lawsuit claimed constructive dismissal due to the creation of a hostile sexual work environment. The goal of having the police come to our place of business was to embarrass the company and me.

It turned out that the police officers were off duty; yet, they were allowed to serve the papers as agents of the court, in uniform, carrying firearms.

It worked. I was mortified, and when it hit the front page of the local newspaper, I was humiliated. I thought of leaving my position. The suit sought $3 million in damages from both the company and me. The legal battle that ensued took three years.

We could have settled, and probably for less than $50,000, but I insisted that we fight. My integrity was on the line, and the subject matter was so morally concerning to me that I felt I needed to clear my name.

I am not sure what the final cost in dollars was, or how many total man-hours were invested, but both sums were significant. When it ended, we won and paid nothing; but I lost, personally, and so did my team and my company. The distraction of the lawsuit was more debilitating than the raw cost in dollars. It paralyzed the organization. The tragedy was that every twisted claim in the suit had been fabricated.

I had known after her first day that the employee was a bad fit. If I had acted when I should have and terminated her employment, all of the turmoil, cost and mental anguish could have been avoided.

For those who are wondering, the newspaper did print an article confirming that the company and I had been cleared, and that the lawsuit was found to have no merit. Of course, that information was not printed on the front page. No – it ended up on page 18, just under the Word Jumble.

Another approach would have been to settle, but that is no bargain either. Settling sends a message that the company will pay to keep things out of court. While $50,000 may not sound like much to a corporation, it is a significant amount of money to some. Worse yet, a settlement can often be construed as an admission of guilt.

Ask Herman Cain, the brilliant businessman whose 2012 presidential bid was thwarted by allegations. I have no inside knowledge of the validity of claims of sexual harassment against him, but his background as a turnaround leader would make him ripe for such complaints – even if he had done nothing wrong. The media tore through him. They seemingly could not fathom why his company would have settled for $50,000 had he not been guilty.

It's important to know that settlement checks – both large and small – get written with great regularity and have no bearing on the facts of the accusations. Genuine claims will result in awards for many times more than a settlement amount.

I am sure there are plenty of examples where legitimately harassed and exploited employees kept their mouths shut and suffered greatly at the hands of amoral supervisors and managers. Nevertheless, those occurrences do not justify the countless contrived claims filed out of anger or spite. In fact, the sheer regularity of invalid claims makes those that are valid less credible. This is a true tragedy on both fronts.

Exceptions to the Misfit Rule

There are some who end up classified in the bottom 10 percent of the workforce who are truly individuals who have either been put in a bad situation or are struggling. These people are candidates for rehabilitation, but a delicate balance must be achieved, which requires a jointly agreed-upon development plan and close monitoring. Typically, 90-day plans are developed and executed. In almost all cases, if the individual's performance has not vastly improved after the first week or two, the person is not worth keeping on the team.

Do not allow your associates to use the "We have to keep them for a full 90 days, because that is the length of the probation" excuse. Ninety-day probations are simply the **maximum** amount of time allowed for rehabilitation. If employees working under a probationary period do not improve dramatically in the first few weeks, they are either incapable or unwilling to meet the minimum criteria for the position.

Yes, there might be some risk of losing a potentially good performer by acting swiftly. In my view, the benefits far outweigh the risks. Cut bottom performers from the team in a timely fashion and watch your team cheer.

Many people struggle with the concept of differentiation. I have found that it is best explained by reminding folks of when we picked teams in elementary school. Everyone lined up, and the two captains picked alternately. Someone was always first, and someone was always last; that too was differentiation.

Differentiate Everything

Differentiation should be applied to everything we do. Formal differentiation of customers, projects, and products will achieve great results. It is a simple exercise, once you get comfortable with it. We differentiate all the time: when we choose to order the sea bass instead of the steak, or we decide to go to Movie A instead of Movie B.

If you can get your IT team to prepare reports that do the work for you, it makes formal differentiation quicker and easier. Then there is the question of what we compare our customers, projects, and products against. I advocate that a good start is by asking, "Does it make money, and if so, how much?" If the evaluated entity is a money-loser (or our old friend, the wealth dissipater), we simply need to remove it from our business model.

There will almost always be one bundler or complicator on the team who will passionately object, claiming that the process is very risky. They will cite strategic implications to impede the completion of the exercise. Remember, just as with the employee exercise, a customer or brand finding itself on the bottom of the list is not automatically removed. There will be a chance for rehabilitation – but as with employees, make sure there is a plan and that it is closely monitored. There is simply bad business, and it should be exited from your portfolio. If you are not actively differentiating your accounts, brands, and SKUs (product items), I'll wager that you have some losers in the portfolio.

When you complete the exercise, you will probably feel stupid, angry, and embarrassed, all at the same time. That's OK; it's a great character builder.

Prioritization and Organizational Capacity

Prioritization is simply a form of differentiation. When you prioritize, you make a choice. One opportunity is more important than a second opportunity, and so forth. It is important to recognize that, in addition to deciding what you are going to tackle first as a team, there is a limit on organizational capacity.

Far too often, companies overextend the organization's capacity to complete work. I have found that most organizations severely overestimate their capacity. But remember – it is much more important to do three things well than to do five things poorly. In a business where opportunities abound, it takes great discipline to limit the ones that you attempt to tackle. It is too easy to say "yes" to the additional opportunities; prudence urges us to say "no."

Unclear Objectives Create Confusion

Once the organization has chosen what is to be accomplished, each team should examine its role in making sure the organization is successful. Oftentimes, the team will find that its objectives are in conflict with the organization's priorities.

At one time, I worked for a company that sold both branded and private-label products. Private-label products existed for two reasons. First, they helped cover overhead and, in some cases, they helped the company retain a strategic customer.

Clearly, the branded-product business was the top priority, but evidently no one informed the private-label team. When the private-label team committed a significant amount of product to a customer, the capacity was outstripped. We ended up cutting orders to our branded-product customers because the capacity did not exist for both products. Shortly afterward, the private-label and branded teams were consolidated, to avoid a repeat occurrence of the problem.

The top priorities of the organization must prevail; a team's objectives always must be configured to meet the organization's broader needs. Simply stated, if there is a conflict between the team goals and the broader organization's goals, the organization must override the team. It is certainly appropriate for teams to stretch and produce peripheral work, but it must not interfere with the successful delivery of the organization's top priorities. There must be total clarity on this subject.

The same principle can be applied to individual goals and work plans. They must first be designed to deliver the team's commitment to the organization, and then to deliver the individual's commitment to the team. This is a cascade effect – it should flow up and down through the organization throughout the years.

The corporation's top priorities dictate the department's work plan; which, in turn, dictates the individual's work plan. The individual's work plan fuels the successful completion of the departmental work plan; which, in turn, fuels the successful delivery of the organization's top priorities. If you commit to follow this discipline, it will become part of the culture of the company and soon be an automatic core competency.

It is a reality that no department, and no individual, is great at everything. In fact, all of us might be at a different point on the journey to competency. Recognizing the realities of the competence continuum is vital to learning.

Four Stages of Competency

Successful realization of competency has four stages. It is important that every company comprehends each of the four stages and be objective enough to understand which stage they are in. Each competency requires us to go through the four stages. Oftentimes, the earliest stages are the most difficult to identify, because "we don't know what we don't know."

Stage One: Unconscious Incompetency

In the first stage of competency, we are not competent, and we do not even realize it. We may not be aware that a future competency is something we would be interested in or that it even exists as an activity. Or, we may not realize something we have competency experience in is applicable to our business. We are Unconsciously Incompetent.

Think about riding a bike. At some point in our childhood, we see a bike for the first time. We are intrigued but do not have an understanding. Once we observe bike riding or hear our friends talking about it, we become aware that it is for enjoyment and transportation. We then might say, "I'd like to try that." But before we are introduced to the bike for the first time, we definitely are not conscious about bike riding. It is a fair bet that we are also incompetent about how to ride.

Stage Two: Conscious Incompetency

Once we have decided that we want to attempt to do something, we move to Conscious Incompetency. We attempt to learn, and often we will struggle.

In the case of bike riding, it might require training wheels. It might result in a few skinned knees or a bruised ego. Stage two can take on many forms; and, depending on what it is we are attempting to accomplish, may take a great deal of time.

In bike riding, most pass stage two. This is not true in business. For some reason, businesses tend to lose patience. It might be due to quarterly pressures, but more than likely, it's a lack of commitment from top management. Think about the bike riding analogy. Why do most of us persevere when learning to ride a bike? I think it comes down to two words: peer pressure.

When we get stuck in stage two of a particular competency, we eventually lose interest and decide that whatever we wanted to do was not that important after all. I have often wondered, if businesses could learn to harness peer pressure, how many important initiatives could have been accomplished?

Business uses management by objectives (MBOs) to deliver its goals. This system is an effective tool, but we often fail to see it through. We tend to want to soften our positions because we convince ourselves that we need to be more understanding or sympathetic.

Equally important in business is a filtering system. We do not allow ourselves to pass through stage two when the thing we want to master really is not at the core of our goals. From my personal life, I would draw the example of golf. For years, I was consciously incompetent. At some point, I decided that the investment to get from stage two to stage three was far too great. So, I threw my clubs away.

If I had recognized early on that golf was not central to anything I needed to do in my life, I could have avoided a great deal of expense and frustration. If you have ever played golf poorly, you know the frustration. I enjoy watching golf, but I believe I have picked up my last club, and I celebrate that fact.

Stage Three: Conscious Competency

Assuming we make it to the third stage, we evolve to the state of Conscious Competency. We are able to successfully engage in whatever activity it is that we have chosen to tackle, but we still need to continually remind ourselves of each step in the process that allows us to remain competent. When I first learned to drive, I had to have my hands on 10 and 2, and as I recall, a firm grip on the steering wheel. Some who were around during my early driving days might question my competency then, but there is no question I was careful in each turn and in every acceleration or braking action.

When businesses achieve this level of competency, they start to reap the rewards of the discipline and effort invested. Yet, far too often they tend to lose their resolve and regress, falling far short of what could have been.

Stage Four: Unconscious Competency

It takes continued practice to maintain Conscious Competency, but over time, if the discipline is continued, we smoothly transition into the final stage, Unconscious Competency.

We are good at doing something and we do not even have to think about it. It just happens. Think about the bike riding analogy or driving a car. We get on or in, and go. We never give it a thought. Imagine how powerful that would be in business, if we only invested the time and effort to get to that level. The paradox is, we **do** invest the time and effort but we often just do not follow through. If we had stuck with the plan and stayed on course, we would have invested less time, less effort and less money, and ended up with superior results.

Ask and You Will Receive

It has always amazed me that people in business tend to be afraid to ask for what they are looking for, particularly when it pertains to customers. We spend huge amounts of resources preparing for customer summits. We become anxious and plan for confronting an unyielding monster on the other side of the desk. When questions are asked, our minds race to try to figure out what the customer is really asking.

Difficult People Are Often Playing a Role

I recall visiting a customer, a major retailer. I was completely unnerved – my feeling stemmed from a combination of having extensively prepared for the meeting and a fear of inferiority. This company's buyer had developed a legendary difficult status within the halls of my organization. He did not disappoint; he was a complete and utter bully. I walked out of the meeting wondering how any human could be that difficult.

Ironically, I ran into the person several years later at an industry share group session. He had retired and was consulting. I found him to be an extremely affable individual. After a bit of time, I had mentioned that I had called on him when he was with his former company, the major retailer. Before I could get the next sentence out, he stated, "I bet you thought I was a complete jerk."

I lied and said, "No, just a bit challenging."

He revealed he had undergone intense training at his company to learn how to put vendors out of their comfort zone. He added that the strategy was intentional, and it was believed at that particular retailer to be a superior and financially advantageous tactic.

Fear Not

When dealing with yet another account, I was faced with a genuine dilemma. They were a key account – my largest – but they ordered in three-quarter truck quantities. I had implored my sales team to try to have the trucks filled, but they had been unsuccessful in their endeavors.

I went to a meeting that included executives from both companies; our team did a great job, and I was feeling extremely confident. When the meeting was ending, the customer's senior level executive and decision-maker thanked us, and asked us if there was anything else she could do for us.

In a moment I will remember for the rest of my life, I said, "In an effort to keep your cost of goods down, could you help us by ordering full truck quantities?"

I cringed as I awaited the reply. "Sure, that sounds reasonable," she said.

That question and response was worth millions of dollars to my company and saved countless barrels of oil. "I guess we simply had to ask," one of my co-workers said as we returned to our car.

But there are also those customers who exploit vendor weaknesses. It is a strategic imperative for them.

When I worked at a large consumer products goods company, the sales team was so adept at making excuses to customers that it had become a core competency. We were known in the industry for our ineffectiveness. We had come to believe we were a substandard supplier, and it permeated our collective persona. I was meeting with another major retailer and was blindsided by a barrage of threats. The buyer remained professional, but I walked out believing that this man was one of the harshest people I had ever met; I felt that our business was in severe jeopardy. Frankly, for the first time in my career, I began to question my instincts.

I changed jobs three months later. My first sales call with my new employer was in front of this same man. I walked into the room and shook his hand, secretly hoping he would not remember me. After the introductions, he could sense my nervousness. He then advised that he remembered me, and apologized for the rough time he had given me. He revealed that he always was that way when dealing with my previous employer because he got more from that company when he put them on the defensive.

I have seen this scenario play out over 20 times in my career. While I am sure there are some individuals that are more difficult than others, the vast majority are great people who, as I like to say, "put their pants on one leg at a time."

A company in alignment will present effectively to the most discerning of customers, provided they are transparent, honest, and deliver results. Buyers are no different than the rest of us. They want to be successful and will make their assignments as easy as possible. A vendor that helps them achieve these objectives will win, but it starts with internal alignment across your organization.

Plain and Simple, People Lie

There is an uncomfortable truth that few people talk about openly: people lie. Some do it occasionally; others do it frequently. A few seem to struggle with telling the truth at all. People lie to gain advantage, avoid consequences, or shape how others see them. Most lies are small and relatively harmless, but chronic dishonesty is different. It destroys trust, and trust is the foundation of every effective team.

When you identify a chronic liar on your team, the best course of action is to remove them quickly. The chaos they create is devastating; and in my experience, chronic dishonesty is rarely corrected. Allowing someone who repeatedly violates trust to remain on the team will slowly poison the culture.

Even people who are generally honest will sometimes lie, particularly when they feel they have been wronged. I have seen this happen repeatedly when an employment is terminated. Facts are quickly reshaped, narratives change, and accusations can suddenly appear.

For this reason, leaders must act decisively and carefully when exiting employees. Documentation should be clear, communication should be direct, and standards of conduct must be unmistakable. Behavior that could be interpreted as discriminatory cannot be allowed. Even actions that seem harmless in the moment can later be reframed by a disgruntled employee.

Over the years, I have developed a few simple rules to help reduce disruptions that threaten to complicate leadership and team dynamics. Trust is the foundation of every great team. Once dishonesty enters the culture, the damage spreads. A leader's job is to protect trust without hesitation. One vital axiom guides me: if someone lies about the small things, you cannot trust them with the big ones.

Unbridled Zealotry Is a Risk

I have found that a type of person who often exhibits inauthentic personality traits are zealots. They tend to be among the worst when it comes to engaging in what I call "self-justified" dishonesty. They preach to others, while – under the guise of their "the end justifies the means" agenda – they weave the tallest of tales. As long as it is "for the cause," they rationalize the lying as acceptable behavior. Often, they have a huge blind spot when it comes to their fanaticism.

When I refer to zealots, I am not referring to religious partisans; however, those individuals do exist and can fall into the same traps as all ideologues. But zealotry can find its way into almost any area where misplaced passion can overtake normally well-intended individuals. Little League sports are a great example. One only needs to visit ball fields on Saturday afternoons to see overzealous parents transform into foul-mouthed maniacs.

Zealots in the workplace are not rare, but rather quite common. While that judgment might seem a bit extreme to some, I have found that many simply cannot control themselves.

The Rule of 100

Emotion debilitates companies. The smallest situation can create emotional outbursts that have no place in life, let alone in business. Whenever an associate becomes emotional, I will ask them to take a deep breath and calm down. I ask them if the situation is going to matter in 100 years. The answer is always "no." Then I follow up with questions about 10 years, five years, and then one year. Most of the time, the answers are "no" and "no" and… "no."

Once we frame the "disaster" in the proper perspective, we can better determine an approach to fix it. Removing emotion from charged situations allows us to more objectively seek a solution. That, of course, assumes that the situation can be fixed. One should also ask the question: "Can anything be done about it?"

There is an exercise that I find extremely powerful when coaching others. I instruct them to write down the 10 things that are the biggest problems in their lives. I then have them insert those into an envelope. I promise that no one will open the envelope other than them, and I advise that we will review them in one year. It is often very powerful to mail the envelope to the participant in a year's time.

In almost every case, the participants had completely forgotten about the exercise. Moreover, those seemingly insurmountable issues that plagued them a year previously have been replaced by new challenges. The exercise is an enlightening and liberating experience.

It has many applications. It can be used for goal-setting or to develop introspection. And writing a letter to yourself that you have a third party mail to you in a year can be quite enlightening.

One of my favorite quotes is from Sir Winston Churchill: "Those who fail to learn from history are doomed to repeat it."

If there is nothing that can be done about the situation, it is best to put it behind you and then shift to determining what can be learned from the experience. The real tragedy of failures is that we often make them a **double** failure – by failing to learn from them.

The Rule of 90-10

Another wonderful quote, from Lou Holtz, the former Notre Dame head football coach, frames our next rule. "Life is 10 percent what happens to you and 90 percent how you respond to it."

Bad things happen to people and businesses all the time… and so do good things. But for some reason, most of us tend to focus on the bad. We need to give good and bad equal billing. When something good or bad happens, how we respond to it is what's most important. Frankly, if you can learn to respond unemotionally, yet remain passionate, you will end up with the most positive outcome.

First, when we encounter a bad situation, we need to understand what the root cause is. Why did it really happen? Far too often, we do not dig deep enough and find symptoms or red herrings. The danger here is that we risk bringing Winston Churchill's quote to life. We simply discover the first symptoms and then stop.

When something terrible occurs, we can choose to react negatively or positively. Or, we can also choose not to react at all. I had an employee call me and tell me he had been fired. He was fairly emotional, and I advised him to calm down and state what exactly had happened. He ranted for a good half hour, but when I probed him for details, he really was unable to provide much. Immediately I saw what appeared to be a classic emotional-outburst misunderstanding.

I completed a cursory investigation. It turned out that he had been counseled by his superior that he was not a good fit for the job he was in. A different position was being considered for him, and the superior wanted to work with the employee to find the best fit. However, during the session, the employee got frustrated and resigned, burning a few bridges.

I conducted a follow-up session with the employee. We walked through the steps in the process, and the employee realized that he had reacted to bad news in a very poor fashion.

He acknowledged resigning, and admitted that he had stopped listening the minute the phrase "not a good fit" was uttered. After our chat, he realized that what could have been a minor setback, and totally within his control, had turned into a major life-altering event. Unfortunately, his behavior during the session was considered so outrageous that we could not reinstate him under any circumstances.

Since we like good things so much, we really do not analyze them when they happen. I find that lack of examination to be a major missed opportunity for an improved, simplified life. We want good things to be repeated, so we should understand the root causes of why they occur. We should use the same diligence to examine good events as we do when bad things happen. Learning what makes good things happen allows you to put yourself in position for good things to happen again. It's certainly not a guarantee, but it is well worth the effort.

As Henry Ford said, "If you always do what you've always done, you'll always get what you've always got." It is up to you to choose how to react – negatively, positively or not at all. You are totally in control of how you decide to respond.

I would eliminate any negativity from your thinking. Focus on the positive, and learn the benefits of not reacting at all. You will alleviate 90 percent of the stress in your life if you adopt this approach. And applying it to business will bring significant benefits for your career.

To close this section, I will go back to John Wooden, one of my favorite leaders, for another quote. "Things turn out best for the people who make the best of the way things turn out."

The Rules of Fishing

I love to fish. It is one of my favorite hobbies. I mostly freshwater fish, but enjoy saltwater fishing, as well. I fish for everything from pan fish to sailfish. I use live bait, artificial lures, and flies. I have learned that, depending on what species you are looking for, you use different equipment and go to different waters to find specific types of fish.

Nothing could be easier. You select the proper equipment, and fish where the fish are. If you do not catch anything, you move to the next spot. If one type of bait is not working, you can change it up and try a different type.

Business is just as simple, but we regularly overcomplicate matters by trying to find complex solutions to easy challenges.

One of the companies I have had the pleasure of leading in my career was struggling to find candidates for positions in the factory. These were unskilled and semi-skilled labor positions. We placed advertisements in newspapers and had no success. We then turned to temporary agencies and got plenty of people, but their caliber was below expectations. Nevertheless, we repeated this process over and over for more than a year. We continued to be disappointed, and the turnover was debilitating to the business.

The Right Bait and the Proper Equipment

We assembled a team to attempt to understand the situation and find a solution. We found that our starting wage was too low, and our benefit package was too expensive. Management loved the benefits, but it cost the company an extra $1.50 an hour. And, compared to a more basic plan that cost significantly less, the benefit package was not attractive to the hourly wage earners; they wanted every available dollar in their pockets.

Most of the people we sought were young, single, and healthy. Young, healthy people rarely think about insurance or getting sick. They are thinking about having fun, doing the things they like to do. They think they are bulletproof. Our team immediately developed a new, scaled-down menu of benefits as an option, allowing all employees to opt in for, you guessed it, $1.50 per hour. Existing team members were offered the option to trade down for, you guessed it, $1.50 an hour pay raise.

When the team presented me with that solution, I initially thought they had lost their minds. But they were resolute and convinced me to allow them to follow that course. It worked extremely well – we were able to attract more candidates, and I replicated that solution later in other companies.

Nearly every manager remained on the more comprehensive plan, and nearly every existing hourly associate opted for the increase in base pay.

Fish Where the Fish Are

We decided we ought to go to where the people we sought spent their time. We canvassed all the local high schools for upcoming graduates. We also put ads up at youth centers. Finally, we found out where our competitors' employees liked to spend time after work, and put ads up there.

The First to a Hungry Fish Catches More Fish

Finally, we realized that the best people are taken first, and that it is far easier to grab someone who is unemployed rather than try to wrestle someone away from their current job. We found that our screening process simply took too long. We know that speed matters in business, but we didn't think of that factor in hiring.

We realized that speed matters when hiring as well. We also found that there is a finite number of potential employees. A small percentage is of "A" caliber – they are the elite prospects, and they are easily identified by all the companies seeking employees. It's no surprise that the A's go first.

Once they are gone, your potential employee pool is diluted. An extended and arduous employment process eventually has you deciding between "C" and "D" performers. Most, if not all, of the "B" players are gobbled up by the competition.

We sought to speed up the process, and were immediately barraged by naysayers in the company, who felt compelled to expose what they referred to as reckless and irresponsible hiring. Despite the challenge, we implemented a new process that allowed us to have a candidate go from applicant to employee in less than three days.

Everyone went on probation for 60 days too, which allowed for the opportunity for more robust screening. Since we did our homework early and only selected what we thought were "A" performers, not one single person failed the more intensive scrutiny of the evaluation during probation.

We found that if we fished where the fish were, and if we used the right compensation as bait and set the hook quickly, we caught many more fish. This rule, "Fish where the fish are," can be applied to many challenges in business.

As is the case with fishermen, we found that getting to the target fish first was a huge positive. I guess that's why fishermen have such big engines on their boats. Speed does matter in fishing… and in business.

The Rule of A, B, C

The transitive property in mathematics states that if A = B, and B = C, then A = C. Applying this simplest of all mathematical rules to business will allow for speed by eliminating mistakes.

This rule works well when trying to determine if there are errors in reports or analysis. It is also good for tracking units. I find it particularly helpful when faced with accounting for inventories.

Systems rarely make mistakes, but people make them regularly. People unintentionally transpose numbers with great regularity. In a fast-paced environment, like shipping or receiving, simple transposition errors can result in significant issues.

I can't begin to share how many times I have reviewed inventory reports and found significant errors. The easiest to find are negative numbers. You simply cannot have a negative on-hand balance. I have been in more discussions over this topic than I care to remember. Typically, people will defend their numbers until we find the source of the error.

Impossible Measurements Are… Impossible

Another frequent example of a mistake involving the A, B, C rule is impossible measurement. You cannot have more of something than will fit into the vessel that holds it. For example, you cannot have ten gallons of gas in a five-gallon gas can. That example may sound ridiculous, but similar ones play out in the real world regularly. Such examples of impossibility can either overstate or understate value; and, once corrected, they can create unpleasant surprises that have significant impacts on the bottom line.

Once, during a pallet audit, I was told there were 40,000 pallets on the books in a particular warehouse. However, I knew the warehouse could only hold 25,000 pallets. A quick walk-through suggested that the warehouse was not nearly at capacity. I engaged in a spirited debate about the pallet inventory, and afterwards we discovered the administrative snafu. I guess it was the so-called "new math."

Another great application for the rule of A, B, C is ingredient inventory accounting. I have been involved in dozens of plant operations throughout my career, and all have had unexpected and unaccounted-for ingredient losses. But the root cause is often an input error; at some point, an extra zero is added, or a duplicate entry is made. When we investigated, we usually discovered that the inventory had been overstated; the storage unit for that ingredient was incapable of holding the quantity recorded in the inventory.

For example, we have a bin capable of holding 10,000 pounds of flour, but the books show 15,000 pounds on hand. Instead of implementing a system that catches the error at a more convenient and controlled time, we find out the error when the bin runs empty. Now we have two problems. First, we have overstated the inventory. Second, and more important, we have shut down our facility because we are out of ingredients.

Using the approach that impossible measurements cannot exist can keep you free from material losses. I have taught that approach over and over; but amazingly, most people cannot grasp the concept. And individuals will get very animated when attempting to justify their work when obvious errors are clear to anyone who is not so invested in the work.

These kinds of extremely simple rules abound, and should be applied with great regularity.

Precision Should Never Trump Accuracy

The same is true for reports. Check for errors. An analyst who was amazingly adept at Excel presented me with a complicated multiple-tab analysis that demonstrated a significant savings opportunity for the company. After I briefly reviewed it, it just did not feel correct to me.

I dug into the sheet and found amazing details. All the supporting facts were well justified, but I still felt it was wrong. The math just did not seem to add up. I sent it back to the analyst and asked if he would recheck it. Meanwhile, I continued to examine the analysis myself and found a cut-and-paste error in one of the columns. That simple error created a $3 million miscalculation in the anticipated savings.

If the report had remained unchecked, we would have made a very poor decision. The interesting fact is that not only did the analyst claim to have checked his work, two levels of management below me had reviewed it as well.

Something like this happens almost every day, in almost every company. If you feel I have overstated this point, I would challenge you to look harder. It is happening, and it's costing you both time and money while adding complexity to the situation.

If A = 1, and B = 1, and B = C, then C cannot = 8.

The Rule of Green Light, Yellow Light, Red Light

I used to play a game as a child with the neighborhood kids. It was called **Green Light, Yellow Light, Red Light, Stop.** We played late into the evening on warm summer evenings. At that time, I had no clue that the colors of this game would provide a key principle to help guide me through my business life.

I encourage everyone to consider using a color-coded system to track projects and results. **Green** is "go" – all projects that are coded green are approved, and/or on track for successful completion. It's a pretty easy connection to make, as green lights all around us are "go" signals.

Yellow is slow or "watch out." These are ideas or projects that may not be clear winners, or they may be at risk of falling behind. We use yellow to draw attention to the need for additional evaluation or support. Once properly evaluated, we can make the decision to either give the project a green light or discontinue it.

Red lights are attention getters. Red means "stop," or that failure is imminent. If there is a red light on an opportunity, it means stop working on it. Either move on to another task, or find out what is causing the activity to be classified as red, so you can correct the root drivers of failure. If an existing project gets a red light, it means that we will not meet the objective, and immediate action needs to be taken.

Using this color-coded system allows the team to visually understand where focus and attention is needed. It also allows everyone to know exactly what should be worked on, and what should not be worked on. Throughout my career, I have been known to lead meetings that outlaw talking about green lights as long as reds and yellows exist. It's all about focus.

In meetings, the team can focus on how to turn red and yellow lights green. Far too often, team members get caught up in dwelling on the positive. There is a time and place for that, but it is not in a meeting where time and resources are limited. Focusing on the most important red and yellow lights makes the most productive use of the team's time.

Rules Within a Rule

There are a few underlying rules that help make the **green, yellow, red system** an even more effective tool. Allow any member to change a light on a project from green to yellow or from yellow to red. This will empower every team member and create a sense of ownership. Once a person knows that he or she is empowered – under justifiable circumstances – to put the brakes on, he or she becomes a more willing advocate for change. In my experience, the need to know that the power is available is much more important than actually executing that power. Rarely have I ever seen the lone wolf flip his or her switch. Yet, when they have, I've been thankful.

At the same time, only a full team consensus should be able to change a red light or a yellow light to green. Too many times, project leaders think they can wiggle around challenges; they believe they will hit their objectives, only to fall short. If the complete team green-lights something, there will be no finger-pointing later.

Unless you are color-blind, the **green, yellow, red system** is a wonderful tool for managing your business. You can use other visual stimuli if you like, but a disciplined rating system is powerful.

The Rule of the Duck

It has been said, "If it looks like a duck, walks like a duck, and swims like a duck, it's probably a duck." This simple rule sounds obvious, but we often fail to apply it to business.

Management asks for a detailed analysis of a situation that everyone knows will demonstrate the obvious; nonetheless, the request is made. The results come in as expected, and management's curiosity is satisfied. No big deal, right? Actually, it is a huge deal, because two things occurred. Firstly, valuable time was wasted; more time was taken for the analysis than management anticipated. More importantly, staff members became disgruntled. They misinterpreted the request for the report as management being out of touch or not trusting their judgment.

The duck rule also applies to people. They will usually act the way they have in the past. Reliable people are almost always reliable, and unreliable people never fail to disappoint. Pretending that the duck will become a superstar is an ill-advised endeavor. It just doesn't happen.

The Rule of Digging Until You Can No Longer Dig

"We just need to dig our way out of this problem," is a regular phrase. I agree that there are times when you simply need to fight through an issue. But far too often, we just keep digging and digging and digging. Digging makes us feel good because we are throwing resources against the problem.

The question should be: "Why are we digging, and how will digging solve the problem?" The reality is that we chose to dig our way out of the problem without having any idea what caused it. I offer the following approach as an alternative: Identify the root drivers of the problem, and then determine if digging is even required.

In the most extreme cases, you will employ a digger while you perform the evaluation. The digger might be digging in vain, but once we understand the drivers of the problem, we can apply an appropriate response. One response might be to dig while we solve the dilemma.

A classic example that involves digging is the job of reconciliation. Over the years, I have observed teams of people whose sole job is to reconcile differences between two sets of numbers. Their goal is to make sure both sets of numbers are the same. But as they find differences, they dig in to understand what created the difference.

Once the culprit is discovered, the error is corrected. The reconciler then moves on to the next discrepancy. This process is repeated day after day, and month after month. It has always amazed me that these people who reconcile numbers never attempted to change the behavior that created the situation.

Tragically, these types of jobs exist in businesses around the world, and senior managers are often unaware of the dysfunction. I would challenge leaders to unbundle this type of activity. Put down the shovels, and seek to understand the root causes that create the need for diggers – and find ways to remedy them.

The Rule of Too Much Water

When teams are overworked or are not functioning at a high level, they tend to spiral out of control. Or, at a minimum, they spiral to a place of great stress. Typically, management's gut reaction is to throw more people at the problem. In some cases, additional resources are warranted. In other situations, the lack of disciplined conduct by the team is driving the inefficient behavior, only making it appear that additional resources are needed.

When additional resources are warranted, the question becomes, "What amount of incremental resources is required?" Tragically, those mired in the situation will almost always overestimate the number of resources required. This overcall is a result of the uncontrolled situation that they see; it is paramount in their minds. In many cases, they do not intentionally ask for excessive resources; rather, they fervently believe the requested resources are needed.

I came up with a demonstration that almost always gets this point across and often gets folks literally jumping out of their seats. I call this exercise **Too Much Water**. I simply get three empty glasses and a large picture of water. I start by filling one glass to a reasonable amount. I describe the glass as a resource, and the water is the work. Predictably, team members in the room nod their heads in alignment with the exercise. Next, I overfill the second glass until it starts to run onto the table. I continue to pour until what appears to be an insurmountable amount of water is running across the table.

The team members and I usually agree that when there is too much work for the available resources, it feels like the uncontrolled running of water across the table. Next, I take a paper towel or two and mop up the water and squeeze it into the third glass, which usually only fills that glass one-quarter full.

From time to time, I hear complaints that some of the water has fallen on the floor. I usually offer to repeat the exercise by proposing to dump all of the first glass of water onto the table, so the team can determine whether what was originally spilled was more or less than the contents of the full glass. I have yet to get any takers.

Once the team believes that the under-resource situation is not as severe as it might appear, much better decisions can be made about the level of resource required to resolve the dilemma. If you prefer not to use water for your demonstration, marbles make a good substitute.

When 50 Percent Is More Than 100 Percent

"I want it all," is a fairly common sentiment in business. Of course, getting it all is extremely beneficial; but frequently, businesses are incapable of achieving that outcome without help or support. A common option considered by company leaders is to hire a consulting firm or an advisor, and cover their hefty price tag.

Let's say that a business owns a brand that is struggling; the company is faced with a dilemma. *Do we throw more money at it? Do we cut our losses? Is it worth anything? Do we sell the brand?*

The previous questions come into play, and retained advisors provide their input. A decision is made to kill or sell the brand, and the company moves on to the next hurdle.

One important question is frequently left unasked. Might there be some entity with the capability to help make the brand successful – an entity that also may be interested in sharing the brand with my organization?

Too often, companies kill brands and allow them to languish in the bottom of a filing cabinet. Worse yet, the company will sell the brand at a below-market value, creating a new competitor.

I recommend that careful consideration be given to collaborating with a new partner who is willing to share the risk in exchange for some equity. As I see it, there is little downside. Provided you have properly vetted your new partner, there is tremendous potential to create wealth using this approach. In addition you have just added a passionate advocate for the brand; one who is motivated to make it successful. Even better, this new resource is not part of your regular team; therefore, it does not really create a drain on the organization's capacity.

If orchestrated properly, such a partnership costs the original owner nothing more than a portion of the potential profits. This reality has led me to the conclusion: 50 percent of a big number is more than 100 percent of a small one. Don't get caught up in the percentages. The concept of bringing resources into an appropriate opportunity and sharing the equity is one worthy of great consideration.

Following the rules in this chapter will help you on your journey to unbundled bliss. They are straightforward, but require discipline to use day in and day out. Over time, you will become unconsciously competent in their use.

I admit that they seem overly simple – and they are. Their simplicity is what makes them so powerful and effective.

Combustion Check – IGNITE RULES FOR SUCCESS

Before lighting the fuse on your next strategic effort, ask yourself:

1. Can you see how applying the rules of this chapter to business and life can simplify processes and streamline outcomes?
2. What would happen if you embraced differentiation, understanding that it is a multi-year effort to fully ignite it? Do you have the resolve to see it through?
3. Are you committed to stay the course, persevere through challenges, and reap the long-term rewards?
4. What additional rules would fuel further success and expand your ignition potential?

Answering these questions ensures that your approach burns with clarity and purpose, fueling long-lasting impact in both business and life.

10

Time: Using Fuel Efficiently

Do not count every hour in the day.
Make every hour in the day count.
– *Alfred Binet, psychologist*

Have you . . .

Ever felt like there is never enough time?

Ever felt pressured by aggressive timelines?

What if . . .

You could become a master of time management?

You could make time your competitive advantage?

Time is our best friend and our worst enemy. Depending upon our perspective, we either have too much time or not enough. Things either take too long or don't last long enough. Things either take too long or don't last long enough. Unfortunately, time carries with it much more dire implications.

Of all the challenges we face in business, one constraint stands apart: time. We can manage resources, change strategies, develop people, and overcome obstacles – but we cannot stop the clock. Time moves forward regardless of our actions, making it the one limitation over which we have absolutely no control.

Good News, in a simplified world, we can master time and make it our friend, and create a competitive advantage in doing so. Allow others to do battle with time. Speed matters in business. Every journey starts with a step, hopefully in the right direction. If we view each task as a step on the journey, we give ourselves permission to commence.

We first need to understand how much effort is required to complete a specified task and what the benefits or rewards are. In our daily lives, we have to make these calls with great regularity. It happens quickly and without much thought: the gas gauge is on empty and there is a gas station at the next intersection. We pull in, get fueled, and are on the road again with little thought or effort.

We can apply this same philosophy to simple tasks in the workplace. Remember the example from Chapter 4 where the employee was asked to make the phone call, and he chose to complicate it by adding sticky notes and other superfluous activity? He spent significantly more time and effort in thinking, planning, and in making sure he remembered to make the call than he did in actually making the call.

Move all of the small tasks out of the way as soon as they are assigned. Making a list and checking and rechecking it is fine for longer-term projects, but single-step tasks simply need to be done. Don't put them on a list. If they never land "on the plate," they will require less time because they never have to be "cleared from the plate."

We live in a world of smartphones, iPads, and 24/7 availability. The excuses for not completing the small tasks and allowing them to bundle are simply unacceptable. If we want to make time our ally, discipline is a must. When small items are handled with ease and speed, we create time to address the more complex matters.

The Four-Square Grid

When deciding on how to make time your friend on larger projects, it is good to use a four-square grid where each quadrant clearly depicts the time required, along with the impact. The quadrants track combinations of Low Effort, High Effort, Low Impact, and High Impact. Items that go into the Low Effort/High Impact quadrant simply need to be done immediately.

The same is true for most Low Effort/Low Impact projects. While these projects have much lower impact, the effort required is so small that we ought to just get them done and move on.

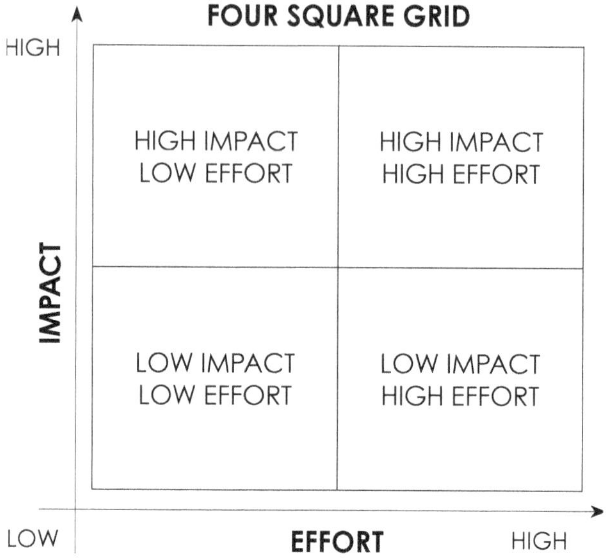

Figure 5: Classic Four-Square Grid

Each Quadrant Has Unique Characteristics

The High Effort/Low Impact quadrant is a simple "Just say no," unless it is a directive that cannot be avoided. Your first course of action is to try to understand the rationale of the request; ask direct questions of the person who requires the work to be completed. Next, you should ensure that the requester understands that what he or she wants demands a high effort and nets a low impact. Once the facts are on the table, one of four things usually occurs:

- The requester has no idea of the effort required and cancels the request.

- The requester knows an easier way to get what is required, and educates you on how to complete the assigned work with less effort.
- The requestor educates you on the real impact of the work stream, which moves the work to an adjacent effort/impact quadrant.
- The work stream is regrettably something that must be completed due to a commitment. Hopefully, this is a rare exception and is only allowed if absolutely required by a client or customer.

In an unbundled/simplified world, other rationales should not exist. Unfortunately, there are some other exceptions. The government is a regular source of creating High Effort/Low Impact work streams. Can you say "tax audit"?

Unbundle High Effort / High Impact Projects

The High Effort/High Impact projects need to be unbundled into subtasks. When you unbundle the tasks, each step takes less effort. Once your unbundling is done, you can start the journey.

A great example of such unbundling is a new product rollout. At first glance, it might appear to be a daunting task that will require a huge time sink. But once we look at the project as a group of subtasks, it becomes much more straightforward and manageable. Each team responsible for each subtask should be able to address its area and consider the internal customer-provider relationship. Once you adopt this lens to look at the project, solutions become extremely clear.

You might try to approach your next complex High Effort/ High Impact project this way. If you struggle, it simply means you have not adopted the correct discipline or you have not broken the project down to its smallest components.

In June 1999, I was appointed the position of Y2K Czar by my employer. I was given the assignment – to ready the company for any technology issues that might trigger on January 1, 2000 – in the middle of a corporate self-inflicted crisis. My predecessor had failed to meet expectations, and the organization feared a disaster. Despite the fact that the Y2K project was behind schedule for more than a year, I felt no pressure, because I knew we had just over six months to complete the readiness assignments. Nothing was imminent; we had plenty of time, or so I thought.

I soon found the project to be so bundled that it was totally paralyzing the team. There was interdependency on top of interdependency. What I initially thought was going to be fairly straightforward began to look extremely cumbersome and unwieldy. We simply did not have enough time to complete the necessary tasks in the conventional or approved fashion.

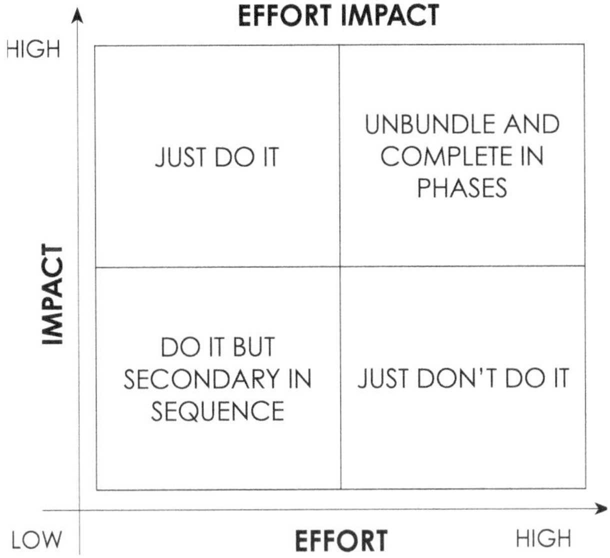

Figure 6: Indicated Actions for Prioritized Projects

Unbundle Pseudo-Interdependencies

As a result of what we discovered, we unbundled and eliminated the interdependencies. We found that the interdependencies were almost all contrived by bureaucrats. We simply broke out each sub-segment and, to no surprise, found that we had multiple parallel paths available. In the end, we completed 24 months of work in less than five months and confidently coasted into the evening of December 31, 1999. My biggest concern was that the power grid would fail. When I saw the fireworks in Sydney, Australia on television in the early morning of December 31, I breathed a sigh of relief.

We had unbundled our internal program. We were highly confident that our systems would withstand any impending cataclysm. So, knowing that we would probably still have power, and that the world would not stop its technological journey, our confidence grew as the day went on.

We did not suffer a single issue with Y2K in our organization. Had we allowed the project to languish, we definitely would not have met the timeline. We probably would have encountered significant adverse ramifications.

The four-square grid is one of the simplest and most easily adaptable analytical tools. It can be used to help prioritize, simplify, and reassure. It is really just one vertical axis, perpendicular to a horizontal axis, that compares two variables so that a set of projects, people and things can be filtered or compared.

Applying the Principles to Management

The four-square grid can also be used to evaluate risk management. One axis is Impact, or the severity of the consequences if an adverse event occurs. The other is Likelihood of Occurrence that the same event will occur. A flood would devastate our operation, but we are 100 feet above the flood plain. So, a flood scenario would fall into the High Impact/Low Likelihood quadrant, and we don't need to waste time preparing for something that will never happen. (If it did occur, we would hope for a visit from Noah.)

When dealing with risk management, it is often important to include a secondary filter. This is particularly important when dealing with High Impact/Low Likelihood quadrant issues. Simply place all topics residing in this quadrant through a secondary filter.

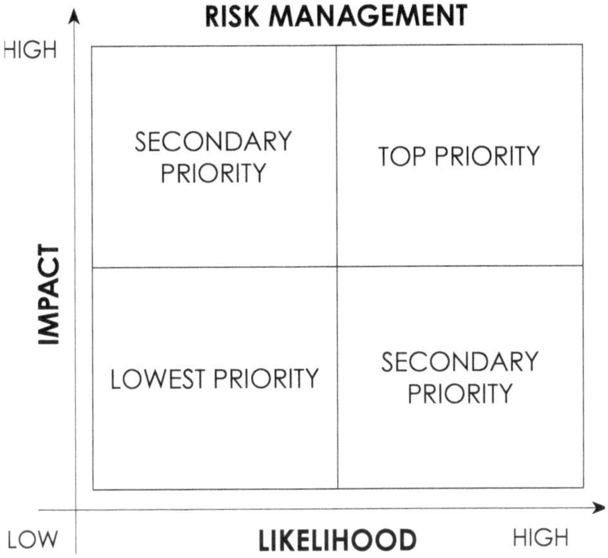

Figure 7: Four Square Grid Applied to Risk Management – Filter One

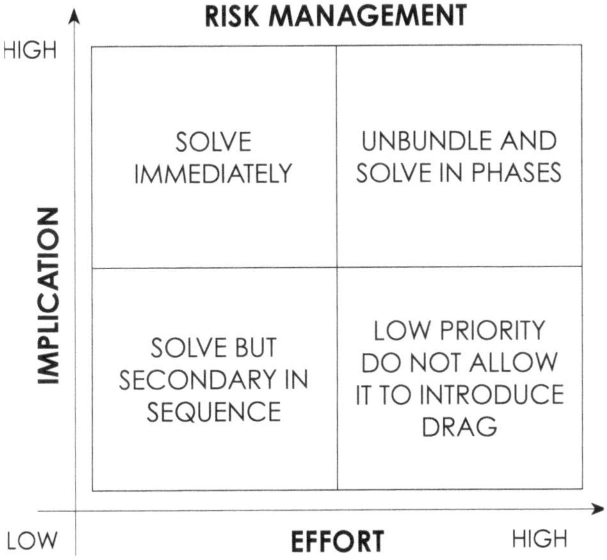

Figure 8: High Impact / Low Likelihood Issues Requiring Further Evaluation

For some reason, many leaders tend to either completely ignore legitimate risks or they obsess over them. Residing at either end of the spectrum is not advisable. It is important that we apply the principles of appropriate risk management to concerns. I am constantly inundated with phrases such as, "...but there's risk." I usually respond, "I agree. There is also a risk that the plane I am flying on tomorrow is going to crash, but I still fly."

The parent company decided to implement a tiered medical benefits program, patterned after the one described earlier in the Rule of Fishing section. Emotion and entitlement caused us to add a top tier that was an extremely comprehensive plan. I found that unnecessary, but agreed, adding the provision that the employee share of the premium would equal the difference between the cost of this new top tier and the middle tier. In other words, the employee who chose the top-tier coverage would pay a premium equal to 100% of the difference to migrate from the middle tier.

There was no scenario where choosing the top tier made any economic sense. The best a person in the top tier could hope for is to experience a catastrophic health crisis, and then it was only equivalent, from a financial perspective to those choosing the middle tier.

In short, I was hoping that no one would elect the top-tier coverage, so the company could eliminate the administrative burden of including that third bundled tier. But amazingly, around 20 percent of the workforce chose the top-tier plan. To this day, I remain perplexed about that, but can only attribute it to the emotion and entitlement in play, as well as a profound failure to understand risk management.

Secondary filters or grids can be used when a third variable needs to be evaluated, or when the sheer number of projects being evaluated needs to be reduced to a manageable subset. Appropriate use of multiple four-square grids help achieve buy-in from the team, because members can visually grasp the relationships between options. Buy-in creates alignment. It also saves time by eliminating unproductive debate.

As mentioned previously, the four-square grid is also great for evaluating people. Performance and Potential are good reference axis lines. I believe that Performance and Cultural Fit axes are equally, if not more, productive.

It's amazing how often we talk ourselves out of doing things because of perceived barriers that are really just small hurdles. We can easily leap over those hurdles once we simplify them. "I can't" or "we can't" is an excuse that typically wastes time and creates complexity, making production or delivery much more difficult. As addressed in Chapter 5, "can't" is pretty much synonymous with "won't," and "won't" simply won't do.

As John Wooden once said, "Do not let what you cannot do interfere with what you can do." That's a powerful statement that, when applied to business, translates into significant time savings. Urge your team to leap over barriers and eliminate excuses. You will free up huge amounts of time.

Analysis Paralysis

When I used Microsoft Excel for the first time, I reveled in what appeared to be a tool that could simplify my life and help me in decision-making. It has proven to be just that, but there is a downside to Excel. Bundlers, who always complicate things, like to employ sophisticated Excel spreadsheets. The data is rich with information, but the complexity is mind-numbing.

The Love Affair with Precision Is a Time Killer

The quest for precision seems to overtake the broader objective of delivering the information to the customer. The cost of precision is a multiheaded beast with an insatiable appetite, consuming huge chunks of time and money.

The time invested creating monolithic Excel templates, documents, or analyses are the tip of the iceberg. They get circulated via email, and the recipients' eyes immediately glaze over, since they have no frame of reference. One of three things occurs:

- The recipient attempts to decipher the information.
- The recipient gets frustrated and asks the author for an explanation.
- The recipient simply ignores the information.

In many cases, it is a progressive reaction. It starts with a failed attempt to understand, followed by frustration, continues with a visit to the author, and often ends with ignoring or discarding the information. In any case, huge amounts of time are wasted, with little or no positive impact. Going back to our four-square grid, this is a High Effort/Low Impact situation that translates into "Just don't do it."

Sometimes the author, proud of his or her work, eagerly dives in to explain his or her masterpiece. That explanation creates more confusion. This process is repeated multiple times, as each recipient has to learn the thought process behind the work. In some cases, there may be an actual benefit generated, but rarely one worth the effort.

Precision Is Often the Enemy of Accuracy

The question of accuracy comes into play. It is quite common for a detailed and precise analysis to lack accuracy, which in turn invalidates all the work. It is certainly possible to support accuracy and precision at the same time, but usually one takes precedence over the other. The cost to successfully get both qualities is great; and when it is required, we simply must make that investment. The fact remains that rarely do we need such precision, and accuracy must always carry a higher priority than precision. The most precise tool, if it is inaccurate, is worthless.

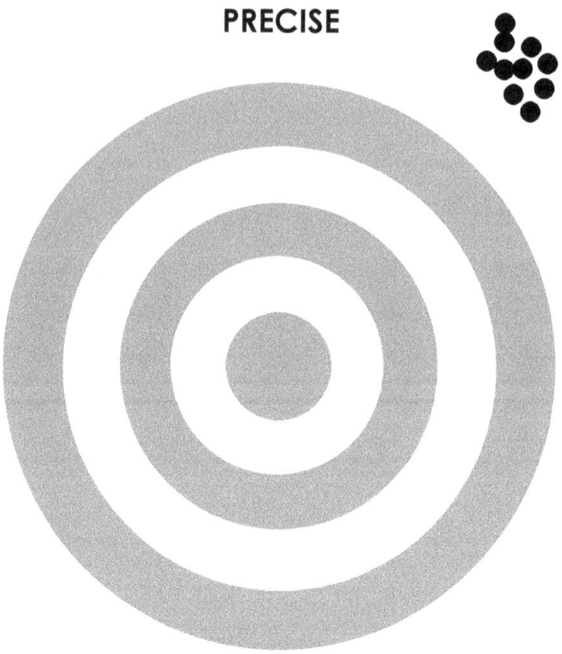

Figure 9: When Precision Trumps Accuracy, We Miss the Target

A great example of the value of accuracy over precision is scientific analysis. There are sophisticated pieces of equipment that can analyze the makeup of materials down to parts per billion, and we can repeat tests to confirm the results. Such results are the epitome of precision. Yet, if the equipment's accuracy is not checked regularly, the data has no worth. In many cases, inaccurate testing equipment creates false results. False results, in turn, can lead to poor decisions, such as the destruction of products that are perfectly good or a change in formula. Often, such a decision will result in a substandard or more costly product, creating quality issues or suboptimal economics.

I have spent much of my career working in the food business, surrounded by production environments. While I do not have a log to refer back to, I would say that when we used precise scientific methods and discovered that products had suspect attributes, most of the time we found that the testing equipment was out of tolerance. In fact, that kind of occurrence is so common that one of the first things typically checked is the accuracy of the scientific equipment.

ACCURATE

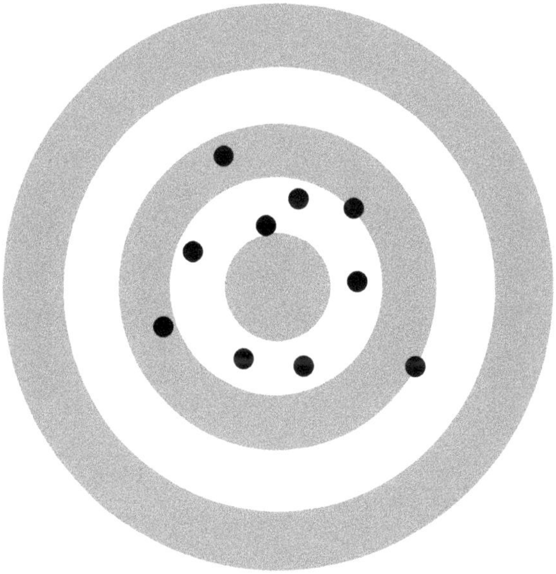

Figure 10: While Not Precise, Favoring Accuracy Hits the Target Every Time

Reports Need Dollar Signs

Another important tradeoff that seems to come with precise analysis is the omission of user-friendly symbols that could help team members understand reports. These include column and row headings, dollar signs, and the consistent use of brackets for negative numbers. This last type of notation may be a pet peeve of mine, but a spreadsheet with bracketed numbers that are, in fact, positive numbers, is misleading. The brackets are particularly frustrating when they are used inconsistently within a single document.

All of these issues create confusion that sucks time out of your organization's world. If you chart all of the time invested in reviewing, explaining, and creating spreadsheets, you will be amazed. And for every man-hour you calculate, there is an amount of time in support that should be included. Time for information technology support, facility support, and human resource support are all required along with analyses. And bundlers traditionally use more support service time than other employees.

Simple Rules for Excel

There are a few rules for Excel users that will make it a much more customer-friendly tool. These rules prevent wasted time and energy, and include:

- For any complex work, include a summary page with simple descriptions of columns and rows.
- Normally, the eyes read from left to right, and from top to bottom. Follow this logic as you process data.

- Use color to direct the user to the most important cells where answers reside.
- Use the freeze panes option to keep row and column headings in place as the user scrolls through data.
- Remember to put units of measure in the descriptions of columns or rows. Millions of $ = $MM.
- Hide rows and columns that may be important to you, the creator, but have no relevance to the end user.
- Carefully consider who your audience is when sending information externally, as sensitive information can be accidently transmitted in the supporting tabs. A savvy user will extract it to their benefit. (Once, I received all of our competitors' pricing when a customer unintentionally sent a file with each vendor's tab included.)
- Remember, how you save your Excel sheet is how it will open when the user receives it. If you are sending a multiple-tab spreadsheet, save it on the tab you want the user to open it in.

Adopting these tips to reports will greatly improve the company's use of data. And, consider the "less is more" philosophy. We do not have to explain something that was never created.

Measuring to Four Places – No More

In general, precision in numbers risks clogging up the system and creating time drag in the organization. In more cases than not, such precision is meaningless.

Let's say that we are buying a material that costs $111.275 a unit, and we buy 10,000 units a year. Total expenditure is over $1 million a year, but each tenth of a penny per unit is only $10 spent in a year. I would argue that the cost to track the tenths of pennies and even the pennies is not worth the time invested.

There are dozens of examples where tenths of pennies could mean a great deal, but more times than not, they are meaningless. A good rule is to measure four decimal places for items that matter and three places for those that are less important. What makes something important enough to add that fourth decimal measurement? Either you are buying a large amount, or you will be buying something with great frequency.

If we are buying something that costs in the tens of dollars and we are buying a great deal of it, then we should measure it to the penny. This level of discipline will result in precision to the tenth of 1 percent. The same is true when we are buying something in the thousands of dollars – the same precision is needed.

The cost to maintain the discipline below a tenth of 1 percent simply does not justify the benefits. As I like to say, "Do the math." When in doubt, go out to four decimal places and never more. You will never be sorry.

Think about buying a home. When did anyone offer to buy a home measured out to the penny? However, once the banks get through with such a transaction, there are columns of pennies that amount to almost nothing.

Even the federal government has moved away from counting pennies on tax forms. Three hundred million of us shorting the government a penny equates to $3 million dollars; that amount covers about two minutes of escalation of the current national debt.

I can visualize the scientists and quality control leads rolling their eyes. I can almost hear the cries of "heresy" echoing in my ears. I am not suggesting that precise measures are not important in some cases. If measuring to "parts per billion" is the standard, then we need to compile figures based on parts per billion. Going out to five decimal places would translate into parts per 10 trillion, however. I would suggest this as ineffective.

I think it is important to readdress pennies, because this has been the biggest pushback that I've had when attempting to explain this theory. If you are buying things that cost a penny, or selling things that sell for a penny, pennies become extremely important. Using the same logic, I would propose you look out three or four places to the one-hundredth of a penny or the one-thousandth of a penny. If you are buying 100 million items that cost a penny, one-hundredth of a penny is 1 percent, or $1 million. Of course, we could offer to give that to the government and cover the debt clock for 30 to 40 seconds.

The only case I can see where five decimal places or more might be appropriate would be the long-range trajectory of an interplanetary vehicle. Since most of us are not in the rocket business, we can leave that kind of precision to those who are.

Corporate Historians

Corporate historians are people who love to regale us with tales of the old days. They can recite chapter and verse of what occurred 30 years ago, going into excruciating detail. Ironically, these folks can be newcomers to your organization who simply apply their own previous history to the current situation.

The first step to rehabilitating a corporate historian is recognizing that there is a problem. "Hi, my name is Elliott Haverlack, and I am a corporate historian."

Learning from history is a great benefit and applying the learning to current situations is incredibly helpful, but not at the expense of the time required to hear the historian through. We need to urge these well-intentioned individuals to stem the storytelling and focus on the facts of the current situation.

It is a very difficult balance. Some of the historian's narrative might be of value. And it is best to avoid the understandable irritation that might be generated by publicly cutting off the historian. A candid, one-on-one conversation with the historian will prove more productive. They will mostly understand when their distraction is pointed out to them discreetly, but they rarely recognize it when they are performing in storytelling mode. A simple code word or gesture will help get them on track.

Corporate historians also tend to add unnecessary detail to current events as well. I recall a historian diving into great detail with a new junior employee on a topic. After 20 minutes, the junior employee said, "You don't need to tell me how to make a toaster; I just wanted a piece of toast."

While the junior employee's message was delivered in a questionable manner, the intent was clear: *Please do not waste my time with information that I neither want to hear nor need to know.*

Stand and Deliver – Time

As discussed previously, meetings can suck the time out of a business. A tool as simple as having employees stand during morning huddles (rather than sit) can easily save 15 minutes a day per person. If there are 10 people at the meeting, you have just created two-and-a-half hours or one-third of a full-time-equivalent worker.

Try a simple test. During your next regularly scheduled meeting, record how much time is spent as people enter the room, get their coffee and settle into their seats. Repeat the measurement at the end of the meeting. I think you will be surprised at the amount of time wasted.

Ironically, you will need to invest some time looking for and eliminating time-wasting activity in your business and your life. You will be amazed at how much time you will find. How we apply that time is the next challenge.

Preparing to effectively use the time you and your colleagues will create is as simple as doing a bit of planning. It is as effortless as answering the question: "What would I do if I had more time?"

Mastering the Pit Stop

In the plant or in an operations environment, preplanning events such as changeovers or shutdowns will save significant time and money. Think of it as a NASCAR pit stop. If you don't think that racers plan and practice, you are wrong. Tenths of seconds matter in racing. Using that type of appropriately applied discipline to a situation will pay big dividends. The operative words here are "appropriately applied."

Do you recall our commentary on Six Sigma? Most applications of Six Sigma are overblown and are time killers. NASCAR achieves a Six Sigma level of performance in a matter of seconds. Tenth of seconds in a race can be the difference of winning or being just another driver in the middle of the pack. It is important that there is a standard in place, and that it is executed flawlessly every time. This does not mean you have to slow down. These are mutually exclusive elements. Treat them as such.

Time is an enigma. How many times have you heard, "I need more time?" How many times have you had too much time on your hands? Of all the things we hold dear, time is the one commodity that is beyond our control. Make it your ally.

In fact, it is probably not a bad idea to include time management as a core competency. Soon, you will be unconsciously competent at time management and your organization's capacity will expand significantly.

Combustion Check – IGNITE INDIVIDUALIZED STRATEGY

Before lighting the fuse on your next project or initiative, ask yourself:

1. Are you capable of eliminating the need for plate-clearing exercises by keeping nonessential items off the plate?
2. Where will you use the four-square grid first? How will you apply it with regularity to maximize efficiency and clarity?
3. Will you always choose accuracy over precision, ensuring your energy is focused on what truly matters?
4. Are you a corporate historian, learning from the past to ignite smarter decisions today?
5. Are you willing to invest the time it takes to create more time, fueling a self-sustaining engine of productivity?

Answering these questions ensures that your strategies ignite with focus, eliminate waste, and propel your organization forward.

11

Negotiation: Guidelines for a Healthy Flame

Let us never negotiate out of fear.
But let us never fear to negotiate.
–John Fitzgerald Kennedy, 35th US president

Have you . . .

Ever become anxious over an upcoming negotiation?

Regretted a contract that you signed?

What if . . .

You could become a master negotiator?

You could revel in the negotiation process and feast off the outcomes?

I have had the pleasure of participating in negotiations for over 40 years and have found there are some very simple principles that are essential to optimizing an outcome. Before you even consider entering into a negotiation, you must plan properly.

Planning for Successful Negotiation

Know What You Want

First, determine what your desired outcome is. In other words, ask yourself: What does good look like? Then, decide how far from your optimal outcome you are willing to move. List all the elements or variables in the deal, and determine which are most important to you and where you are willing to move if need be. Set boundaries for yourself and your team in advance on specific items: "We will not move beyond this point." Write out your position for the team, but never share it with the opposition.

Prepare yourself for the tone and tenor of the negotiation. Will it be a cordial and friendly negotiation, or could it be tense and adversarial? A good example of a potentially adversarial negotiation is a union negotiation. They do not have to be adversarial, but union-management meetings are breeding grounds for dysfunctional emotion.

Educate Yourself on Your Opponent

Find out as much as you can about the opposition. You may think you know them well, but there is almost always something new to learn.

If you do not know your opponent that well, use whatever methods are available to gather as much information as you can on the people and the company, if applicable. Speak with colleagues who may know them from other business deals. Use the internet. Google them.

Adopt a Battle Mindset

Now that your preplanning is completed, you can prepare yourself for battle. I like to frame negotiations as battles. That reminds me that even when the negotiation involves old friends or is extremely cordial, the other side has something to gain from negotiations – as do you. More importantly, you have something to lose, and they will try their best – whether they are cordial or not – to get the best deal possible. Think about a game of chess. You might be playing with your best friend, but if you are not thinking several moves in advance, you are likely to get trounced.

Remain Above the Fray

However, remain above the fray. When emotion gets into negotiations, things usually turn out poorly. You are certainly permitted to **pretend** to be emotional, particularly when the other party has lost their control. But that too can be risky, because you can easily fall into the emotional mode if you're not careful.

Learn to Listen

John Wooden said, "Listen if you want to be heard." That is the perfect advice to apply to negotiations. Those who know me know that I am a talker. In fact, I could be described as a corporate historian from time to time. Nevertheless, when it comes to negotiation, I listen carefully.

People will tell you everything you need to know if you just allow them to talk. Listening will allow you to learn what is most important to your opposition. It will allow you to discern strengths and weaknesses, and it will give you the opportunity to exploit both. The more your opposition talks, the better your situation becomes.

Reading body language and inflections in speech patterns will allow you to ascertain just how important the outcome is to the opposition. I always say, "You can smell desperation." You can hear it in their voice; and you can read panic in their eyes. It all comes from listening; from paying attention.

Make Others Comfortable

Even the quietest and most sophisticated opponents will loosen up once you have helped them migrate to their comfort zone. Realize that you have an immediate advantage if you are fortunate enough to have discussions in their office. Look around the room – what is on the desk, or on the credenza or the walls?

Ask some questions that are relevant to what you have seen in their office; you will quickly learn a great deal about the person. If you don't get any ideas from your surroundings, start by talking about something going on in your life and attempt to engage them. Children –yours or theirs – make great introductory discussion topics.

I recall entering one office for what I was certain would be a difficult negotiation. Upon entering the office, I spied a small University of Notre Dame mascot on the bookshelf. There was a pretty important Notre Dame game on the calendar that upcoming weekend. I wove a reference to the upcoming game into my introduction. My remark precipitated a 20-minute discussion on Notre Dame football.

By the time our formal discussion began, we were inclined to like each other. The negotiation went off much easier than I could have ever imagined. Even more important, our future discussions were cordial and productive.

Please keep in mind that you have to give to get. The more open and real you are, the more comfortable the other person will become. You have the distinct advantage because you are working your plan, and the other person is unwittingly playing along to your benefit. You can give what you feel is appropriate and supportive to your position while you often learn nuggets of great value.

Observe

One of the most overlooked tactics – no pun intended – is observation. You are looking for body language or nervous twitches. We all do them, and they are most often uncontrollable. Not unlike a good poker player who can read your face, a good negotiator will quickly learn to understand his or her opponent by reading these features.

At the same time, you will be giving off your own signs. Don't be concerned – the vast majority of your opponents have never been trained to watch for them. Since you really can't control your own quirks without a great deal of attention, the effort you would have to put into controlling them is probably not worth it.

If you find yourself being read by your opponent, you might want to consider trying a change in tactics. You might want to try some test behavior. Engage in some body language or say something that might be thought of as out of character for you.

Watch the reaction. I always look at this as a low risk/less effort tactic; you frequently learn little, but what you could gain is of great value. It will be just another point of data about the person you are dealing with; you can tuck it away in your memory for future use.

I once sat in an intense, but cordial, negotiation with a prospective partner who held what we thought was a stronger position than ours. One of my superiors joined me, and we were literally desperate to conclude a deal. We were looking for a supply of products, and, frankly, we felt as if we had few options.

During our discussion, everything our opponent said left us feeling as if the deal was far from done. In fact, we almost convinced ourselves that we would have to move to the end of our bottom-line position.

My superior tended to be an animated sort, and was fairly concerned as we drove back to the airport. But I advised him that the deal was almost in the bag. He wanted to know what I heard – he was quite insistent – that made me feel that way I did.

"He has the slightest stammer when he's nervous," I said. "When we left and I shook his hand, he was definitely nervous."

"You are crazy," was my superior's response.

"Trust me," I replied.

The deal was concluded within a week. It took a bit more discussion, but we stood firm and did not have to move our position.

Outline Objectives and Objections

Everyone at a negotiation meeting knows why you are assembled, but it is always best to clearly state your objective and expected positive outcome at the beginning of the negotiation. This should not be a detailed accounting, but rather a broad-stroke summary. This is more aptly referred to as a **precap.** Have your opponent do the same thing, or build on what you stated and add any clarifications.

If you believe that there are some points of the agreement that are potentially objectionable or nonstarters for you, then state them up front. A great example is a non-disclosure agreement. If you are unwilling to move beyond a certain point without a non-disclosure agreement, put that on the table at the beginning. No sense wasting everyone's time.

The reader might think that a non-disclosure agreement is a straightforward and easy item to agree upon. Quite the contrary – several large companies object to non-disclosure agreements. They fear that, due to their scale, they are targets for litigation and believe they can throw their weight around. They do so very successfully.

I was involved in a particularly challenging contract negotiation during the height of the Snickers® "Not Going Anywhere for A While" ad campaign. I knew that this particular deal could be consummated, but there had been some shenanigans and posturing. Moreover, we had an extremely tight timeline.

I entered the room with a box of Snickers® bars. I tossed them on the table and stated, "We are here to get this contract completed and no one is leaving until we do." With that short sentence, everyone knew the purpose of the session, and the expected outcomes. We successfully finished the negotiations in time for dinner.

Once objectives and objections are aired, attempt to get the other party to provide the details of their plan. A good way to do that is to ask, "So, how do you guys see this working out?" That's a great opening line.

Be a Voracious Note-Taker

Record everything you hear. You should have three columns on your paper, for three categories:

- Items that are no problem.
- Items that are a problem.
- Items that can be exploited or newfound opportunities.

Remember, what you do not hear is as important as what you do hear. Usually, people talk about those things that are important to them. If there are important deal points that you do not hear them reveal, attempt to draw them out. See if those points have simply been overlooked or are really unimportant. Make note of the answers.

Point three of our note-taking is an important one. These are things that we learn during the negotiation that you can take advantage of later. It might be a weakness that can be exploited, or something you were previously unaware of that can make the deal more favorable. An example might be an unknown asset or capability that might help your organization.

Take Breaks When You Need Them

If you feel yourself getting trapped, call for a break or a time out. Have an excuse ready, so you don't tip your hand. Regardless, it's always good to get up and walk around.

To insert a needed break, you might make arrangements beforehand to have your assistant or another co-worker interrupt the session. You can agree on a predetermined, unspoken signal that will trigger them to tell you that you are needed. You could have them advise you of an important call or some other matter that requires your immediate attention. Another great tactic is to have your assistant stop in at some point to check on everyone's comfort. For example, they could ask if coffee or another beverage is desired, or if the room's temperature is acceptable.

It's advantageous to gather your team during such breaks and perform a "gut check" on how things are going. You may have missed something that others might have seen.

Exploiting Weakness

There are two distinct and recommended approaches for exploiting weaknesses, and two ways to respond to such exploitation when you are on the receiving end. You should decide how to employ each approach for various scenarios.

My preferred approach is to ensure that your opponent is aware that the weakness or failure on his or her part is a fairly significant concern, even if it is not. You can sympathize with them and promise to try to work around their weakness.

This approach builds the relationship. And – depending on your opponent's personality – it can give you leverage later, because they may feel either a sense of guilt or loyalty due to your perceived generosity. Use all of this to your advantage.

If you are the recipient of such a seemingly kind gesture, accept it politely. However, do not allow yourself to fall into the guilt trap. The gesture is probably sincere, but even though you may appreciate it, it should not compel you to move your position.

Another approach is to become more volatile. Make a much bigger issue out of something than it is. I do not care for this approach, but I will use it if I am dealing with a difficult person or someone who was challenging in the past.

If you choose to adopt this approach, you must be sure not to allow your act to take on a life of its own. If you should actually get emotional, you lose. **Appearing** emotional is a good tactic; **becoming** emotional is not. The key is to have a controlled or purposeful volatility.

Fifteen years ago, I was in negotiations with a very difficult trading partner that I did not trust. I did not particularly like the company, nor did I like the players. I knew they were lying, but that was difficult to prove.

I found their weakness in a single comment. A small part of a much larger deceit was uncovered. I pretended to blow a gasket, and then stormed out of the room with my colleague in tow. I told them I needed five minutes.

Unfortunately, I had not been able to prepare my colleague beforehand, so when we entered my office to "cool off," he was concerned. I turned to him and laughed. "That performance ought to be worth a few bucks," I confided.

We returned to the room and were offered a $1.5-million-dollar settlement. It was every penny we had sought. By the time the meeting was over, we had received our settlement, we had our opponents apologizing to us, and we had negotiated a better deal moving forward.

But sometimes it does not work. During the same period of time, I was struggling with the service of one of the railroads. They had botched a merger, and had literally lost over 100 of their cars with my product on them.

I demanded a meeting and flew to Los Angeles. We met in my company's offices there. When we were all assembled, I started by stating sternly, "Do you or do you not want my business?"

"Actually, no," he answered.

I was totally defused. The respondent was sincere, not flippant. They were looking to lose business in the short term until they recovered from their merger woes. I did get some licks in later on when they were looking for business and reengaged me, but I never felt I got enough restitution for the pain and cost we had endured.

Good Negotiators Are Great Actors

Volatility is a frequent negotiating strategy. If your opponent uses this type of technique, be mindful that it is either an act, or that your emotional opponent is a powder keg. Either way, remain calm, but add some passion to your voice as you apologize – if an apology is in order. If no apology is in order, employ a different kind of passion as you defend your position.

Remember, chances are they are trying to embarrass you or make you feel inferior. As we covered in Chapter One, this is not a problem. Just go with it.

Often, exposed weaknesses are honest errors. Sometimes, such errors are significant enough that they will alter future deal metrics. Simply state, "There is nothing we can do about this other than learn from it." And if necessary, add, "If it is a deal killer, I understand." Hope for the best.

Many times, there are complete misunderstandings that only face-to-face discussions can resolve. In one incident, I led a team into a large customer's building for a service summit. We had a terrible relationship with this particular customer. But from our perspective, all of our service metrics put us in what we thought was an extremely strong position, compared to our competition.

We entered the conference room at their offices. Before we were seated, five individuals from the company entered the room. After an hour and a half of their ranting, we had been verbally beaten up. Still, we kept our composure. We simply chose not to challenge their numbers or perception. We apologized and promised to do better.

My team left the meeting demoralized.

We returned to our car, and I announced, "Tonight we celebrate. They got it off their chest." I added, "And since their numbers are wrong, we have nothing to fear."

The next quarter, we won their Vendor of the Quarter award and changed nothing in our dealings, other than to telephone them regularly. That enhanced the relationship. We solved a huge misperception, gained some friends, and all we had to endure was a bit of embarrassment and an unjust tongue lashing.

Extreme situations may require drastic measures. I was once in a protracted negotiation with an important client that lasted several months. We continued to tiptoe around issues, and he was pushing for a commitment. I continued to express concerns over some early pricing errors my team had made.

I had been assured by my team that the errors had been communicated to the client and were being worked out. The errors were so substantial that my company was prepared to walk away from the deal if we could not remedy the pricing.

We were having dinner to consummate the agreement when I handed my client the new pricing. He flew into a rage and stormed out of the restaurant, leaving his very uncomfortable colleague at the table with me and two of my colleagues. We spent a painful few minutes sitting there until I had had enough. I quietly asked our opponent's colleague to find his friend. I told him, "In five minutes, I will get up – and if I do, we are finished with this negotiation."

It worked. Our opponent returned and apologized, and we were able to resume our discussion. I then apologized to him for our mistake, but also assured him that we could not enter into an agreement under the pricing structure we had originally submitted. I added that I felt justified, as I had been advising him of that fact for over a month. He claimed to have no knowledge of the scale of the problem.

I never found out if his leaving the table was an act or a real outburst. But I did find out that one of my team members had been less than truthful with me. He had never actually sent the information on the pricing errors to the client, and the dinner was indeed the first inkling they had had of the scale of the discrepancy.

I called to apologize, but added there still was not anything we could change. We signed the contract as we had submitted, and the employee who had been in the wrong soon left our company.

Never allow your opponent to unnerve you. If you think that he or she is a person of bad character, stop the negotiations and move on to the next opportunity. But if he or she is simply a bully and just likes to throw his or her weight around? Who cares? Usually, those bullies are trained negotiators who will probably not be handling your relationship in the long run. Smile and take advantage of their formal training.

A Story: Seeds and Rinds

There is a great story I learned along the way that really brings the benefits of cooperative negotiations to life. I do not remember where it originated, but I have used it regularly in working through sticky matters.

There were two companies who were always vying for the same annual crop of fruit. Both of their businesses had flourished, and they were not competitive – or at least, they did not see each other as competitors.

One year, the fruit was in short supply. The two companies, each in an attempt to protect their business, entered into a nasty battle for supply. The price of the fruit increased dramatically, creating economic strife. Each company independently created its own battle plan in an effort to secure more than a fair share of the crop, including spending money to obtain and relocate crops from other countries.

At some point, the two companies decided that they should meet to see if they could find a more reasonable solution. As it turned out, one of the companies was in need of seeds and the other was in need of rinds. One company's by-product was the other company's required resource. I suspect we do not need to cover what happened – you can guess. These sorts of situations occur all the time when negotiating.

Many times, public companies have to answer to analysts on Wall Street. They are willing to cover expenses to create a Wall Street-friendly environment. A great example is return on invested capital (ROIC) indexes. I have entered into a number of very lucrative deals because the other company wanted a better index, which, in turn, would earn them a higher price-earnings (P/E) ratio multiple. Despite the fact that the deal they committed to had a negative impact on earnings, the multiple they sought – and achieved – created a much better market cap for their shareholders.

Some companies have working capital goals or challenges. They will pay a higher cost for you to be the bank. Provided that they are creditworthy, and that the benefit you receive is more than the cost of carrying the working capital, it may be worthwhile to consider that role. Many opportunities can be fashioned when we are creative with negotiations. Do not underestimate the power of seeds and rinds.

Concluding the Negotiations

Hopefully, you have grown to enjoy working with your opponent. Negotiations are all about having fun. They can take place anywhere: on golf courses, in restaurants, in the smoking lounge, in offices, and in conference rooms.

If you simply don't like the person or people you are dealing with, that's a red flag you should consider before you shake hands. If the transaction is a one-time buy/sell deal, how you feel about them is not that important. However, in many deals, you will be working with them for a very long time.

Cooperative people usually remain cooperative, and uncooperative people often stay uncooperative. Consider that fact. If your partner is the uncooperative type, you might want to slip a little "pain money" into the negotiation. "Pain money" is nothing more than a bit of extra margin that helps one "feel better" about a potentially difficult future trading partner.

Ultimately, you'll shake hands, celebrate and get ready for the next phase. Because once the attorneys get involved, the real fun begins.

The Contract

Equally important to the negotiations is the contract. Frankly, a contract is merely a different form of negotiation – but it includes some new actors, the attorneys. With any luck, you have an attorney you trust and with whom you have a great working relationship. I have worked with dozens of them, and finding one you connect with is really a huge benefit.

Good Attorney = Great Asset

I have been blessed with having a key legal colleague at each of my companies throughout my career. They were all legally proficient, but more important, they were cooperative, and individuals whom I considered to be close friends. I knew they had my back, and they never caused a deal to collapse with bravado.

I have seen dozens of attorneys who lack the personality and edge to get deals done successfully. If you do not connect with your counsel, work within your corporate structure to obtain alternative counsel. It is worth the effort. I've dealt with some that I just could not connect with, and I was able to make the changes needed to be more efficient without them. Chemistry between you and your legal counsel is one of the most important aspects of successfully executing effective contracts.

When you are negotiating a contract, remember that in good, productive relationships, the contract will almost never see the light of day after it gets signed and filed. You'll simply conduct business as usual, and only go to the contract when a renewal is due.

I prefer to have automatic renewals with long lead times so that I am never surprised. Usually, the parties forget key dates, and – provided it is in my company's favor – I have intentionally allowed contracts to renew with no discussion. On the other hand, it is important to be aware of key dates like renewal times, particularly when you want out of the arrangement or seek to make changes. On the day you sign the contract, put all the pertinent renewal information into your calendar. It is simple in the computerized world; your reminders are preselected.

All you have to do is a little bit of initial entry work in your phone calendar.

View Contract Wording in an Unfavorable Light

When you are negotiating the wording in a contract, you simply need to view the implications of the verbiage in the most unfavorable light. Remember, you will probably only go to this language if there is a dispute.

Most companies will not intentionally breach a contract, but if they do, you have a distinct advantage when the wording is in your favor. The fear of litigation usually keeps the parties in check. However, courtroom calendars across the United States are still full of cases regarding contract disputes. For that reason, you should ensure that you write in terms and conditions that are as favorable to you as possible.

The more naive your opponent is, the better terms you can negotiate for yourself. For example, specifying something that seems simple, like shipping terms, can avoid significant problems. The term "shipper load, shipper count" means the person doing the shipping is responsible for the count on the load. If you are contracting with someone to ship on your behalf, and if they agree to those terms, they are responsible for the product until you receive it. If the product is missing, you merely have to go back to them for credit.

If you are the shipper, and you negotiate "shipper load, carrier count" terms, you have successfully eliminated any responsibility for the load once it leaves your facility – as long as the carrier has properly signed the paperwork. Obviously, negotiating those terms is a distinct advantage. If you find an error on your part, you should certainly notify your partner, but in the mysterious world of lost or damaged products, such matters usually end up unresolved.

Negotiating a favorable contract with terms and conditions that are difficult – if not impossible – for your new partner to achieve gives you a significant benefit. Obviously, there is no good reason to hold others to unachievable results, but if things get dicey, you have a number of factors on your side of the ledger if you have to go through a litigation. Often, the fear of losing in litigation (due to not meeting agreed-upon terms) will motivate your partner to allow you to resolve the situation to your satisfaction.

Tips for Better Contracts

Some of the most important things to remember about contracts (but are often forgotten) are:

- **Slight language changes can make a huge difference.** Phrases like "commercially reasonable efforts" and "best efforts" have significant differences, as do "negligence" and "gross negligence." You do not have to know all of these rules, but if you see some of these words, point them out to your counsel.
- **Capitalized words in the middle of sentences are defined terms**. Make sure you understand the definition and can live with it. The definition of these terms can also change from contract to contract. Be careful.

- **How and where disputes are litigated is important.** Different jurisdictions have different laws, and the cost to litigate in remote jurisdictions is significant. In fact, your counsel might have to engage alternative counsel to litigate in other jurisdictions. This should not be a dealbreaker; others may not care, and it is worth asking for.
- **Indemnification can be costly.** Understand exactly what you're indemnifying, and understand the language regarding the indemnification.
- **Attempt to get evergreen "never-ending" commitments when they are in your favor.** If they are not in your favor, avoid them if at all possible.

Once the contract is agreed upon and executed, your opponent becomes your partner and friend. Go out and celebrate. But never discuss your strategy, even if asked. In the majority of the cases, the terms and conditions of the contract you just signed will never be tested; but if they are, you will be happy you made the effort to negotiate favorable terms.

I have had others question my strategy from time to time, claiming that the investment of time and expense to get contract terms correct is not worth it. I would counter that once you get good at it, the investment is very little. And if things go awry with the contract, think of the time and money you will save by having made that modest investment.

I was having coffee with the new chief operating officer of a partner of mine; we have had a cordial, productive relationship. He asked me where I learned to negotiate contracts.

"Just learned it along the way," was my answer. "Why?"

"I've never seen anything like it," he replied. "You have all the power and control. I never would have signed this thing. It is the worst contract I have ever seen."

"I'll take that as a compliment," I answered, and added, "I guess I should be thankful you weren't around back then."

"Absolutely, but I have to live by it," he lamented.

"It only runs for another 10 years." I laughed.

"At your sole option," he grumbled.

We laughed and went on with our discussion. This relationship has been a very strong one, and there is little reason to be concerned, but he clearly knew that his position was a weak one. That knowledge alone could keep a number of issues from bubbling up in the future.

Contract language is a great deal like mayonnaise on a sandwich. If you want it, you can always add it, and there is no harm. If it is already spread on the sandwich, and then you decide you don't want it, you are out of luck, as it's impossible to remove. It permeates everything. If you are like me and hate mayonnaise, then it makes the sandwich intolerable. Unfortunately, I have lived with mayonnaise contracts, and they are not very palatable.

The Acquisition

Acquisitions are another type of negotiation. I have had the great pleasure of being involved in many acquisition negotiations. The most important advice I can give to someone considering an acquisition, or a divestiture for that matter, is: Do not fall into the trap of "deal heat." Deal heat occurs when you lose objectivity, and the appeal of wrapping up the deal overrides making a good choice. Even though you might be the most anxious person in the world, you must appear cool and confident. Once you tip your hand, you either spend too much if you are buying, or receive too little if you are selling.

There will always be other deals. If you have done your homework, you know the worth of what you are selling or buying. Move on and live with the consequences. The future tends to either make us look smart or stupid. I'd rather look stupid while avoiding an acquisition or divestiture than look stupid having done a bad deal.

Know What You Are Buying

When you are acquiring a company, it is important that you understand that you are usually buying three things:

Brands, Intellectual Property, and Book of Business – Valuing these can be a bit tricky, but is fairly straightforward. You run into challenges when you either overvalue or undervalue the future earnings potential of these assets. Each of the subcategories will have a bit of subtlety to them, but you are valuing earning potential.

Hard Assets – These are buildings, equipment, and other tangible items that have an appraisable market value. Valuing a hard asset is as simple as having an appraisal completed, and then discounting it for the sunk costs that have no real value other than for allowing operations to continue. Sunk costs include infrastructure, operating systems, and installation (or potential removal) costs.

Please be sure to consider environmental risks with the acquisition of hard assets. They can be extremely costly. Keep in mind that your predecessor may be grandfathered in on an item and that status may not continue after a change in control.

Human Capital –People are often the most overlooked asset in an acquisition. We tend to think about how to eliminate people and find synergy. Eliminating positions and combining job responsibilities is a huge benefit in an acquisition, but one of the worst mistakes you can make is to underestimate some of the individual talent you have acquired. Good people are in high demand. Do not allow your ego to minimize what you have just acquired. Some of the acquired workforce may be a better fit, or more talented, than some of your current team members.

Think about it using a sports analogy. Even the worst team in the league has talent that almost any other team in the league would love to have. Remember, employees of the company that has just been acquired are nervous; they are concerned about their future. If you do not address that issue properly, you will start to lose talent. And, unsurprisingly, the best and brightest are the most employable. Therefore, they are most likely to fill other positions at other companies, leaving you with the lower end of the workforce – the "C" and "D" players. You will be left with the worst of the marketing, sales, and finance teams, and so on. What you paid for has slipped out the back door, and you are left with the liability of poorer performers.

How you handle employee communications will speak volumes. The conduct of your veteran workforce after the acquisition will have an impact too. Take the human factor into consideration before signing on the dotted line.

People: The Most Overlooked Acquisition Asset

I was involved in a major acquisition almost 30 years ago. As a young, inexperienced junior executive, I jumped as directed, and adopted a scorched-earth type of strategy when it came to the acquired personnel. So did all of my counterparts in the other departments.

The synergies of that particular deal created a profound economic windfall, and for two years we feasted on the spoils of war. We even referred to ourselves as Vikings. We had pillaged and we gorged ourselves with huge bonus checks.

We were so convinced we were superior that we simply did not see the error of our course. We woke up after two years in an unfathomable position. All of the top talent was gone, and we were left with a disgruntled team of refugees. The people who remained were, frankly, the least talented and most unmotivated of the acquired workforce. Ultimately, it was necessary to offer lucrative severance packages to exit those individuals.

While we maintained cost synergies well into the future, we oversaw a significant decline in market share, because our best marketing and sales talent – who knew and understood the brands – had fled. We never admitted it, and I only understood what had happened after careful reflection. We had made the fatal error of not understanding the value of talent. Even worse, we had underestimated the chaos that acquiring poor performers would have on our business.

The entire business unit, including our preexisting business, ended up being sold off.

To be fair, I had left the company long before that divestiture, so I really have no basis in my opinion other than as a shareholder of the company. Nevertheless, I watched the share price get cut in half, and only after several years of struggle did it start to rebound. Of course, management spun the facts and trumpeted their wonderful effort in building the share price. But even after over a dozen years, the share price has still not reached what it was at the time of my departure.

It is a must to understand the value of all three asset classes in an acquisition. If all three exist, then properly valuing and caring for them after the acquisition will deliver optimal results.

Due Diligence

An extremely vital part of an acquisition is **due diligence**. Due diligence is the painstaking process of ensuring that what you think you are acquiring is, indeed, what you are acquiring. As with anything being sold, there is a great deal of marketing and gamesmanship to present the business in the best light possible.

There are a number of laws that protect acquirers from blatant fraud, but it is always best to dig deep and uncover all the skeletons prior to the consummation of the deal. Even with all the focus I have placed on it during my career, I have yet to be involved in an acquisition where I felt that the due diligence had been complete enough to protect the company.

Maybe someday I will fully understand the due diligence lapse, but without any additional data points, I have to accept the fact that it is a painful and tedious process and prone to being poorly executed. Perhaps my perceptions stem from the fact that we had the wrong people performing the due diligence. Performing due diligence is a great assignment for bundlers who remain within your organization.

A good deal can easily become a bad deal if due diligence is not handled properly. Following the guidelines outlined here will deliver the best results possible for the conditions.

Stupid Is Smart

I wanted to end this chapter with a story about a great friend and mentor of mine. This individual was the epitome of the "Southern Gentleman" – he even had a thick Southern drawl. He taught me an approach to business that I had not previously contemplated; he was the first to tell me that business is simple.

"You Yankees complicate it," he would say. "Y'all think because we talk funny that we are stupid."

I had been assigned to lead a new facility that had been part of an acquisition by my new employer. It was my first assignment in the Deep South. Almost immediately, I became friends with the gentleman that had run his family business and had sold it to my employer for $89 million.

As part of one of the most intriguing negotiations I had ever heard of, he had retained an office for himself and an assistant for five years. His office was down the hall from mine, and I took every opportunity to visit with him and glean morsels of wisdom that I use in my life to this day.

The original sale price was to be $86 million, but a snag had occurred during the due diligence process. My employer sent in a team of attorneys and experts to ensure that everything we were buying was as represented. Included in the sale was a tract of land that had frontage on the Gulf of Mexico. It had been a cannery years earlier, and had since been shut down.

In those days, before the bright lights of waterfront casinos, gulf frontage in that part of the United States was considered not particularly valuable. When our team of experts completed their evaluation, they claimed that they had discovered significant environmental risk where the old cannery had been, and estimated that it would cost the company $3 million to remediate it.

The team brought the fact to the negotiating table. Evidently, there was a bit of behind-the-scenes debate. My employer announced that they would make the acquisition, but would extract that piece of land from the transaction.

I would have loved to have been in the room when my friend more than likely placed his thumbs under the thin suspenders he wore, leaned back and said, "Well, you see boys, my family and I had figured that piece of property to be a $3 million problem. We'll keep it, but the price just went to $89 million."

I do not know all the details, but the final transaction price ended up being $3 million more than the original deal, and I remember one of my superiors lamenting that it was the first time he had ever paid money **not** to buy something.

I always figured it was a combination of being outsmarted and "deal heat." But the higher sale price was also a result of the egocentric superiority complex that large companies fall into when dealing with people they consider less sophisticated.

Here is the rest of the story. My friend's family cleaned the site up for less than $500,000. A few years later, when gaming came to that part of the United States, my friend leased the property to a casino for a lucrative amount. To this day, I believe his family continues to own the property and receive substantial revenues from lease payments.

I learned many things from that great man, but nothing more important than to listen. Let the guys who think they are smarter than you talk themselves into all sorts of problems.

It's all right to be the dumbest guy in the room. Sometimes it even makes you a bunch of money.

Combustion Check – IGNITE NEGOTIATION

Before lighting the fuse on your next negotiation, ask yourself:

1. Are you willing to do the preplanning work required to fuel a successful outcome?
2. Can you remain unemotional, keeping the flame of rational thinking burning bright?
3. Are you willing to listen actively, allowing insights to ignite better solutions?
4. Do you have an attorney you trust, a co-pilot to manage legal sparks safely?
5. Can you resist the temptation of "deal heat," keeping the fire controlled and strategic?
6. Can you remember the people, understanding that relationships fuel long-term success?

Answering "yes" to each point ensures that your negotiations burn with clarity, control, and lasting impact, sparking outcomes that light the path forward.

12

Leadership: Conducting the Flame

A man who wants to lead the orchestra
must turn his back on the crowd.
– *Unknown*

Have you . . .

Ever struggled with the pressures of leadership?

Ever experienced a leader who crushed your spirit?

Ever crushed the spirit of someone under your direction?

What if . . .

You find the secret fuel to ignite fires within the next few pages?

You could emerge as the leader who inspires, reassures, and rewards?

An old friend and mentor of mine used to describe leadership as follows: The leader is the conductor of the orchestra. Your job is to bring all the instruments together to create beautiful music. You can't lead the orchestra if you are trying to play the piccolo. Go and find the best player of each instrument and teach them to create beautiful sounds together. Conductors conduct; musicians perform. Some musicians become conductors, but to be successful, each must stick to one role at a time. So it is with leadership.

While the musician vs. conductor comparison does not completely describe the role of the leader, it is a good description that gets to the core leadership concern. You cannot really teach leadership. You are either predisposed to be a good leader, or you're not. But, you can teach leadership skills to help develop an individual who has the innate ability to become a great leader.

The Best Performer Often Makes the Worst Leader

I have learned that just because an individual is a good performer, they are not necessarily equipped to become a good leader. I've learned that the hard way. Countless times, I have either promoted – or allowed others to promote – the best performer of their area of expertise into leadership positions. Almost always, they have failed. So, being the best at what you do does not make you a great or even good leader. In fact, I have found that the very best experts often make poor leaders.

I have isolated some intangibles that a person must possess to become a great leader. You do not have to be great at every one of the attributes described in the paragraphs that follow. Still, a leader should be able to embrace them and understand the importance of each.

A leader must also have the maturity to recognize if he or she is lacking in any of the attributes required to be successful. Lack of perfection in an area is not fatal. But the leader must enlist a trusted team member for help, who is great at the attribute where the leader is not as good.

To begin with, there is one attribute that you must have before you can even consider becoming an outstanding leader. I suspect that many "successful" leaders do not have this attribute or forgot its importance long ago. Too many leaders simply get caught up in the world of limousines, five-star hotels and first class travel, and tend to forget the basics. This attribute I'm speaking of is a game-changer. Without it, you simply cannot successfully lead an organization. That attribute is... **humility**.

Humility

All of us were brought into this world with a single breath of air, and we will leave the same way. Along the way in life, we get to experience many different encounters and opportunities. Many of us are more blessed, or luckier than others, and things seem to fall into place. Some have the drive to overcome the obstacles in their lives. And others are satisfied with just participating in the experience. We are all a bit different, but we all come from the same humble beginnings.

Somewhere along the way, some of us start to think we are better than others. This idea seems to typically manifest itself in sports at an early age. The football quarterback becomes deified by the students at his school. The most talented cheerleader holds the same status. Receiving such overt adoration at a young age makes it difficult for one to remain grounded in his or her skin.

If they are lucky or talented enough, those school "stars" can transition their skills into a lifelong advantage. But more often than not, it does not work out that way. As the high school years fade, so does the elite status that many began to believe was their birthright. How many times do we notice that the former star athlete or one-time homecoming queen is struggling, as they lose their status and become just plain old folks?

Many leaders face the same challenges. When they lose their positions, their identity follows. Moreover, if they do not possess a good measure of humility, their teams see right through them. The team may very well execute each transaction flawlessly, but without a real connection between leader and team, the journey will always be rocky. It should not be a popularity contest, but rather an understanding between leader and team that, as people, they are equals – no matter what their titles might be.

It is important that we do not confuse the concept of equality as individuals with the superior position the leader holds within the organization. The leader is the final decision-maker. While understanding the power of humility, he or she can never allow themselves to become friends with members of the team. Being reachable by the team is encouraged, but the leader must maintain a level of distinction between their position and those of the team members.

Treating your fellow teammates with dignity and respect does not mean that you should go out to the bar and drink with them. Ensuring that you make the next pot of coffee when it's your turn should not be confused with interactions like passing internet jokes around the office. Seeking an employee out to ask about their sick parent or how their son or daughter's sports team did over the weekend is a far cry from gossiping about the new woman in accounting or the old guy in sales. If we have our humility box checked, we can move forward and review those other attributes that make leaders great.

The Equitable Hard-Ass

The first thing you need to be able to do if you want to be a great leader is to make unpopular decisions. Remember, leadership is not a popularity contest. It is incredibly difficult for just about everyone to make tough calls, particularly when those decisions directly affect their people. Unless you don't have a heart, you are probably going to agonize about those decisions.

If you don't have a heart, you have no business being a leader.

So, it's a given that making tough calls will turn your stomach inside out and probably will result in sleepless nights. You are not unique; there is no crime in being afraid or sympathetic. The crime is committed when you allow your fear or sympathy to slow your decision-making process or change your decision to the detriment of the company.

You must act swiftly and deftly. Get the tough call behind you and move on with life. While it is certainly permissible to talk compassionately about the difficulty of the decision, shirking responsibility and passing the duty onto others is unacceptable. You need to take responsibility, and then clearly and concisely explain the rationale for the decision. If you cannot clearly or concisely explain it, you are not ready to make the decision.

Consult Key Advisors

Before you make any decision-related announcements to the broader internal and external audience, consult with your key advisors. Make sure they understand the rationale for the decision. Seek input on how to communicate or message the decision. But avoid allowing the conversation to spiral into challenging the decision. In most cases, if not all, you will have received vital input from your key resources regarding crafting the best messaging approach.

The more negatively you believe the decision will be received by your team, the more important it is that you have your key leaders on board with you. Even if they personally disagree with the decision being made, insist that they endorse it publicly. Nothing creates more angst in an organization than when fellow leaders question a decision with other team members.

It's OK to say, "I don't expect you to like this decision, but it is the best thing we can do under the circumstances." I have found that it is the second and third layer of management that normally causes more difficulty than the lower-level employees. People are much more resilient than many leaders expect; and, provided that the communication is forthright and the rationale is explained, team members will understand. There is no correlation between liking a decision and accepting it.

Impartiality During Tough Times

It is of vital importance that you and your closest team members exhibit total impartiality with all employees. You cannot be perceived as being inequitable. In fact, you need to demand that your top executives lead by example. Nothing kills morale more than when executives communicate a tough decision but exclude themselves from the implications of that decision. This kind of scenario plays out regularly when executives announce a drastic cost-cutting program – including wage freezes – but are then spotted dining at a top-tier restaurant soon afterward.

Once, after a very difficult year, I had to announce that there would be no raises or bonuses for the vast majority of my organization. Nevertheless, I had decided to provide raises for the lower-level pay grades, because I felt that they and their families would experience hardship without a slight increase. But a significant percentage of the employee base did not receive raises, bonuses or profit sharing.

As you can imagine, the decision was unpopular, but almost everyone understood the reasons for the decision. But I was incredulous when, shortly afterward, a couple of our executives decided to go on a recreational junket. When they returned, I challenged them and found that there was no good reason for the excursion. Fortunately, we dodged a major internal outcry from the staff, but the risk was severe.

When you need to make an announcement that people may not like, you should communicate it directly to your team, and face-to-face when possible. In some cases, you might need to use trusted representatives from your executive team to assist. There is nothing worse than hearing bad news from a third party or via email. Hiding behind emails should be outlawed in all organizations.

Honesty Is the Best Policy

Also, total transparency is vital when announcing a challenging decision. Tell everyone on the team why the decision is being made; make sure they understand that you have carefully considered many options. Also, tell them how the decision will positively impact the future. Do not fall into the trap of attempting to spin the story to make the situation sound nicer than it is. Almost everyone sees through such facades, and it will erode your credibility.

When an organization makes cuts to benefit packages, it often ends up being a textbook example of how a company attempts to shroud and spin bad news. If the organization has decided to change a benefit program because it is struggling to cover the rising costs of health care, then tell the broader team exactly what the decision is. Explain why the decision is being made. Attempting to get the team members to believe the change results in a better benefit package will not work, and there will be more damage when the full story is revealed. If you think you can succeed with this type of messaging, you're wrong – and it will cost you.

If it's bad news, then tell them it's bad news. Over time, your candor will earn you the admiration of your team. They may hate the decision, but they will respect you for your honesty.

The Ear

We have covered the importance of being a good listener in some previous chapters. "Lend an ear," as I like to say. There is no more underrated quality that makes leaders great than the ability to listen and hear. Everyone claims to be great at listening, but do we really hear?

Hearing means you transform your listening into action that demonstrates comprehension. This is important when you are attempting to connect with every level of your organization.

To be a good ear, you must understand that leaders need to be in touch with all their people. You must understand that what excites you may not excite your employees. Frankly, you might be trying to decide what artwork you want in your ski chalet while they may be figuring out how to put food on the table next week.

Every leader will be exposed to some uncomfortable topics, including ones that most people do not like to talk about. How a leader addresses these topics will suggest the quality of leader that they are.

I am one of the fortunate ones. I came from the lower middle class and know firsthand the struggles of the working class. Every day, I remind myself that I am blessed; I have been lucky enough to have been born in a country where I could realize my dreams. For those who have not lived that kind of experience, it can be much more challenging to understand and to be able to truly empathize.

Team Connections Make You a Better Listener

Being able to identify and connect with almost everyone in my organization has been a blessing. I lived it and loved it. Regardless of your socioeconomic past, we are all able to learn how to connect with our employees, but it takes a discipline few are willing to follow. It means actually working at the job that your lowest-level person completes, every day of his or her life.

That does not mean just spending a day in the field and then going out for a nice lobster dinner afterward. It means getting your hands dirty for up to a month, doing the actual work that you are asking others to do. Understanding what their day-to-day is like will allow you to truly empathize with their struggles.

It's incredibly enlightening and rewarding, if you are willing to do it. Of course, you will have your regular work to do during the same period of time, so the time on the floor might come in spurts of two- or three-hour increments. But two or three hours on the packaging line or in the receiving pit will give you a perspective like no other.

Once connected with your team, you will realize many things that may have escaped you before. You will learn that the vast majority of employees in your organization work only to maintain a standard of living that allows them to strive for a better life for their children. They are deeply committed and loyal, but they rely on you as the leader to make the right decisions. The paradox is that they have no idea what it is you actually do.

When you connect with your people, they will come to you with their problems. It is dangerous territory, but if managed properly, this communication is very powerful and can be a huge advantage against unproductive behavior.

The Silence Is Deafening

One of Colin Powell's quotes on leadership is, "The day soldiers stop bringing you their problems is the day you have stopped leading them. They have either lost confidence that you can help them or concluded that you do not care. Either case is a failure of leadership."

We can apply this same sentiment to business. If your employees stop sharing their thoughts and concerns with you, you are failing to lead. Allowing your people to think you're incompetent or uncaring is not acceptable. This applies in life as well. My father, who passed away when I was in high school, always said, "Wherever you go, son, remember where you came from, and never forget you put your pants on one leg at a time just like everyone else."

There is another side of being a good listener. It is understanding that, due to the success you've had as a leader, you have huge influence that spreads across the organization. You may not feel any different, but many people will be intimidated by you and your position. Consequently, you must make an extra effort to connect.

When I held my executive position at a major consumer product goods company, I had two significant experiences that molded me into the listener I am today. As background, I was considered by most in the organization as a man of the people. I loved everyone on my team, and I felt that they returned the same affection to me. I made it a point to visit with everyone on a daily basis when I was in the office. I knew their families, and they knew mine.

The first experience came one day when I was walking around visiting with my team. An employee asked me a question to which I did not know the answer. I asked her to stop by my office, and

I would find the answer. An hour later she had not shown up. I stopped by her work station and asked her what happened. She said, "I don't know where your office is."

I was completely shocked and embarrassed. I escorted her to my office, and we had a nice chat.

The second experience came when the company decided to have an ice cream social; the executives were going to prepare cones for the employees. I overheard one of the employees say, "It should be fun with Elliott, but I am not sure the others even know how to serve ice cream."

Contrary to the first lesson, that statement marked a very proud moment for me, personally. Unfortunately, and more importantly, it was an indictment of the broader organization and its leaders. I knew my fellow executives well, and they were great men and women. Regrettably, the most important people, our team members, had no idea.

Make time to connect with your people. If you have facilities that work multiple shifts, make sure you take time to visit with all shifts regularly. You may have to put it in your calendar. As mentioned in a previous chapter, it sounds simple, but you might find it quite difficult.

I had a female employee who I had placed in a newly expanded leadership role. I added a weekly plant walk-through as part of her management business objective bonus program. She was a wonderful and candid individual, and said she was offended by my suggestion. She explained that she had every intention of doing a walk-through as part of her new role. She added that if I thought I needed to pay her for that, it seemed to indicate a lack of trust. I let her know that it had nothing to do with trust; I advised her to just look at it as "easy money," if that made it more palatable. At the end of the year, she admitted that it was among the toughest things she had ever been charged with.

Actions Signal That You Listened and Have Heard

Leaders learn how to listen and hear. Through their actions, they demonstrate that they have done both. Find a way to incorporate this skill set into your leadership style. If you think you are already great at it, ask yourself: When was the last time that someone who you don't frequently communicate with came to your office, and told you something you didn't want to hear? If that hasn't happened somewhat regularly, then you have not learned to connect.

The Coach

Leaders are great coaches. They use candor and discipline, along with confidence-building reassurance, to develop their teams. As covered in the differentiation section, all people are created equal, but all employees are not.

Even the best teams will have some members that are more talented and others that are struggling. Aside from the intended action of the differentiation program, the coach must be viewed by team members as unbiased and equitable.

Coaches need to have the courage to remove people from the team who are not great team players, even if they are potential superstars. Leaders should also have the acumen to push team members to the next level. And they should push the best and the brightest as hard, if not harder, than the weakest.

The Best Coaches Embrace Variety

Great coaches know that the best teams are an amalgamation of individuals, who each have their own unique skills, experiences and capabilities, and are brought together for a common purpose and goal. Coaches realize that the results of the entire team far outweigh the individual performances of team members.

Individual Praise Is Best Given in Private

Coaches are careful to recognize individual performances, but they are also quick to publicly frame those achievements through a team lens. Save individual praise for one-on-one sessions. Great leaders develop and encourage maturity in their best performers, so they embrace individual performances as quiet victories. People on your team who have the character to understand and thrive using this approach can become leaders of your organization.

Correcting Behavior – Always in Private

At the same time, even the best and brightest will struggle from time to time. Great leaders will "coach up" when team members need it. Leaders will also promptly coach out poor behaviors, in one-on-one sessions.

The Team Trumps the Individual

Too often, recognition is given only to superstar individuals after astounding performances. Great coaches realize it is important to cultivate an environment where all employees are acknowledged for giving their best. This practice will increase morale and prompt team members to do their best work every day – not just in larger, prestigious initiatives. Even failures should be celebrated, if the person truly gave their very best. If you are in the business of inflating already-bloated egos of a few elite performers, you're not coaching at the highest level.

A Collection of Great People, or a Great Team

As a leader, you should step back and ask yourself two questions. First, ask, "Am I leading, or am I part of a group of talented individuals who have been thrown together as a team?" Or ask, "Am I leading, or am I part of a great team who has members who are talented?" The latter structure is far more powerful and will win more reliably. As John Wooden said, "Winning takes talent, to repeat takes character."

The Great Simplifier

Leaders have the uncanny ability to be great simplifiers. The more complicated a challenge, the harder the leader works to reduce it to the most basic terms. Simplification, of course, is critical to creating the environment where combustion thrives.

Simplification starts with elimination of variables. I have always loved math, and the easiest way to describe this concept is to look at algebraic equations. Most would agree that a math problem with one variable is fairly easy to solve. When we introduce two variables, we need significantly more information, but as with the single-variable equation, it is a relatively easy solution.

When we get to three-variable equations, we start to add a level of complexity that requires much more information and effort to solve. It may not be accurate to describe the complexity in moving from two to three variables as logarithmic. But it is certainly much more descriptive than using the direct three-divided-by-two model, which falsely assumes that the three-variable equation is merely 50 percent harder to solve.

In business, the biggest challenges will probably have dozens of variables, all independently moving in their own directions. In many cases, the problems are so complicated that it seems necessary to find the root cause. Unfortunately, there can be many root causes – and along the way, red herrings will move the team in the wrong direction.

Great leaders direct their team to try to hold as many variables constant as possible and then to examine the situation through a single variable. By doing so, the team can quickly discount those pseudo-root causes and focus on the key driver or drivers.

Leaders must be careful to avoid falling into the trap of getting too immersed in corrective action. They need to be a source that remains above the fray and watches vigilantly as the team searches for a solution. The old adage, "You can't see the forest for the trees," is a cautionary statement when it comes to the leader's role. He or she must remain out of the trees.

But far too often, teams become invested in false theories created from complexity. A watchful eye, not mired in the details, can save significant time and expense. The leader needs to assume this role, if warranted. In the best of circumstances, the leader will fulfill this role without fanfare, and the team will marvel at the leader's ability to arrive at the solution or provide guidance.

Simplification does not only come into play during problem-solving. It is vital to enhancing the organization's capacity to take on more assignments and still deliver optimal results. When faced with solving a problem or deciding on the path to take, the power of simplicity pays huge dividends.

The Teacher

Leaders are great educators. Leaders use failures and victories alike as teachable moments. They find creative ways to make sure that their team and its individual members learn from history. They apply living, breathing educational tools that can be used far into the future.

Leaders are particularly adept at teaching others how to learn from a key experience; to apply that experience to other opportunities or hurdles. Something that worked in one situation may be the perfect solution in another.

A great tip for leaders: Place reminders in your calendar far in advance to periodically reeducate your team members. I find it amazing how many times during my career that I felt I was experiencing déjà vu. Unfortunately, it was much less about déjà vu and a great deal more about forgetting that we had already encountered the same situation.

As with all great teachers, leaders must not only be willing to be educated. They must seek out opportunities to broaden the scope of their learning. Leaders should be inquisitive, constantly challenging the experts. They will dig into details to find new solutions.

Leaders are always looking for opportunities to learn. They are adept at applying learning to multiple scenarios. I believe that a day that I do not learn something is a lost day. I look for educational opportunities everywhere, and sometimes I find them in the strangest ways.

I was attending a holiday party at one of the companies I oversaw and had to drive around 100 miles to Branson, Missouri. I arrived late and was ushered directly to the podium. I actually had become quite ill and could barely deliver my speech. But I started by telling the team that I try to learn something every day, and on my way to the event, I learned three important things.

First, I learned that the roads through the Ozark Mountains have more twists, turns, and steep grades than any road I had ever driven on. Second, I found that if you miss a turn, it might be 10 or more miles before you can turn around. Third, and most important, it **is** possible to get motion sickness while driving a car.

Obviously, that was a bit of humor to start a holiday greeting. Still, if I had known about those three facts prior to that morning, I would have certainly felt better, been on time, and endured less aggravation.

If you are not seeking to learn, you are probably missing out on many educational opportunities.

The Risk-Taker

Everyone loves a good action movie. It is always exciting to watch the lead actor or actress successfully traverse unparalleled risks to achieve a goal. Good leaders in business are a bit like action heroes or heroines; their risks are very different and much more controlled, but no less exciting.

A leader who must have all details proven to them before making a decision creates a very boring environment, and that tends to demotivate the team. Certainly, taking wild, irresponsible risks is not advisable, but going with your gut and challenging conventional wisdom creates an exciting environment where opportunities abound.

Companies where risk-taking is not encouraged may routinely deliver positive results, but at the same time, they may be leaving material amounts of revenue and profit untapped. They operate in a malaise, waiting for others to create disruption in the marketplace.

It is not easy to determine which opportunities to chase, but I have used a couple of rules to guide my decision-making. The first rule is, if the opportunity is 50 percent or more attractive from a return on the investment than the average of the portfolio or the expectation of the shareholders, then it should be further evaluated with a bias to proceed.

For example, let's say that you lead a private company, and the shareholders seek a 20 percent annual return on investment.

A new project – it could be a new product launch or a capital investment – is estimated to create a 30 percent or better return, all factors considered. Because the project meets the criterion, it is definitely worthy of a complete evaluation.

Growth and Excitement Move the Needle

The same is true with publicly traded companies. Your stock trades at a historic price earnings ratio (P/E). General market conditions may affect this average for the companies traded in your sector, but your company will either trade at a premium to or a discount to the average. The higher the P/E, the better market cap you have created for your shareholders.

There are two ways to generate a higher market cap. The first way is to create more earnings; and the second way – often overlooked by many leaders – is to create an environment where you can move the needle on P/E. Our earlier example of Apple and Microsoft is a great one. During the months of March and April 2012, Microsoft was at a P/E of 11.2 while Apple enjoyed a P/E of 17.4. If Microsoft could have commanded the same P/E as Apple, their shareholders would have enjoyed a more than 50 percent premium in share price, creating $140 billion in market capitalization with not a single extra penny earned. Said another way, Microsoft would have had to deliver almost 50 percent more net profit percent to deliver the same return to its shareholders as Apple.

Handicapping the Risk

Companies that take measured risk and create disruption in the marketplace are rewarded with higher-than-average valuations, but they must become proficient risk-takers in order to do that. If we use our portfolio model of a 50 percent better return than average, we allow ourselves room for some mistakes.

The second filter in determining your confidence level is that the decision or investment is the correct one. If you are more than 67 percent confident, the investment would probably trigger a decision to go forward. Let's assume that your gut is right; that two-thirds of the time, applying the 50 percent premium factor, your exact historical performance is delivered. In effect, the downside risk is very low if you apply these two filters. In a sense, you have hedged your bet.

The time and expense you have saved your company is significant, and you can now investigate other opportunities. Simply stated, you have just created a much more effective organization with greatly expanded capacity.

Risk-Taking Watch-Outs

There are two very important watch-outs when taking risks. The first is that your key stakeholders must be passionate about the risk to be taken. Lack of passion will probably doom the opportunity to a failed status.

The second watch-out is to make sure you do not become so invested in an essentially bad opportunity that you waste resources and money trying to chase it. Nevertheless, remember that you are going to have some failures if you follow this risk-based approach. It is best to have preset targets and benchmarks prior to commencing, and to watch them closely. If you do not meet important deliverables, have the maturity to either change on the fly or kill the project.

Knowing When to Accept Defeat

In my years in business, I have seen quite a bit of money and time wasted trying to turn poor decisions into good ones. This approach is rarely successful. Leaders erroneously examine the investment and try to save it. But when we look at it as a sunk cost that we will probably never recover, and make a decision based on the facts, we might very well take a different approach. I have fallen into this trap more times than I care to remember. I refer to this trap as the "death spiral." We will cover the death spiral in more detail in a future chapter.

The best way to examine these bad situations is to ignore the historical investment. Look at the factors in play, and ask yourself, *Would I be doing this with what I know today?* If the answer is no, turn your attention to what you can salvage or learn from the experience.

Great leaders take risks, challenge the status quo, and go with their gut. Hiring a bunch of experts to tell you how to proceed is like giving them your watch and having them tell you what time it is.

There is a time and a place for consultants. Evaluate your core competencies and consider engaging outside experts when you are out of your area of expertise. When an issue you are struggling with is not a core competency, that is the time to look at hiring an outside advisor.

Here is a great quote from Ralph Waldo Emerson that applies to risk-taking: "Do not go where the path may lead; go instead where there is no path and leave a trail."

The Visionary

Great leaders inspire their teams with their view of the future. Not unlike a great artist, a leader can see the end product before the first "brushstroke" is placed against the "canvas."

Great leaders passionately engage in bringing their future to life and to embedding a vision into the fabric of the entire organization. When every member of the team understands and embraces the vision, the resulting enthusiasm transcends most – if not all – obstacles.

The leader, surrounded by a talented group of experts, can lead that team along the path required to breathe life into the vision. And then each team member, employing his or her own unique talents, can work in concert with the broader team to successfully deliver that vision.

Realization of a vision is often a long journey. Many roads can be taken. Great leaders allow the team to explore many routes along the path, giving guidance along the way. Where one path appears to be fraught with obstacles, the leader will make changes on the fly and suggest alternatives.

One watch-out, implied earlier, is that we can become too invested in a particular method or path. We will then make poor decisions that are focused on using that specific path, rather than on completing the journey as a whole. Great leaders know that it really matters less about the path taken, and more about arriving at the destination successfully.

The Cheerleader

Every team needs a cheerleader. Cheerleaders can be the official, uniformed variety; they can be fans in the stadium; or they can be the proud grandfather or grandmother on the sidelines. In whatever form they take, cheerleaders keep the team pumped up when it is on a roll, creating momentum that fuels success. There is no more powerful factor for success than confidence, and nothing creates confidence more than momentum.

When troubles appear to be insurmountable, cheerleaders are there to encourage the team. Everyone loves a comeback, and most often comebacks start with a single play that creates momentum. That momentum is fueled by confidence-boosting cheers.

In business, there is no better cheerleader than the leader. The leader needs to be a prominent advocate for the team and the team's goals. Getting the team excited about the company and what it stands for will drive individual team members to go faster, leap higher, and be stronger.

In fact, every Olympic medal is inscribed with the words *Citius, Altius, Fortius*, which is Latin for Faster, Higher, Stronger. Great leaders understand that embedding that kind of mindset into the organization delivers huge benefits.

While no one on your team may be an Olympic athlete, we can adapt the sentiment to our business. We can create a culture that cheers on our "business Olympian" to perform beyond everyone's wildest expectations.

Over a decade ago, I had the honor of being invited to a Walmart team meeting. As a vendor, I felt very fortunate to have been on the invitee list. The session was more like a pep rally than anything else. When I left, I felt motivated and empowered, and I was not even a member of the team. The memory of the power created in that room has stayed with me throughout my career.

Leaders know when to cheer and when to let the cheering subside. The biggest risk to adopting the cheerleading mentality is that, if the leader is not careful, the cheerleading can become undisciplined and some intangible benefits can go away. Keep everything in check through a balanced approach.

Maintaining a perspective and recognizing that there is truth in the saying "There can be too much of a good thing" is extremely important. The same is true with "We are wallowing in our sorrows." I usually try the balanced approach – things are never as good or as bad as they seem at the time. Moderating the approach means being more positive during times of struggle, and being a bit more measured when things appear to be going overly well.

If cheerleading isn't your thing, then be astute enough to engage a natural cheerleader as a close advisor. Surrogate cheerleaders are acceptable, as long as the leader endorses their cheering.

Leadership Snippets

Seek to Understand: While we as unbundlers will strive to keep emotion out of the workplace, it is inevitable that some will slip in from time to time. When an employee comes to you with an emotionally charged topic, make an effort to understand why the emotion is so high. Chances are, once you understand the person's perspective, you will be able to much more easily address the concern. Many compare the escalation of emotion as climbing the rungs of a ladder. The leader must be skilled at helping team members to come down from the top of their emotional ladder; the leader also should ask questions that probe into the root causes of the emotion.

Assume Positive Intent: When handling a sensitive matter, begin by assuming that the motivations of those involved are genuine and positive. Your team member assessments can help you understand how different personality preferences may shape the situation. This is especially important when you're dealing with people you don't know well. Unfamiliarity can create space for skepticism. Educate yourself on the issue, and if you discover that the motivation is not as it appeared, respond appropriately. As Ronald Reagan said, "Trust, but verify."

The Best Performers Are Often Their Own Worst Critics: That statement is one that I have found to be very accurate. As such, attempting to embarrass or chastise a team member publicly rarely works. Keep coaching sessions positive and private. In fact, if you have a top performer who is struggling with the implications of a bad decision, remind him or her that the only person who never made a bad decision is the person who never did anything. You might even want to introduce some levity into the situation by sharing a pertinent story from your past. If you are honest with yourself there are plenty to share.

Have Fun and Don't Take Yourself Too Seriously: If you are truly capable of becoming a great leader, you need to make sure you are enjoying yourself. Your team will notice it immediately. Equally important, you must be able to poke fun at yourself. The ability to have a good laugh at your own expense is a great attribute.

Profile In Leadership Disaster – The Crusher

There is an incredibly wise saying: "People do not quit their jobs – they quit their bosses." When I first heard that, I thought it was inaccurate, but after more than 40 years in business, I have found it to be extremely valid. In my case, the primary motivation for each of my resignations was my relationship with my boss.

The more noteworthy of the two was my resignation from an executive position at a major consumer product goods company. I had been on the so-called fast track there for years, but quickly was derailed when I met **The Crusher**. Yes, that was his nickname, and he reveled in the moniker.

He would have said that his nickname was a result of being a tough and decisive manager, and because could make the hard call like no one else. The reality is, he earned the nickname from his team because he **crushed** the dignity out of almost everyone he touched.

My company was consolidating operations, and I was given the nod to lead a team. The team was over 200 people strong, and they were housed in a dilapidated building. When I had my initial meeting with the team members, I found them to be completely demoralized and unmotivated. Poor working conditions, coupled with poor leadership, had contributed to poor performance.

These folks were wonderful individuals, but they had been crushed under the weight of totalitarian leadership. The Crusher was both feared and reviled by most, if not all, of the team members. He was known for regular deceit and for being completely detached from the team. In fact, he had led this particular team for almost a decade, but had never entered the building where he expected them to perform.

In classic abuser fashion, he would **beat them senseless** and then afterward would send them **guilt gifts** to make amends. A $50 gift card was supposed to make up for a 12-hour Saturday shift created by his neglect.

He violated almost every principle outlined in this chapter:

- His arrogance was like no other that I have ever experienced, and it's fair to say that he didn't connect with the team since he had never darkened the door of the building where his people worked.
- His dishonesty was well known throughout the team. At one point, I contacted him to quell a rumor that had the team concerned. He assured me that the rumor was false. As the words came out of his mouth over the phone, an

announcement confirming the same rumor was being typed by his assistant for distribution.

- He was so disconnected that coaching was not possible. He resided in an office so far from any of his people that he was simply not accessible. As I recall, you had to actually walk through his assistant's office to gain access to his. Remember, you must be visible and reachable to be a coach.
- With The Crusher, nothing was simple. In a moment of frustration, I once asked him if I had to prove to him scientifically that the sun rose in the east.
- In fairness, I must admit that I learned a great deal from this man. All of it was what **not** to do. In that light, the experience was educational.
- Everything was done "old school" with The Crusher. He had the experience, and no one dared challenge his beliefs. The only risk he ever took was to treat his people so poorly that they ought to have revolted.
- There was no vision beyond the last month's results and the anticipated results of the next month.
- You simply can't be nicknamed The Crusher and be a cheerleader. Enough said.

The reader is probably thinking, *Elliott just doesn't like him; he's got to be exaggerating.* I can assure you: Yes, I do not like him, but I also assure you that, if anything, I am understating his inadequacies.

To illustrate the sincerity of my critique, I advise the reader that I left the company in the early summer, having only been at that location for four months. But that December, I received a heartfelt Christmas card from one of the teams. Each member had signed it and added touching comments. The one that crystallized the situation for me was, "Thanks for the chairs."

When I had arrived at that workplace, the employees had been sitting in broken chairs for who knows how long. There simply wasn't a budget to repair the chairs; it was a ridiculous but true situation and I immediately remedied it.

So, how did The Crusher stay in his position so long, you may ask? The answer is simple. He managed the expectations of the executives and delivered regularly. I don't believe his superiors embraced his methods, but they turned a blind eye, favoring **acceptable results** over great leadership.

What's the problem with someone like The Crusher? Plain and simple, short-term and even longer-term results are often misleading. Had this individual been a great leader, how much better could the results have been? I assure you they would have been superior.

So, whatever happened to The Crusher? I heard that the company finally could not endure his methods, and he was put out to pasture in a role at some remote location.

I had worked for that company for 11 years. I had met some crusty guys along the way, but never anyone like that. I knew The Crusher was a misfit and was amazed he had been able to remain in his position.

So, The Crusher is a great example of someone who delivers, but does not share the company's values. This is a person who is allowed to create havoc to the detriment of the broader organization.

Unfortunately, there are Crushers in leadership roles in companies throughout the world. Is there a Crusher in your business? My advice is: Muster the courage to **crush them right out of your organization**. Your people will love you for it, and your company will flourish.

The Leadership Playbook

Being a truly successful leader takes a blend of humility, courage, discipline, flexibility and desire. This combination is extremely hard to find. I believe that many of the best leaders never rise to the highest levels because they lack the self-confidence to try, don't attach themselves to a mentor, or do not fit the mold mandated by the establishment.

Truly great leaders find other individuals who have the right positive attributes and mentor them as leaders of the future. I like to refer to these individuals as raw clay, waiting to be molded into masterpieces. One of the most important pieces of advice that any leader can give to a developing leader is: Adopt your own style. There is a tendency for junior employees to attempt to mimic the mannerisms of those they respect. But I find that simply copying a mentor's behavior rarely, if ever, is effective. To be a great leader, we each have to create our own persona.

There is nothing as gratifying for a leader than to witness the transformation of junior employees into outstanding leaders. These people are the future of your business and of businesses yet to be created.

Combustion Check – IGNITE LEADERSHIP

Before lighting the fuse on your leadership journey, ask yourself:

1. Do you embrace the theory that the best performers are often not the best leaders, and are you willing to ignite your leadership potential anyway?
2. Do you have the humility to lead, keeping the fire of respect and influence alive?
3. Are you willing to connect with your people, fanning the flames of engagement?
4. Will you listen and truly hear, allowing insights to spark innovation and trust?
5. Do you have the courage to make tough or risky calls, fueling the organization's forward momentum?
6. Can you fulfill the role of cheerleader, igniting energy and morale across the team?
7. Are there Crushers in your organization, and are you ready to remove them before they snuff out the flames?

Answering "yes" to each point ensures that your leadership burns bright, guiding your team with energy, clarity, and unstoppable momentum.

13

Inefficiency: Hard Truths That Feed the Fire

The era of procrastination, of half-measures, of soothing and baffling expedients, of delays is coming to its close. In its place we are entering a period of consequences.

– Winston Churchill, former prime minister, United Kingdom

Have you . . .

Ever questioned the status quo?

Became exhausted with the inefficiency inherent in the system?

Wondered why you see incongruent behavior repeated and championed?

What if . . .

You could embark on an enhanced journey constructed through innovative ideas?

You could strip away all the outdated and ineffective rules?

Traditional businesses create environments that result in inefficiency, wasted time and wasted money. They make use of items and systems that cause sleepless nights, burning stomach acid, and illness. One of the tools used in business is the "deck." This is not your backyard area for relaxation. Rather, it's a presentation, consisting of words and supporting visuals.

Traditionally, a deck was used in formal presentations, but deckmania has created an environment where decks are employed to pitch even the most mundane ideas. This can lead to inefficiency.

For those unfamiliar with the term "deck," it refers to a collection of information and charts that are collated and bound together into a book-like item that is used to relate the point or points that the presenter is trying to make. Yes, the explanation of a deck might be as tedious as the creation of one.

Not long ago, I was challenged by one of my team members to become more involved in the safety program. I reached out to the manager in charge of safety, and asked him to put together a deck for my review. Within 48 hours, he was in the hospital with what appeared to be a heart attack.

The word spread throughout the organization: "Elliott gave Carl a heart attack." I felt a mix of regret and confusion as I wondered what was so wrong with what I had asked. Could my request have brought on a possibly life-threatening event? I was on an extended business trip at the time, and by the time I returned, Carl was home and in good health. It turned out to be more about stress than anything else; the mere mention of a deck had him panicking.

Decks Can Be a House of Cards

I have always been a straight shooter and a person who tried to minimize decks, but even my rather benign and nonchalant approach to decks seems to have created drag in the organization.

I have lived with presentation decks for most of my professional career. I have come to believe that the resources invested in decks, along with the cost to print and collate them, could be much better utilized to drive the business forward.

A Place for Everything, and Everything Has a Place

As is the case with many of the examples in this book, there is a time and a place for decks and presentations. Decks help tell a story and bring clarity and life to a topic, but I believe that they are way overdone in business.

While I was a member of two management boards as part of a major consumer product goods company, we set aside two full days every month to presentations. Each department leader would present his or her deck regarding what happened in the previous month and what would happen in the future. Those presentation days were long and arduous. Moreover, it took a day to prepare for each meeting, and I calculated that I spent – on average – four of the regular 22 workdays per month preparing for, listening to, delivering, or following up on decks.

Wasted Paper = Wasted time = Lost Opportunity

As sure as a full moon reveals itself every 28 days, once every month the entire board met at 8 a.m. sharp to begin our business review or deck presentations. I remember one July morning;

I was responsible for coaching a new vice president, and as we settled in our chairs at 10 minutes to 8, I leaned over and mentioned that the sunset would look beautiful from the boardroom window. He looked at me and laughed, not believing that any meeting could last 13 hours. As the sun set that evening just after 9 o'clock, he agreed it was a wonderful sight. This was not an exception, but rather the rule.

Incidentally, we all carried in 15 copies of our deck, each weighing about a pound, and we left at the end of the day with 15 different decks, each weighing about a pound. In some ways, the most beneficial part of the day was the exercise we got by lugging the decks around.

Excruciating Details Left Behind Create Risk

Another favorite deck story comes from a different work setting. We were preparing for a meeting with a major customer, and we decided to review our presentation deck. It was 94 pages long.

We had only a 30-minute time slot to visit with the customer. How could we deliver a 94-page deck in such a short period? The answer was, we could not. But that did not stop us from keeping the deck intact and moving two-thirds of the slides to the dreaded Appendix. Appendices themselves create a huge risk. They are not reviewed during the meeting; and if the customer – either internal or external – decides to review those pages later, questions are created.

Whoops

Frequently, the sheer bulk of a deck creates challenges. We were making a final run-through of a deck for a presentation to an important new customer. Late in the morning of the presentation, we found three slides that somehow had a competitor's logo on them. Imagine the fun we would have had explaining that to our prospective customer. We had a hard enough time explaining the mysterious disappearance of pages 19, 20, and 21. I don't think the customer believed us when we said our secretary was the famous Rose Mary Woods.

Since Ms. Woods' fame might be waning at this point in time, I will share her story. She was President Richard Nixon's secretary, and she was purportedly responsible for erasing taped conversations that were relevant to the Watergate scandal. That scandal ended Nixon's presidency.

The conclusion is this: decks are a house of cards. They may look very beautiful and ornate, but they are extremely time-consuming to construct and do not withstand much force. Usually, the constructor spends more time preparing the deck and making sure it looks good than actually addressing the reason for the deck.

While there is a good reason for a deck when used appropriately, I advocate minimizing the size of decks and their use in general. Re-deploy the effort used to construct a deck – instead, plan the successful delivery of the objective with as few props as possible. There will be major time and effort saved, and the environment will thank you for using less paper.

Going Deckless Delivers

The most successful meeting I have ever had with a key customer – who had been the recipient of the previously referred to 94-page deck on a different day – was when I walked in with a one-page document, printed on both sides. I explained that I was attempting to be sensitive to their sustainability efforts by not wasting paper. The buyer then advised that she hated decks, and added that she preferred a one-pager supported by dialogue.

We actually had a great meeting with good eye contact, and a much greater understanding of each other's requirements and hot-buttons. The result: We made more progress in one meeting than we had made in the previous half-dozen deck-filled sessions.

Another risk of using decks is that many buyers, in an attempt to get favorable treatment by vendors, often circulate sensitive and confidential decks to the competition. I have been the recipient of dozens of such deck copies in my career. While I have never been slipped one of my own by a customer, it would be naive of me to believe that one of my decks hasn't ever found their way to my competition.

The Tsunami Factor

In 1995, I coined the term **the Tsunami Factor** to describe how corporate headquarters' decisions often adversely affect field operations. Failure to understand implications of decisions can play havoc with the executors.

To understand the Tsunami Factor, we need to review some facts about the tsunami itself. A tsunami is created when the ocean floor shifts due to an earthquake. When the earth shifts vertically, the force generated starts a swell in the ocean. The swell might appear to be just another wave out in the depths of the ocean, but it is carrying significant force.

Since the location of the earthquake is several miles deep under the ocean surface, there is a vast area of water to absorb the energy. As the ocean floor rises toward land, the energy is concentrated in a much smaller area. When the wave approaches land, it crests, releasing energy – and causing devastation.

The story has been told that, many times, Japanese fishermen would be out at sea and would return home only to find their villages completely destroyed. Yet, they themselves never felt the tsunami that may have passed beneath them earlier in the day.

My knowledge (or lack thereof) of the science behind tsunamis can be attributed to my college geology professor. His instruction brought my studies to life, and he was an approachable and competent educator.

Self-Created Corporate Tsunamis

The same effect can occur with some decisions made at the corporate level. The directives may sound fairly innocuous, but when they make their way to the field, the impact creates devastating results. I began using the Tsunami Factor term when my company, a manufacturer of pet food, made the decision to offer one of our big customers a particular product for a promotion. The customer was so intrigued by the promotion that they asked for two pallets per store.

Champagne bottles were uncorked at the corporate office. It was a huge win for our company. But as it turned out, no one had bothered to check with the field personnel before the deal was finalized. The customer had more than 2,000 retail outlets, which translated to 4,000 pallets – over 120 truckloads of product. To be sure, that was a sizable amount of product, but on paper it appeared very doable.

Unfortunately, the product was sole-sourced from a small factory in northern Minnesota. Their plant could conceivably manufacture the product in a reasonable amount of time, but that company's town had not seen 120 truck shipments in a week in its history, and there was no storage space for the product within 100 miles.

It began to look like an impossibility; alternate plans needed to be made. We had to secure outside storage in a Minneapolis warehouse for over half of the product, along with arranging for secondary freight movement. Both actions resulted in higher costs for the factory and the logistics teams. The workforce had to put in an obscene amount of hours.

The dust finally settled and the shipments were successfully delivered to the customer. Everyone at the corporate office seemed satisfied with the incremental volume and the execution of the program – until the accountants figured out the net profitability.

We had actually lost money on the program, even when examined through a variable cost-spend lens. On the positive side, we fed a great number of dogs, and we made an important customer happy. On the negative side, we lost almost $100,000, we wore out our equipment and our people, and stuffed the marketplace with too much product. Our demand fell to less than

50 percent for the next four weeks, causing us to temporarily lay off part of the workforce.

When planning at the corporate level, it is vital that we consult directly with the internal stakeholders. In addition to the confusion and wasted money, corporate Tsunami events cause a major loss of confidence. Personnel at multiple levels will question the competency of the leaders of the organization, exacerbating the situation.

The Corporate Seagull

A corporate seagull is not much different from the bird we love to hate. The corporate version is a leader or a team – often an entourage from the corporate office – that swoops down into a site, makes noise, consumes time and resources, leaves a mess, and then disappears. A seagull-like scenario can occur when senior leaders visit retail stores, plants, or distribution centers. There is unnecessary preparation and widespread anxiety. Most of this chaos and stress can be avoided if the organization has a culture rooted in trust. Trust reduces fear-driven behaviors, and visits from leaders will be productive rather than disruptive.

Self-Awareness Prevents Seagull Behavior: Leaders must recognize how intimidating they can appear to frontline teams. Genuine, approachable behavior immediately lowers defenses and increases the visit's value. And when people feel comfortable, they share real information, instead of rehearsed talking points.

Transparency Neutralizes Seagulls: Be clear about why you're visiting. There should be no secrets; no hidden agendas. Engage people at every level with a smile and ask simple, sincere questions. If you don't genuinely care, don't visit; leadership without authentic interest is worse than no leadership at all. Transparency also means giving immediate, honest feedback to the site leader. Praise and criticism should be delivered respectfully and in the right setting, and not saved for a post-visit ambush.

Seagull Behavior: The worst leadership move is pretending that everything looks great during a visit, and then returning to headquarters with a negative report. This destroys trust, triggers more intrusive visits, and creates division between corporate and field teams. Recovery from a trust-breaking visit can take months – and sometimes it never fully happens.

Success: If your goal is to help the site succeed, ask about their biggest challenges and listen. If they won't open up, it's a sign that they don't trust you. That's a cultural problem you own. But when offering help, be honest about what you can and cannot do. Candor builds credibility; vague promises destroy it. If your goal is not to help and learn, don't visit. On the other hand, poor leadership at remote sites complicates visits; however, that problem must be addressed quickly. An ineffective or untrustworthy site leader is one of the most damaging personnel issues a company can face.

Build a No-Seagull Culture: A culture that rejects seagull behavior encourages openness, early warnings, and collaborative problem-solving. In a seagull-infested culture, secrecy becomes the norm, and the people most capable of fixing problems flee to less tainted waters. When the best depart, we find ourselves left with the dregs… and even seagulls will reject that fare.

The Corporate Lemming

Another interesting creature is the Corporate Lemming. Real lemmings are rodents that live in Norway, and the popular belief is that every few years, they make mass migrations to the cliffs adjacent to the sea, and jump off and drown themselves.

Corporate lemmings do not drown themselves; rather, they hang on to their careers by becoming "yes-men" and "yes-women." They agree with the leaders on almost everything, except maybe their allegiance to a sports team. They never offer critical advice and provide little or no service other than to reassure the leaders how great they are. Of course, they can also provide commentary on the leader's insightful decisions.

This breed of lemming does not cast itself off a cliff – unfortunately – but it can certainly help drive the entire organization to its doom. As it is with most personnel issues, it is the leader's failure that allows such ineffective individuals to remain in their roles. Worse yet, they often clog up executive slots, because some leaders enjoy having these ego-boosters around.

FOB Alert

Another name for these lemmings is "Friend of Boss" or FOB (or, substitute the boss's first name for the term Boss and replace the "B" with the boss's first initial). If I were the boss, the term would be "Friends of Elliott" or FOE. FOEs are truly foes to a productive work environment. Whether you refer to them as lemmings or FOBs, they spell trouble for the team.

AOK (Acronym Overkill)

Note to Reader: "Overkill" is one word, but it ruined my acronym, and we simply cannot tolerate that, as it kills my point.

Businesspeople love acronyms. I suppose they save time, and the rationale for them is sound. Certainly, they save multiple keystrokes versus typing out the entire term, but they have become so overblown and overused that I question their effectiveness. In many cases, different branches of your own organization may use the same acronym for different tools or procedures. Additionally, some team members bundle acronyms to make themselves feel important, or to make themselves sound more qualified or educated.

Acronyms Can Create Confusion

One of the acronyms I lived by for a big portion of my career was **CRP, Continuous Replenishment Program**. It arrived on the scene with great fanfare as the solution for problems with the ordering cycles between my company as a vendor and our key trading partners. In a nutshell, we did their ordering to save them additional administrative costs.

Almost every conversation that related to customer ordering started and ended with CRP. It was the topic of books and seminars, and businesses cropped up to support CRP plans.

Fast forward 30 years, and CRP is still with us. But the fanfare has subsided. In fact, when I Googled CRP, I found multiple CRP definitions. Here are the first 10:

- California Republican Party
- Cleaved Radioactivity of Phosphopeptides

- Child Resistant Packaging
- Center for Responsive Politics
- Certified Reliability Professional
- C-reactive Protein
- Conservation Reserve Program
- Capital Resource Partners
- Certified Relocation Professionals
- Corporate Realty Partners

In addition, there were at least five different references to state and local government projects or programs. I did not find the intended definition, the one I am familiar with. There was no mention of this once-ubiquitous term. The story of CRP is a very basic example of how acronym overkill can create confusion to your business, both internally and externally.

Again, the appropriate use of acronyms can be helpful, but the acronym explosion is confusing. I recommend that corporate leaders poke fun at the overuse of acronyms in an attempt to curtail them. A great example is a scene from the movie *Good Morning Vietnam,* where Robin Williams describes an upcoming dignitary visit using mostly all acronyms:

"Excuse me, sir. Seeing as how the VP is such a VIP, shouldn't we keep the PC on the QT? 'Cause if it leaks to the VC he could end up an MIA, and then we'd all be put on KP."

I think this typifies the point.

Buzzwords and Name-Droppers

Every generation has its buzzwords. We had "groovy" in my generation, and my children used "coolage." Then there was “crunk,” followed by “fo’ shizzle.” Thankfully, all have disappeared from our lexicon, although I have heard that “coolage” might be making a comeback.

Business is no exception; we grab buzzwords and overuse them until we exhaust everyone with them. I have always found it odd that almost all business leaders tend to follow the trend and grab onto these words. I suppose it helps give us credibility with our peers and makes us feel more “in the know.”

Bull**** Bingo: A Fun Respite

A problem is created when we become so ingrained in the use of buzzwords that people around us notice that the buzzwords feel more forced than natural. This leads to games like Bull**** Bingo (a more acceptable term is Buzzword Bingo) being played during company meetings.

This game is much like regular Bingo, but instead of numbers and letters, buzzwords are inserted into the grid. Each card is different, and the first person to create a line when the speaker utters the next buzzword wins. It is fairly unproductive behavior, but it keeps attendees awake during long, arduous speeches.

I referred to the Continuous Replenishment Program (CRP) in the acronym section. It was the definitive customer relationship buzzword of the 1990s. It, along with Efficient Consumer Response (ECR), has all but vanished from business commentary today. It is true that some of the building-block principles from the programs remain, but the pomp and circumstance has vanished.

As Promised, TQM Revisited

The most conspicuous example of a buzzword gone bad is the overblown use of Total Quality Management (TQM). Corporations around the world invested astounding amounts of money to market TQM programs within their organizations. Many felt that a failure to promote and implement TQM was a precursor to failure itself.

The bloom is off the rose, and you hear almost nothing about TQM today. While the principles are in many cases sound, the money invested in TQM really never paid off for most corporations that implemented it. Results were crafted to appear to be noteworthy, but the reality is that most – if not all – of the perceived benefits could have been delivered without the fanfare and expense. At the height of the TQM insanity, a corporation I worked at actually had an entire department dedicated to TQM. This group delivered absolutely no results. It served only to waste the organization's money and annoy the employees. It was an utter disaster. Finally, the program was disbanded without any official word. We simply went through a cost-savings effort, woke up, and the TQM team had disappeared.

The TQM program is a prime example of the outrageous bundle. Projects were mandated, had to be placed in special templates, had to involve cross-functional teams, and had to deliver results (or be manipulated to appear to deliver results). Finally, cross-functional teams had to attend sharing rallies where they discussed their success on stage. In one case, a team spent $50,000 to prepare their sharing rally performance. That expense did not include the hundreds of man-hours invested in preparing for the performance.

There is no question that buzzwords and management fads can be very costly and easily go awry. More often than not, there is a better way to get the desired outcomes without the expense and disruption. Leaders should carefully unbundle buzzwords and fads, and examine all alternatives.

Do You Know Who I Had Lunch With?

Name-droppers likewise waste time and cause disruption. Usually, these folks are consultants who evidently feel that their credibility will be enriched if they can squeeze the names of at least 10 notable influencers into their presentations. They state things like, "When I was having lunch with (insert name), and I floated this by (him or her), (he or she) thought it was very powerful."

I continue to be perplexed as to what such references mean to me or my company. If the consultant has a "powerful" idea, I think the team is more than capable of evaluating an opportunity on its own merit. We do not need validation from someone in an unrelated field who just happens to be popular.

Do You Know Where I Was Last Week?

Name droppers also repeatedly drop names of venues, and mention events and exotic-sounding cities. We had such a person make a presentation to our team. In addition to getting completely off track and spending over two extra hours prattling on about irrelevant topics, he exhausted us with his endless mention of names and venues.

At one point, he commented very nonchalantly, "The next time you are in London…" There were 24 of us in the room, and I believe 21 had never been to London. If any of us did have any interest in traveling to England, we definitely had no plans of visiting his recommended venue. This particular speaker was successful in disengaging almost all of the participants and severely eroded the effectiveness of his session.

We had a great deal of fun at the speaker's expense when, the next morning, our CFO arrived at Session Two wearing a Hard Rock Café London T-shirt. I can assure you that our CFO had never been to London, and was not aware of the irony of the shirt when he chose to wear it. It was great comedy relief.

Know your Audience!

It is important that we as leaders recognize the audience we are addressing. If we have a "four-syllable word audience," then proceed with the use of four-syllable words, acronyms and buzzwords. They are totally appropriate in these situations.

But more times than not, we are speaking to audiences who prefer straight talk. Most in the audience may not even understand the buzzwords and acronyms. We end up turning off our intended customers. It seems to be a much safer, clearer approach to use a one-syllable word if it effectively sends the message, instead of using the four-syllable variety.

Some time ago, one of the men I admired greatly was giving a speech to marketing team members, who were with a company that we had just acquired. This man was known for giving inspirational speeches, and I absolutely loved listening to him engage an audience. Among his best references were sports metaphors, and he could deliver them with passion and energy.

Unfortunately, this time, his audience was composed mostly of females who not only didn't care for sports, but found the use of sport metaphors offensive. He completely bombed.

He made the fatal error of not understanding his audience, and it cost him. His intended outcome was to inspire the team to relocate to our headquarters, which was in a different city. We attracted almost none of the team members.

Unions: The Failure of Management

Note to the Reader: This deep dive into unionism focuses specifically on labor unions. In the interest of full disclosure, my experience with unions has been almost exclusively within labor union environments. I have little direct experience working with professional unions. Accordingly, the observations, lessons, and guidance that follow should be understood within the context of working with labor unions and should not necessarily be applied to professional union environments.

Unions are the bane of companies. It really is not the contract, the wages, or the benefits that are the biggest issues with unionized workforces. It is the time and energy wasted in dealing with the day-to-day requirements of the union bureaucracy, and in the negotiation of the union contract. Remember, management is busy trying to run the business. Meanwhile, improperly managed union members have plenty of time to watch out for errors made by management and pounce on them, creating confusion and conflict.

With the exception of some of the public unions and trade unions that are preordained by our left-leaning government, the vast majority of unions exist due to poor management practices. When a union does exist, and the relationship is strained or the union is running roughshod over management, it is almost always due to weak management.

I absolutely despise unions, and would do almost anything within reason to avoid having to deal with a unionized workforce. I find it amazing that most every businessperson I know tends to agree with me, but they are unwilling to publicly state that they are a union-free business or explain why their business is union-free to their employees. As for me, I like to scream it from the highest hill in town.

Mistreatment: Breeding Ground for Unionism

Why do employees vote to unionize? It's usually because they have never been educated on the pitfalls of unionism, or because they have been so mistreated by management that they do not believe that management cares about them. However, just having to go through the disruption of a union campaign is so debilitating that it can cripple an organization's progress for years. A successful unionizing campaign can even lead to the dissolution of a company.

Productive and regular two-way communication between the workforce and management is the first step in being able to successfully avoid a union organizing attempt. When employees feel like management is not listening to them, or that management does not care, the time is ripe for an organizing campaign.

'Union-Free': Part of Your Corporate Playbook

Two key parts of a program can help an organization maintain its union-free status, and they are often overlooked. The first part starts with regular and formal communication with the workforce. Advise them why your company has chosen to be union-free. A good beginning point is to explain that your company likes to speak directly to its employees and hear directly from them in return. It's also important to explain that the costs associated with supporting a union put a burden on the company and employee alike.

Proper Hiring Practices

The second part of the program is to have a formal hiring plan that detects a possible pro-union bias in prospective employees. It is against the law to discriminate against a person due to his or her feelings on unionization, but you can ask questions that may draw out signs of their bias. When a candidate speaks about topics like seniority, bidding jobs, or stewards, there is a good chance that he or she has been a member of a union or is biased toward unionism. In addition, the prospect's work history on a resume or application can be helpful.

Having been a member of a union, or even sympathizing with union activity, is not a crime. Nor should all candidates who might have that experience or tendency toward unionism be automatically screened out of the hiring process. However, it is one data point to consider during your evaluation. Again, you cannot overtly engage in this type of screening, so do so carefully.

I would always have a couple of standard questions that I included as part of my interviewing process to get candidates to loosen up – and to distract them from rehearsed answers. One was to think about a person they admired, and – without divulging the person's name or relationship to the candidate – to explain what admirable attributes that person had. Almost every candidate immediately revealed the person's name and relationship, which I always found interesting.

One female candidate answered that she admired her boyfriend because he had led a union organizing campaign, which brought the company he worked for to its knees. I screened her out of the process for other reasons, but I found the stupidity of that statement astounding. I have interviewed thousands of people in my career, and it is amazing what you learn by merely asking questions.

Watch for Union Activity

A union organizing drive usually starts with a few union advocates, either internal or external, casually mentioning a local company with a unionized workforce. Conversations veer toward how much better that company's benefits and wages seem to be. It typically starts during informal sessions in the break room or after work at the local bar.

Watch for small pods of employees who immediately clam up when a supervisor enters the room. In fact, it is a good idea to enlist your front-line supervisor as your "canary in the cave" when it comes to getting an early read on pro-union activity. As with any crisis, when faced with a union organizing campaign, lost time is your worst enemy.

As federal administrations change, so does the government's attitude toward unions. By the time this book goes to print, it may be easier for unions to infiltrate your organization. As of this writing, the process that leads to formal union organization activity is fairly straightforward. You, as management, will initially be notified that a minimum of 30 percent of your workforce has signed cards stating that they have a desire to learn more about organizing the workforce.

Do Not S.P.I.T.

Once you have been served notice that a formal unionizing campaign is underway, you are under the microscope. Union advocates will be watching closely that you do not violate any of the standards that you have to follow. I usually refer to this scenario as "not being able to **SPIT**."

If you "SPIT," you will be hit with a National Labor Relations Board (NLRB) unfair labor practice (ULP) complaint.

The "S" in "SPIT" stands for **Spy**. You cannot assign superiors or other internal or external resources to watch for pro-union activity. You cannot attend, listen to, or record any union organizing activity.

The "P" stands for **Promise**. You cannot promise anything to any employee for their vote against the union, nor can you make any promises that working conditions will get better if the employees choose not to unionize.

The "I" stands for **Interrogate**. Simply stated, you are not allowed to ask any employees any questions about their feelings about the unionization of your company. However, you are allowed to listen to them if they ask you questions or decide to tell you about the activity.

The "T" stands for **Threaten**. You are not permitted to make any implied or overt threats, such as suggesting that the company is going to close or that anyone will lose their jobs.

Sometimes, union operatives will attempt to spin the facts to make it look like the company personnel have violated the standards, when they have not. Certainly, there are instances where companies and their management people either intentionally or unintentionally break the rules. But more times than not, companies follow the rules, because the penalties are stiff.

Astoundingly, the union organizers are permitted to do all of the above – and they do so regularly. Granted, they do not publicize spying and threatening, but it is a regular part of the informal grassroots organizing campaign.

Companies are allowed to educate the employees and explain the company's position on advocating for a union-free status. Usually, it is a good idea to hire an expert on the subject to help the company fight the union's campaign.

You've Got Yourself a Union – Now What?

After the union's campaign is concluded, a vote is taken. If 50 percent plus one of your workforce votes "yes" and the vote is certified, you are on your way to becoming a unionized workplace. Each state has its own rules on the next steps and how the union representation will be handled, but you will have to start negotiating a contract.

There are a number of maneuvers that your company can take to try to invalidate the union vote or to delay the inevitable. Unless you have real, credible evidence that something occurred that is consequential enough to invalidate the vote, I recommend that you avoid the legal moves and begin negotiation.

One thing that management often overlooks is that when negotiating a contract, everything is on the table. The union organizers will try to start negotiations with everything staying in place as is, but that is only a ploy. Obviously, if you become unreasonable, you will never get to a contract. You will then be forced into mediation, which only serves to waste more time and money.

Once you have a contract agreed upon, seniority and what is called "past practice" become the new standard. Another ploy of union operatives is to attempt to implement the past practice standard to a date before finalizing the initial contract. The fact is this: if it is not spelled out in the contract on day one, it is totally management's discretion whether to continue any previous policies or procedures.

Intense Discipline Nullifies Union Power

Day one is the beginning of a very important discipline for all management. Every time management does anything that is considered a "favor" for any employee, it becomes "past practice," and the company can be obliged to offer the same favor to every employee. Weak supervision or ineffective managers create untold chaos for the company because they gave favors to employees they liked. You simply have to say "no," and invoke the union rules as your guide. This should be a zero-tolerance standard. If your supervision is too weak to live up to this standard, those managers will have to be reassigned or exited from the organization. Remember, "past practice" lives forever – or at least until it can be negotiated out of the next contract.

When I supervised union shops, it was the easiest management assignment I had, once I got the rank and file under control. I never had to make any tough decisions regarding employee relations. An item would either be required by union guidelines, or those same guidelines would preclude me from doing what was asked.

Learn Contract Language

I observed an interesting anomaly. In most of the union shops where I managed, the shop stewards carried a small version of the contract with them, but none of the supervisors did. In fact, most of the supervisors had never seen the contract. But I always had one with me or nearby; imagine the look on the steward's face when I reached for my copy of the contract as he reached for his!

Unfortunately, I worked in unionized facilities where management-employee relations were so strained that it disabled the company's operations. There was real hatred between the two groups, and it was extremely counterproductive for both sides. I have also worked in environments where union-management relations were extremely productive. Management generally claims that poor relations are the fault of unreasonable local union bosses; nothing could be more inaccurate.

Remember that it is management's responsibility to ensure union bosses do not get out of control. If they try, simply don't allow it. Keeping things under control is accomplished by a few simple actions:

- Maintain honest and productive communication with union representatives.
- Have zero tolerance for management slippage in discipline when dealing with union personnel.
- Understand what the hot buttons are, and earn the respect of the rank and file.
- Engage in savvy negotiation.

Easing Management-Union Conflicts

At 6-foot-5, I rarely meet a person who has as large a frame as mine. However, once I found myself face-to-face with a formidable cigarette-smoking Teamsters business agent named Bill. I was the newly assigned transportation manager at the company, and I had decided to meet with what had been described as an unreasonable, violent, and lazy union driver workforce.

It was to be a social event to get acquainted with the team, and no elected union officials were to be present. But, in strode Bill; immediately, I knew he was trouble and intended to showboat for his guys. I greeted him, and he came right at me with a threat.

It was rumored that the drivers, who had never pumped their own diesel, were going to be required to do so by me.

I asked Bill to schedule a time when we could meet to discuss his concerns, and added that this was a social event. Bill would not back down, and insisted that I acknowledge his demand. I finally answered his demand with one of my own, stating that his drivers would pump fuel, and that they would like it. I then quietly left the room.

Within two weeks the matter was settled, with all drivers pumping fuel, but I did consent to provide one pair of gloves per month at company expense. The drivers soon learned that I was a new type of manager, and I wanted to work with them. Previous management had abused the drivers, and the drivers had returned the favor.

Management controlled the schedule, and the drivers executed it. But previous management had so disliked the drivers that they appeared to intentionally give every driver a haphazard schedule. That had made the drivers' personal lives very difficult. But, in exchange for pumping fuel and some other even more important concessions, I created a schedule that allowed over 50 percent of the drivers to have three days off in a row. The schedule also reduced the cost per mile by over 40 percent. As a result of the mutual benefits created, union-management relations flourished.

Within a year, we had such a productive relationship that union executives would call me at home and advise me when troublemakers were creating potential chaos. It was a quintessential win-win. The company won, the union looked like a hero to the rank and file, I had very few headaches, and the drivers had a much better quality of life. In addition, the drivers were much more pleasant to other employees at the remote sites where they delivered.

Remain Union-Free if Possible

By all means, avoid having a union shop when you can, but if it is inevitable that your workforce will be unionized, make sure the relationship is as productive as possible. I have worked with five different unions and 11 local chapters. I never lost a grievance and never had a strike.

The Death Spiral

Regularly, business leaders become so invested in a decision that they tend to lose objectivity. Once objectivity is gone, additional poor decisions follow in an attempt to salvage or defend the original one.

A great example is a new brand launch. All the appropriate homework and planning was done, and the execution has been sound. Yet, the launch is falling short of expectations. In fact, the brand is losing money well beyond the most conservative estimates.

Teams are assembled to determine how the brand can be salvaged. Plans are created and executed, along with significant investment of both human and financial resources. The brand continues to flounder.

Teams are assembled to determine how the brand can be salvaged. Plans are created and executed, along with significant investment of both human and financial resources. The brand continues to flounder.

Teams are assembled to determine how the brand can be salvaged. Plans are created and executed, along with significant investment of both human and financial resources. The brand continues to flounder.

Those previous three paragraphs are intended to be identical, as this is how the process of reaction unfolds. There is no crime in fine-tuning and reworking programs. In fact, it is encouraged. However, the tendency to spiral into reactionary and unproductive chains of work streams, with the sole goal of saving the unsavable, is ill-advised and dangerous.

It's reminiscent of a pilot spiraling his or her plane down toward the earth in an exhibition, with the pilot intending to pull the plane up before crashing. Unfortunately, death spirals in business are not for the entertainment of the people at the local air show. Rather, they are unproductive and expensive, often damaging a company for months or even years.

Continuing with poor judgment to salvage a bad situation usually occurs because of a misconception that the investment so far is so great that it must not be lost. Other times, the pure egotism – or fear – of the decision-maker fuels the unproductive behaviors.

It is important that we have the maturity to examine the bigger picture and make informed decisions. We must ask ourselves: *If we had not invested the money, or if we were not psychologically invested through ego or fear, would we make the same decision?* Said another way: *If we knew then what we know now, would we make the same decision?* If the answer is "no," we should explore options available to unwind the decision – while creating the best long-term outcome for the organization and its shareholders.

It's OK to fail. It is not acceptable to throw away good money and time to chase a failure.

The Overlooked Competitor

In business, we are taught to understand our competitors and to have a strategy to cause them as much grief as possible. They, in turn, are taught to do the same to us. I had one senior executive who liked to say, "Kick them until they are down, and when you have them down, stick a garden hose down their throat until they drown."

We attempted to do just that as we played the turf warfare game with all of our competitors. Fighting for share, every step of the way… it was a real slugfest. Unfortunately, it's easy to overlook the competitors that are the real threat. For example, we were competing in the ketchup business, and when salsa overtook ketchup as America's favorite condiment, we felt a bit stupid.

Not Your Competitor? Think Again!

Whatever your business, there is probably a competitor that you have not thought about. They are out there, taking your market, unchallenged. All the children who spend their spare time playing video games would be doing some other leisure activity if gaming systems had not been invented. What leisure activities would they be engaged in if gaming was not an option?

While you could not have avoided the invention of video games, could proper marketing against the activity have stemmed its growth and created a bigger market for other recreation-related industries? Emerging trends are often allowed to capture a segment of a market without any challenge from the established players.

Are kayaks a competitor to canoes? Are pet rabbits and hamsters (and their owners) competitors to the dog and cat food business? Is home cooking a competitor to the restaurant business? I think the answer to all three questions is a resounding "yes."

Inconvenient Probably, Reality Absolutely

I suspect that this chapter has annoyed many readers. It is not intended to indict, but rather to get us to think about some of the inefficiencies that our behaviors create. Unfortunately, we cannot completely eliminate many of these realities. Admittedly, it is far more difficult to manage the use of something than it is to eradicate it all together. As such, special care must be employed.

We live in a world composed of a full spectrum of color. It is helpful, when we can make many of our decisions black or white, but that simply is not reality.

A great example is unions. There are plenty of examples where unions serve a great purpose. Academia and civil service are two examples. This acknowledged, I remain convinced that it is always better to be able to talk directly to your team members and the third parties introduce unneeded complexity and are ripe for creating confusion.

All things in moderation. There is a place for all the inconvenient truths, but we need to recognize the consequences of their use and decide when and where their use is appropriate. It's a delicate balance, but one that can be managed with the proper amount of vigilance.

Combustion Check – IGNITE COMMUNICATION

Before lighting the fuse on your next communication effort, ask yourself:

1. Are you willing to minimize the use of decks, letting ideas burn brightly without unnecessary smoke?
2. Have you ensured that your energy flows efficiently or have you created corporate tsunamis with destructive waves?
3. Are you committed to reducing acronyms and buzzwords, keeping the air clear for meaningful ignition?
4. How can you create a no-seagull zone (eliminating those who swoop in, drop chaos, and leave) so your team can sustain a steady burn?
5. Do you recognize that poor management creates the opportunity for union activity, and are you ready to stoke proactive engagement instead?
6. Who is your unexpected competitor? How will you fuel your vigilance and adaptability?

Answering these questions ensures that your communication ignites clarity, alignment, and energy across your organization.

14

Crisis: Controlling the Flare

It takes 20 years to build a reputation and five minutes to ruin it. If you think about that, you'll do things differently.

– *Warren Buffett, investor, philanthropist, former CEO*

Have you . . .

Ever been embroiled in a crisis that was completely avoidable?

Ever lost sleep or become distressed over the mishandling of a crisis?

What if . . .

You could create a mindset that crisis management is a core competency?

You could create a resource with a NASCAR pitcrew standard of speed and excellence?

For many years, my brother served in the United States Air Force as a missile control officer in both the Titan and Minuteman programs. He told me very little about the details of his training, but he did share that he had been trained to execute orders without hesitation if and when a crisis came. Further, he related that his job consisted of regular training sessions; during those sessions, he and his co-commander were unaware if it would be another to-be-aborted drill or the start of a nuclear conflict.

I have always thought that his job was the quintessential example of working in constant crisis. If we, as individuals and business leaders, could prepare for crises in the same way that the military prepares its men and women for war, we could avoid a great deal of dysfunction that often surrounds crises.

Let's face it, a crisis is nothing more than potential for a full-blown conflict or disaster. It can have an impact of varying degrees – it can ruin your business at one extreme or become a mere footnote in the company's history at the other. It is **how you handle the crisis** that can make the difference where the crisis lands on the scale of impact.

Get Really Good at Dealing with Crises

If you are leading a vibrant and edgy organization, chances are that you are heading into a crisis, are in the middle of one, or are just coming out of one. Frankly, they are part of the game. It is certainly best to plan so that unnecessary crises are avoided, but to think you can plan your way out of all crises is a fool's errand. At the same time, training your team on how to conduct itself during a crisis can soften its impact.

I was once asked what I thought was the biggest challenge that would face my company in the future and my answer was, "Something we don't know about today." My belief is, if you know what is coming, you have a very high probability of dealing with it. It is the unknown factor that creates the havoc and catapults the organization into crisis.

Since we cannot avoid crises, we need to learn to become extremely competent at dealing with them. In fact, the saying, "Use your peace time wisely," is never truer than in dealing with crisis management.

Crises can take many shapes and forms. They can come in the form of force majeure (extraordinary or unforeseeable) events, public relations missteps, customer relations issues, or human resources conflicts. While each crisis has its own unique components, they all have things in common. First, they suck energy and time out of the organization's capacity; and second, they all come with some level of pain.

Plan for Crises to Manage Them

As with most things, appropriate planning is the most important part of a good crisis management program. In dealing with crises, time is a huge factor. Even an hour or two can make a significant difference when in a crisis.

Proper planning includes the creation of a core crisis management team. The names and contact information for all members of the team should be documented. And, part of the plan should include a hierarchy or communication-chain protocol.

When a crisis hits, your team's reaction should be like that of a pit stop crew in a NASCAR race or like officers in a military maneuver. Every stakeholder should know his or her role. There should be a preplanned protocol for each action.

Depending on the size and scope of the crisis, the team should generally have the ability to assemble within the hour. Each crisis classification should have a distinct course of action. To keep roles and responsibilities crisp and clear, the team should periodically practice crisis reaction and management skills.

There are a number of essential elements of a plan; some may not be readily obvious. Others, however, are extremely easy to complete and should have the status of "Just do it."

The Media Is Watching

There is a significant risk that the media might become involved while you are dealing with a crisis. Assume that the media will see every action you take in the most negative light. So, every employee should be advised not to speak to the media under any circumstances. That guideline should be confirmed in the company's media policy, which should be part of a broader employee code of conduct. Every member of the workforce should sign off on it.

Another rule that should be enforced is a no-recording-equipment policy. A sign should be posted at each of your locations, in a prominent place, that clearly states that no video or audio recording is permitted on your property. With that policy posted, you can avoid the possibility that the media will enter your place of business with cameras or recording devices, or stand outside on your property using that equipment.

When a crisis flares up, the media will not be your ally. The public loves to hate businesses and their leaders, and the media is a willing facilitator of that emotion.

Who Is Doing the Talking?

As part of your crisis plan, you should have a company spokesperson. He or she can either be an employee or a professional consultant on retainer. Also, you should designate at least one additional spokesperson, in the event that the primary spokesperson is unavailable. You may even choose to have multiple spokespeople, each for specific types of situations. For example, it might be the human resources professional who speaks to the media regarding employee-related issues, or perhaps a head research scientist who explains product performance issues.

Regardless, each person who will potentially act as a spokesperson for the organization should go through media training. Media training is a fairly straightforward and relatively inexpensive investment, and will easily pay for itself during one crisis. Media training may also reveal if your preselected spokespeople have what it takes to effectively represent the organization.

In the midst of a crisis, you absolutely don't need a PR gaffe to exacerbate the situation. Having people who can weather the storm of the media during a crisis is extremely important. For serious crises, definitely engage a public relations professional to coach your spokespeople before any interviews. You should prepare mock questions that are likely to be asked, and rehearsed answers.

When the media contacts your organization, it is usually best to confirm their contact information, and then return their call promptly after you have had a chance to prep your spokesperson. The worst thing you can do is allow someone to speak to the media without an agreed-upon company position. Almost as problematic is to not respond at all to media inquiries. Failing to respond irritates the media. To the public, the media will relay your non-response as, "We attempted to contact the company, but they did not return our calls." The public will draw its own – negative – conclusions.

One morning after putting coffee on, I reached for the morning paper. Below the fold, I saw a headline and read something to the effect that one of my company's executives was accused of wrongdoing. I read further into the article, and I was alarmed to learn it was me.

The company and I immediately went into crisis mode. No one at my company had any clue that such a story was going to run. We were aware that we were involved in a frivolous lawsuit, but we had no idea that the media would be releasing a story. It was a fairly small town, and it was in pre-internet days, so the story was confined to the local community.

Sleazy Attorneys Try to Embarrass Companies

The complainant's sleazy attorney, in an attempt to embarrass the company and me, slipped the story to the newspaper. He anticipated that he could use the publicity to get a quick settlement for his client while lining his pockets. The newspaper, which didn't seem to understand our company's value as the area's fourth largest employer, appeared to revel in attacking the company and its people. They were eager to print the story on their front page.

Despite the fact that the company was a member of the Fortune 500, our division had no formal crisis management plan or team. It cost us, and me, dearly. In an attempt to help explain the company's side of the story, one of the executives contacted the newspaper for an interview. During his discussion with the reporter, our company spokesman stated that, if there had been any wrongdoing, it was on the very low end of the spectrum and unintentional.

The next morning, the newspaper headline read something like, "Senior Company Executive Confirms Wrongdoing." The situation went from manageable to catastrophic for me, and put the company in a very difficult position. There is no question that the executive was well-intentioned, but he had not been trained properly, and it cost us in the press.

This story might sound familiar. This is the same lawsuit discussed in Chapter 9. If it is not familiar, you either skipped Chapter 9 or have chosen to disregard it. Either is unacceptable. It is not only important to illustrate why we should not let malcontents stay in our company; it is also critical to demonstrate the perils of speaking with the media without proper training and preparation.

Failure to Plan Is a Plan to Fail

Much of the chaos could have been avoided if we had implemented a crisis program. Moreover, had we adopted many of the other principles outlined in this book, we could have avoided the entire unpleasant event.

Today, with the advent of the internet, what typically was a controllable problem years ago is potentially a worldwide maelstrom in minutes. For that reason, another element of your crisis planning program should be a daily review of the internet for any stories involving the company name, brands, facilities or key managers. Such a review is easily done by preparing Google Alerts. You can also hire a company to provide that service for you. Either way, a business simply cannot afford to have the world know about bad press before its owners and executives do. Far too many companies have dug their heads in the sand and refused to understand the implications of an online world.

Create a Crisis Playbook

Additional planning includes the creation of a crisis playbook. It outlines each step of the process for each type of crisis. When preparing the playbook, involve all stakeholders. And, an annual refresh of the playbook is recommended, as are real-time updates for communication tree contacts when roles change.

A bit more difficult to execute, but also worthy of major consideration, is the development of a contingency planning protocol in the event of a force majeure event. Most companies fail to plan for these types of events, and find themselves forced into a scramble mode when a disaster occurs.

Oftentimes, you can work with others in your industry who may not be direct competitors to have a catastrophic planning reciprocity agreement. These types of agreements will offer some stability when a crisis hits.

When a crisis occurs, having as many controllable factors in place as possible allows the crisis team to focus on the actual issue. As with the simplification example in Chapter 12, the more variables we can hold constant, the easier it will be to come to a successful conclusion.

Minimize Variables

It's important to hold as many variables constant so that the team does not chase red herrings. Quickly focus on and frame the scope of the crisis. Using the meeting tools in Chapter 6 will go a long way to bring a sense of normalcy to the crisis. Utilizing those tools will allow the team to effectively get to the solution.

The following are a few simple rules that will help resolve current crises and prevent potential problems in the future:

- Make sure your receptionist or other personnel who greet people are well-trained on identifying phone calls or visitors who might be the source of a potential issue.
- Make sure your receptionist or any others who might make initial contact with visitors has a keen sense of how to respond to questions, and knows to contact the appropriate personnel immediately.
- Conduct the same training with all of your consumer affairs personnel.
- Educate your entire team on the perils of leaking company information outside the parameters of the organization.
- The vast majority of crisis events should be confined to a very small team of people, and great care should be taken to ensure that confidence and communication is held tightly.
- During larger and unavoidably public crises, make sure the company's messages are clearly communicated to the entire team on a regular basis. Failing to do so will leave

team members to engage in speculation, which leads to uncertainty and fuels the crisis.

- Insist that crisis team members limit discussions to formal meetings, and mandate that the information in those meetings remains private. Only the approved company messaging should leave the room.
- Request that all team members ask questions. Any rumors should be brought to the crisis team's attention.

The Fear Factor

When a crisis hits, the sense of uncertainty that comes along with it tends to fuel fear. It is human nature to imagine the worst outcomes. As the leader, it is your responsibility to manage that fear factor. This does not mean deceiving team members. It means shouldering the responsibility and the risk internally, as appropriate for the circumstances.

Fear fuels panic, and when panic ensues, all control is lost. Crises are exacerbated by uncertainty. Remaining unemotional – while demonstrating your sincere concern – will speak volumes to the team assembled around you. It is also essential that you purposefully guide the team through the tumultuous waters of the crisis.

Inevitably, someone on the team will take Chicken Little's "The sky is falling" position. This is a real challenge for you as the leader, and you simply cannot afford to allow that pessimism to taint the team's attitude. At the same time, you cannot be seen as flippant or nonchalant about the risks facing the organization. When that "Sky is falling" belief is expressed by a team member,

I would advise that you call a break from the meeting. Engage the concerned individual one-on-one, explaining that you are well aware of the severity of the situation. Reassure them that, if they allow the opportunity, their issues will be addressed. Also, urge them to use a controlled tone and tenor in their voice during meetings, and to phrase their concerns in question form.

I Am on the Bridge

Another important responsibility of the leader is to be very visible to the group during crises. I like to think of the television show *Star Trek*. Captain Kirk was always on the ship's bridge during the worst crises that faced the Starship Enterprise. He never seemed to sweat. He was in his chair, issuing commands to the team around him. Everyone on the ship and everyone at home knew who was in charge. It should be the same way in business. The leader is making the calls, and he or she must make those calls deftly and calmly.

If the crisis becomes public, it is important that you are even more visible. In fact, you should make an effort to be seen throughout the operation to answer any questions that concerned employees might have. You should avoid getting into protracted discussions, but when the team sees you on the premises like they have seen you in the past, it will help to allay most of their fears.

The leader is the key resource in minimizing the impact of a crisis. The leader is responsible for making sure that team members are used efficiently to resolve the matter. Remember, things are rarely as good or bad as they seem at the time.

Keeping everything in perspective – while preparing for the worst possible outcome – will often generate the best results.

The After-Crisis Critique Is Essential

When the crisis is over, everyone will breathe a huge sigh of relief. But that is the time when the leader must push the team to the next level and insist on a postmortem review. Recognizing that, after a particularly agonizing crisis, team members are understandably mentally exhausted, it is natural to want to relax. The leader must avoid that inclination, and insist that the crisis has not been fully resolved until a postmortem report has been completed.

Many advise waiting a few days prior to conducting the postmortem to allow team members to recharge and reenergize; but in my experience, that thinking has a couple of very adverse consequences. First, people tend to forget details in a very short time frame. Getting all the accurate information recorded right away is essential for preparing for the next crisis (or better yet, avoiding the next crisis before it happens). Second, as time goes on, incomplete postmortems tend to remain unfinished.

The leader must innately know how far he or she can push the team. Each crisis will have its own unique sequence, but the postmortem must be completed within a reasonable time. Failure to complete a postmortem is an invitation to fail. **Some of the best learning on how to handle a future crisis** will come from completing a full and thorough review of the recent crisis. The postmortem should include responses to the following questions:

- What was the root cause or causes of the crisis?
- Have root causes been eliminated or addressed?
- What did the team do that was helpful?
- What could the team have done better?
- How can we improve our crisis team?
- How do we learn from having gone through what we just did?
- What learning can we apply to other facets of our business?
- What action do we need to take now?
- What action do we need to take in the future?

If we take the correct approach to crisis management, we can emerge a stronger, more capable organization. Since each crisis has its own idiosyncrasies, results will vary. Your goal must be to minimize any negative implications and maximize the learning.

Sailing into the Wind

When I was a young boy, my uncle taught me how to sail. He had an Albacore sailboat, which is a versatile craft – it's used by novices and skilled sailors alike. They are widely used in competition for their speed and agility. While I never shared his love of sailing, I did marvel at the boat's ability to sail into the wind.

Accomplished Sailors Know How to Tack

If you are a sailor, you know that it is easy for a sailboat – if controlled properly – to reach a destination that is directly upwind. However, it takes skill and patience. Using a method known as tacking, the captain and crew can use unfriendly weather conditions to their advantage.

When tacking, you are navigating the boat in a zigzag pattern from port to starboard (left to right), and repeating that maneuver until you reach your destination. At no point are you actually moving directly toward the target, as the wind will simply not allow the boat to travel in that direction.

I have applied this tacking metaphor to business in many circumstances. I struggled with where to insert a reference to sailing into this book; it applies to many areas throughout the business world, from the tactical execution of an intended strategy to crisis management. It seemed most appropriate to include sailing, specifically tacking, in this chapter, as navigating a crisis could be considered the epitome of sailing into the wind.

The Best Way Might Not Be Direct

It is logical to assume that the fastest and best way between two points is a straight line. Unfortunately, elements like competition, adverse market conditions, capital constraints, and other unconstructive factors rarely allow a company to take that direct path. As such, we must use tactics that will allow the team to achieve its long-range goal, although the tactics may appear counterproductive in the short term.

Scenario planning of how to **sail into the wind** is an important exercise for teams to go through, because failing to understand the implications of each move creates confusion. That confusion can lead to chaos, or to team members questioning the leader's decision-making. No, the leadership has not lost their minds; they are simply intentionally tacking to the port side, because conditions will not allow the team to move in its desired direction immediately.

No sooner will the team get used to the new direction when the leadership decides to tack to starboard. The same risks of miscommunication and lack of trust can be created here unless there was proper coaching. To add to the complexity in business, "weather conditions" can change rapidly. You must be ready for any next tacks that changing conditions might dictate.

In **business tacking**, it pays to prepare for the execution of multiple future tacks. It is equally important to not become too committed to a tack that you might have taken. Being nimble allows you to have a clear advantage.

Most Everything Requires a Tack or Two

I cannot think of a single important endeavor in my business career, or in my personal life for that matter, that did not require a tack or two along the way. Some of them, I thought about in advance and was ready for; others caught me by surprise. In many cases, I simply got lucky. When you unbundle your life, you can make luck a reality that works for you. No longer is luck a flip of the coin; rather, you have created your own coin with two heads… and you always call "heads."

When you have simplified your life and business, you have more time, energy, and ability to make on-the-fly changes a reality. Fewer adverse things occur, because you have tipped the odds in your favor by proper advance planning. When adversity befalls the team, you embrace it, fix it, and move forward.

Combustion Check – IGNITE CRISIS MANAGEMENT

Before lighting the fuse on your next crisis response, ask yourself:

1. Are you willing to accept that not all crises can be avoided, and prepare to control the burn instead of denying the spark?
2. Are you willing to invest the time and resources to create a crisis plan, ensuring your fireproofing is in place before flames ignite?
3. Are you willing to hire or train experts to handle the media and then keep your own impulses in check, letting the controlled flame guide the narrative?
4. Are you capable of showing the resolve required to guide your team, keeping the combustion steady under pressure?
5. Will you learn to sail into the wind, navigating the sparks and heat of crisis without losing momentum or direction?

Answering "yes" ensures that your organization channels the fire of crisis into controlled energy and turns challenges into forward motion.

15

Efficiency: Streamline the Fuel

After climbing a great hill, one only finds that there are many more hills to climb.

– Nelson Mandela, former President of South Africa

Have you . . .

Ever felt encumbered in the complexity of life and business?

Ever yearned for a moment of peace and solitude to recharge, refresh and renew your spirit?

What if . . .

You could adopt a level of curiosity that demands excellence?

You could discover simple solutions that meet objectives?

You could enjoy the time you create and the goodwill you extend?

As the leader of the business, it is your responsibility to ensure that the foundation of the business is constructed so that it withstands the storms that might form in the future, beyond your time at the helm. I refer to this as "chain reaction combustion."

Chain reaction combustion is defined as: A self-propagating chemical process where the products of a reaction initiate further reactions, sustaining the overall combustion process. When we apply this concept to business, it means creating a self-propagating culture. That culture's value systems create an environment that intuitively sustains itself, leading to long-term success and well-being.

The concepts and tools presented in this book are the building blocks for optimized performance, which leads to superior results. Choosing to adopt a bias for simplification will yield significant dividends. It is a journey that has a start; but frankly, it does not have an ending. Plan to commit to instilling a culture of continual exploration. Business is not static; it is a living, breathing entity that requires constant refinement and nourishment.

The approaches detailed in this book may sound daunting. Significant and continued investment is required, but once we've reached the state of unconscious competency, the effort is continued with ease.

What Does Good Look Like?

The first question that we must ask ourselves is, "What does good look like?" In my travels as a consultant, I find that teams loaded with talent become so focused on the day-to-day that they often fail to think about their goal.

We must challenge ourselves to define "good." Moreover, we must challenge ourselves to ensure that our definition of "good" is aspirational and sustaining.

A great example of this exercise is managing product yield. Throughout my career in consumer product goods, the end product ended up being a subset of the inputs. The volume of the inputs minus the volume of the finished saleable product is referred to as yield loss – or in some cases, it is called scrap. One of the goals of any entity should be to minimize these scrap numbers; to keep them at the lowest level. The question becomes, "What is the optimal level of scrap?"

This might sound like a rather direct exercise, but the nuances involved make it more of a challenge. There are many factors to consider, including line speeds, energy usage, and labor efficiency. The answer might be a bit different for each company, but the overarching imperative would be the most saleable finished goods produced per time increment, at the lowest possible cost.

After part of five decades in the companion animal nutrition space, I do not believe that anyone has optimized the scrap yield dilemma. However, not knowing the optimal target but continuing to manufacture for years is a rather common failing in the industry.

The exercise of understanding what good looks like should extend into every activity in the organization. Everything from optimized operations through company image should be considered, and targets should be set.

Since business is dynamic, "what good looks like" may change due to any number of factors, including competitive set, consumer attitude changes, and advances in technology.

Curiosity

Curiosity is an under-emphasized core value. When failures occur, the drive to understand what went wrong is great. In many cases, the passion to discover the root cause or causes propels the company into a gargantuan effort that consumes much of the organization's capacity.

What if we adopted the same level of enthusiasm when being curious about why things are going **right?** In my experience, it rarely happens; or when it does, it is a restrained journey. Many will say that the expense required to investigate why things are going well is not justified.

We should commit to adopting curiosity as a part of the foundation of the enterprise. What are our competitors doing? What are our consumers thinking? How are my teammates feeling? What is our image in the public eye? What is our image with the competition? What are the priorities of the government? These are a few of the many curiosities we should consider on an ongoing basis.

Education

Hand in hand with curiosity comes education. Curiosity, without education, is a lost opportunity. We should encourage all our team members to become educated and also to educate, with the same level of zeal.

Education can take many forms. There is formal education and informal education; both are important. Embrace an understanding of the correct mix of formal and informal education.

Courage

It takes great courage to stand firm on one's convictions. Can you imagine a time when you will need to decline an opportunity because it does not fit with your values? Can you imagine terminating the employment of your top salesperson because he or she doesn't share the values you hold dear? How about declining new business because your capacity cannot meet the demand, and because taking on the new business might adversely affect existing customer relationships?

Doing the right thing is always the right thing to do. Many confuse their right to do something with doing the right thing. They are very different, and it takes courage to do the right thing – even when it's in conflict with your rights and results in a less favorable short-term outcome.

Business Card Standard

Twenty years ago, I was contemplating rehiring one of our former top salespeople. He had left for greener pastures that wound up being less than fertile, and wished to return. I had elected to confer with other members of the team, and most were lured by the book of business that was sure to come into the company along with his return.

Then, one junior member of the team made a profound statement. "I am not sure how I like having my name on the same business card with this guy." That young man had a point; the salesman's book of business would come with some baggage that the company had long since thrown into the trash heap of history. I made the decision not to rehire that person.

The decision sent shock waves throughout the senior levels of the business; the administrative team was appalled.

So enthralled I was with the notion of the "business card standard" that a few years later, I entered my boss's office and resigned. His surprise was readily evident, and he inquired as to my reasoning. "I was looking at my business card the other day, and I don't like seeing my name on it anymore." A decade-long career was over.

Wisdom

I was reading a book for a class I was taking, and one of the authors referenced the multiple degrees that were part of a specific person's background. I could tell that the author erroneously confused those educational achievements with wisdom. Intellect has no correlation with wisdom, although many educated people happen to have been blessed with wisdom.

Wisdom is the ability to take the proper path when facing the multi-pronged challenges of life and business. True wisdom is on full display when an individual can ignore the noise of life and lead the team to the most desirable conclusion.

Wise people can quickly identify and navigate around temptation. They avoid red herrings with ease. They have the ability to see around corners, and in doing so are uniquely capable of optimizing an outcome. In many cases, the right path might be more difficult.

In the final assessment, the wise person can rise above the fray and see the bigger picture. Having such insight results in sage decisions. Those with great wisdom know that allowing emotions to run amok will cloud one's judgment. Poor judgment, in turn, creates damage that can be fatal to the mission.

Fear

Fear is a normal emotion that affects most, if not all, of us. As you embark on the next chapter of your journey, work diligently to keep your fears in check. It's of vital importance that the leader not allow his fear to manifest itself in poor decisions or to become apparent to team members.

If you struggle with managing your fears, a good executive coach should be considered as a trusted confidant to help you keep such emotions in check. These confidants should be professionally trained, and should be outside resources. If your company will not cover the cost, you should strongly consider two options. First, pay for the resource yourself; and second, start seeking other employment.

There is a great deal packed into this chapter. Take a break to reflect and consider how to incorporate the elements in these pages into the culture of your business and your life.

After the… But!

Every person and every business has a persona. This group of defining attributes is shaped through years of sculpting the soul. Since many of us like to see ourselves as embodiments of the values we hold true, it is understandable that we revel in the positive attributes that define who we are and where we stand.

Every person and every business also has a **"but."** Usually, what comes after the **but** is thought, and not said – or said only in the safety of anonymity. Sometimes these truths are referred to as blind spots; other times, they are known, yet ignored.

Courageous people and defining businesses lean into what comes **after the but**, and in doing so, they enhance their standing in society. They create even stronger and more enduring reputations.

Reflect carefully upon this reality. Take the first step in this illuminating exploration.

What If

People and businesses live in a world of rules, regulations and restrictions. I refer to the obsession with these restrictions as a **"you can't** mindset." There is a place for guidelines and standards, but when they stymie personal or professional growth, they become detrimental.

The **you can't** mindset is tedious, stressful, uncomfortable, and destructive to innovative spirit. But what if… we adopted a **"what if"** mindset instead? A **what if** mindset fosters curiosity and creativity. It breathes life into businesses.

Companies that embrace the culture of **what if** can transform into purposeful visionaries. When they do, ideas flow continually.

To reinforce the **what if** mindset at one of my companies, I outlawed the term **"against"** and any negative responses. If a team member supported an idea, they would say, "I am for this." If they felt the idea needed more thought, they would say, "I wish for this." Amazingly, the **what if** mindset became a cultural igniter and led to a far more productive environment.

A Closing Charge

As we close this final chapter together, I urge the reader to reread its content and thoughtfully consider implementing and championing these initiatives. Adopting them will strengthen your team and create an amazing culture of excellence.

Combustion Check – IGNITE INNOVATION

Before lighting the fuse on your next breakthrough, ask yourself:

1. Are you willing to reflect upon the dynamic nature of business, staying alert to sparks of change before they ignite?
2. Will you commit to learning What Good Looks Like, using it as fuel to accelerate your performance?
3. Are you ready to adopt a curiosity standard, letting questions fan the flames of discovery?
4. Are you committed to education, continuously adding fuel to keep your innovation engine burning hot?
5. Do you feel courageous enough to embrace the principles outlined in this chapter, igniting fresh thinking and burning away old assumptions?

Answering "yes" ensures that you're ready to light the fuse on your next innovation and keep the fire of progress blazing.

PROPER COMBUSTION

The Journey to Significance

Hopefully, I have fulfilled my promise to help you both learn and laugh through the pages of this book. I am a realist, and I recognize that, depending on your circumstances, total transformation may be difficult or even impossible. But if you have discovered even a few kernels of insight that help you lead a better life, then I hope you'll agree that the time you invested in reading this was worthwhile.

Living an **unbundled life** is a long journey, and we may never experience a completely bundle-free state. Yet I can assure you that you can reap the benefits of unbundled bliss simply by taking the first step. If you haven't looked inward and done everything within your control to improve yourself, I urge you to do so. Transformation is much like a chain reaction – one that grows more powerful as it progresses – and reflects a timeless Hermetic Principle: **As Within, So Without**.

I have had my share of disappointments along the way, but I have always stood on my principles. The day of my epiphany came more than 30 years before I coined the phrase *Unbundle It®*; yet, there was no question that I had already unbundled my fears, and the results were astounding.

Unlike personal change, unbundling your business is more of an evolution than a revolution. It takes time, energy, and perseverance. As I have assured teams throughout my career, we are not going to wake up tomorrow to find all our problems magically gone. But if we commit to simplifying our business approach, we give ourselves the best chance to win, and win again. Adopting the principles in this book and applying them thoughtfully will yield shockingly positive results. One size does not fit all, and your organization's evolution into an unbundled enterprise will be uniquely its own.

Each metamorphosis carries its own challenges, but if you have the courage and perseverance to wade through some troubled waters, the benefits will be material and long-lasting. As demonstrated throughout this book, bundles are everywhere and they are incredibly powerful. Uncontrolled bundles waste time, drain money, and sap organizational energy. Controlled or purposeful bundles, properly executed, can release time, generate money, and create energy. Once we understand bundles, we can control them and ultimately become master bundlers.

In the end, *Combustion* is more than a framework. It is an invitation – an invitation to strip away the unnecessary, to release the weight of complexity, and to reclaim the clarity that has always been available to you. When you choose simplicity, you choose focus. When you choose focus, you gain influence.

And when you gain influence, you ignite the kind of success that compounds, accelerates, and transforms.

But success is not the final destination. It is merely the spark.

The real question – the one only you can answer – is what you will do with the fire you've created. Will you use it to illuminate your own path, or will you use it to light the way for others? Will you settle for achievement, or will you reach for significance?

Because…

Success is about what you gain.

Significance is about what you give.

A successful life will impress others.

A significant life may inspire millions.

My hope is that the clarity you've gained, the time you've reclaimed, and the momentum you've built will propel you toward a life that matters – a life where your impact outlives your effort and where your influence outlasts your accomplishments.

This is your combustion point. This is where simplicity becomes strength. This is where your story ignites.

Go forward and burn bright.

Bibliography

Brainy Quote. *John Wooden Quotes*. Internet Study Site. Seattle: Book Rage Media Network, 2001-2012. Internet.

Chapman, Alan. *Conscious Competence Learning Model*. Website. Leicester, England: www.businessballs.com, 1995-2012. Internet.

Collins, Jim. *Good to Great: Why Some Companies Make the Leap… and Others Don't*. William Collins, 2001. Hardcover book.

Collins, Jim. *How the Mighty Fall and Why Some Companies Never Give In*. Crown Publishing, 2009. Hardcover book.

Crosby, Philip. *Quality Without Tears: The Art of Hassle-Free Management.* McGraw-Hill, 1995. Hardcover book.

Dow Chemical Company. *Dow Latin America Mission Vision and Values*. Internet Site. Sao Paulo: Dow Chemical, 1995-2012. Web.

Isachsen, Olaf, PhD and Berens, Linda V., PhD. *Working Together; A Personality-Centered Approach to Management*. Institute for Management Development, 1995. Paperback book.

Lencioni, Patrick. *Getting Naked: A Business Fable About Shedding The Three Fears That Sabotage Client Loyalty*. John Wiley & Sons, 2010. Hardcover book.

Lencioni, Patrick. *The Five Dysfunctions of a Team: A Leadership Fable*. John Wiley & Sons, 2002. Hardcover book.

Society for Conceptual Logistics in Communication Research. "Attribution - Fundamental Attribution Error." Article. 2009-2012. Internet.

United States Department of Agriculture. Myplate.gov. Article. Washington, DC: David Herring, Nutritionist & Webmaster, 2012. Internet.

Welch, Jack and Welch, Suzy. *Winning*. HarperCollins, 2005. Hardcover book.